Between Possibility and Peril

PENNSYLVANIA STUDIES IN HUMAN RIGHTS

Bert B. Lockwood, *Series Editor*

A complete list of books in the series
is available from the publisher.

BETWEEN POSSIBILITY AND PERIL

Domestic Courts and the Selective Enforcement of International Human Rights

Chris Kendall

PENN

UNIVERSITY OF PENNSYLVANIA PRESS

PHILADELPHIA

Published by
University of Pennsylvania Press
Philadelphia, Pennsylvania 19104-4112
www.pennpress.org

Printed in the United States of America on acid-free paper
10 9 8 7 6 5 4 3 2 1

Hardcover ISBN: 9781512826210
eBook ISBN: 9781512826227

Library of Congress Cataloging-in-Publication Data

Names: Kendall, Chris, 1972– author.
Title: Between possibility and peril : domestic courts and the selective enforcement of international human rights / Chris Kendall.
Other titles: Pennsylvania studies in human rights.
Description: Philadelphia : University of Pennsylvania Press, [2024] | Series: Pennsylvania studies in human rights | Includes bibliographical references and index.
Identifiers: LCCN 2024000584 | ISBN 9781512826210 (hardcover)
Subjects: LCSH: International law and human rights—Case studies. | International law and human rights—Colombia. | International law and human rights—Mexico. | International law and human rights—South Africa. | Courts—Colombia. | Courts—Mexico. | Courts—South Africa. | Human rights—Colombia. | Human rights—Mexico. | Human rights--South Africa.
Classification: LCC KZ1266 .K46 2024 | DDC 341.4/8—dc23/eng/20240129
LC record available at https://lccn.loc.gov/2024000584

CONTENTS

Chapter 1. International Human Rights, Domestic Courts 1

Chapter 2. Three-Dimensional Decision-Making in the Domestic Judiciary 16

Chapter 3. Colombia: Balancing Act 54

Chapter 4. South Africa: Majoritarian Difficulties 92

Chapter 5. Mexico: Rigid Reform 133

Chapter 6. Conclusions 179

Appendix 1. Transitional States 193

Appendix 2. Major International Human Rights Treaty Ratifications 195

Notes 199

References 223

Index 241

CHAPTER 1

International Human Rights, Domestic Courts

Expectations

In Colombia, representatives of more than a thousand family groups file individual claims against the government, asserting that the ongoing civil war threatens the families' lives and the existence of entire communities. After numerous lower courts reject the claims on procedural grounds, the Colombian Constitutional Court steps in. It casts aside the potential procedural irregularities, combines the various lawsuits, and recognizes that international humanitarian law requires the government to take action to protect the families. To encourage compliance, the court institutes public hearings, reviews government budgets, and appoints domestic and international civil society groups as monitors to continue applying pressure to the government and maintain links to the court.

After suffering a brutal attack, a woman in South Africa goes to court claiming that the attack represented a profound state failure to protect her rights to equality, life, human dignity, and freedom and security of the person. When lower courts reject her claim, she takes her fight all the way to the nation's Constitutional Court. The outcome is both a legal triumph and a victory deferred. The South African Constitutional Court grants no immediate relief on the merits but agrees with the proposition that police and prosecutors may be held liable for negligence when they fail to prevent a rights violation. It sends the case back to the lower courts with instructions to develop the common law in line with constitutional provisions and international standards. For the individual claimant, however, it will take another 8 years to receive any compensation from the state.

In Mexico, 17 activists are killed and another 14 injured en route to a protest demanding aid for coffee growers. Mexico's National Human Rights Commission concludes that the human rights violations occurred at the hands of police forces, and the Inter-American Commission on Human Rights intercedes with a demand that the Mexican government secure the safety of witnesses. In hopes of holding police responsible for the massacre, a human rights nongovernmental organization (NGO) petitions the Mexican Supreme Court of Justice of the Nation to investigate using powers granted it under the national constitution. Instead, the court seeks to avoid any such role on procedural grounds until it is ultimately forced to act by the president of the republic. Although the investigation concludes that human rights violations occurred, the court struggles to issue a report and fails to provide any remedy to the victims' families. Instead, within a few short years, the court will seek to have its investigatory role transferred to a different state institution in hopes of avoiding a similar politicized role in the future.

These three cases are explored in subsequent chapters, and they share many traits. In each, the litigant turned to a domestic court in search of a solution politicians could not or would not provide; the right in question was protected by international human rights law; and the court was newly empowered as part of the third wave of democratization to protect such rights. Despite these commonalities, the outcomes varied remarkably: a ruling followed by intense judicial oversight, a ruling with no immediate effect, and a nonruling that left nothing but frustration for the litigants and the court itself. How can it be that three courts, all of which were charged by their societies with protecting citizens' international human rights, could land on such varied outcomes? What does this say about our understanding of courts as the one place where rights can be vindicated, as long as there is a law—in this case, international law—enshrining that right?

This book seeks to answer that question by examining the conditions under which courts in democratizing regimes entrench international human rights law. Before delving into that explanation, however, it is important to take a step back to understand why any of the individuals or groups portrayed in the three scenarios described would expect a domestic court to come to their aid when domestic politicians would not. This faith in human rights norms represents a sea change from long-standing notions of how individuals relate to their own state and to international law.

A Golden Age for Human Rights

This transformation in expectations took nearly half a century and was inaugurated by the post–World War II push for global human rights protections. This push went beyond rhetoric to see the burgeoning of an incredibly legalized set of international human rights regimes. The period witnessed the debunking of the Westphalian notion that what happens within a state's borders stays within a state's borders. Whereas the immediate post-WWII trials at Nuremberg failed to prosecute crimes that occurred before the internationalization of the conflict, later treaties rejected this notion of a legal cordon sanitaire insulating domestic crimes from international scrutiny. The United Nations (UN) Charter went so far as to root interstate peace in domestic respect for basic human dignity, making local rights an international concern. Subsequent treaties and declarations, binding or hortatory, proclaimed the duty of states to respect universal human rights. Even the geopolitical standoff of the Cold War did not prevent international human rights from making continued progress, both rhetorical and legal.

For much of the twentieth century, courts promised to play an important role in this process of rights expansion and protection. At the international level, human rights courts and quasi-judicial institutions suggested the possibility of international oversight of domestic political processes. From the European Court of Human Rights to the Inter-American Commission on Human Rights to the International Criminal Court, judicial institutions emerged as would-be protectors of vulnerable individuals and groups. At the domestic level, the ratification of human rights treaties and the establishment of strong courts to protect those rights became a common goal of political reform. This process reached a crescendo with the collapse of the Soviet Union, the end of the Cold War, and the triumph of liberal internationalism. For the first time in modern human history no significant power center acted as a bulwark of illiberalism, and states undergoing regime transitions appeared to all be adopting the same template: democracy and human rights backed by an independent judiciary. Francis Fukuyama's thesis in *The End of History and the Last Man* promised that this represented a common historical end point: the victory of reason and law over power and politics.

Three decades later, however, liberalism's celebration of the individual again faces strong headwinds in the form of resurgent nationalist projects, rising populist rhetoric, and increasingly sophisticated forms of technologically adept autocracy. Individual rights and international law, far from being on the march, retreat before the self-arrogated demands of nation and state. This begs the question: If the motor that drove the expansion of human rights internationally has ground to a halt, does this mean the domestic institutions established to promote and protect the rule of law invariably falter? After all, the governments of newly democratized states ratified treaties and engaged in domestic reform not simply to show support for expanding human rights regimes but also to protect against the real possibility of future backsliding when governments changed hands or when social, economic, or political conditions became less favorable. International law and domestic reform did more than declare allegiance to a cosmopolitan idea of rights; they claimed to provide a buttress for those hard-won rights.

How has that process played out? Have the legalized human rights regimes that were established and embedded during the golden age of human rights succeeded? Has international law become something other than a domestic rhetorical tool, and have courts lived up to the hope so often placed in them as forums for the articulation of reason and law, shielded from the world of power and politics? To answer these questions, I look to those states that partook in the wave of liberalization that began as the Cold War ended. More precisely, I look at the institution most often seen as a nonpolitical protector of legal rights: the court. As states democratized, they by definition engaged in political reform. Where these reforms drew on international human rights law, and where they sought to entrench these rights through the strengthening of the domestic judiciary, have courts played the intended role? Examining these courts teaches us about the success of international human rights regimes and domestic efforts at rights entrenchment. Although courts are not able to single-handedly accomplish democratic transition or prevent democratic backsliding, they do play an important role in the liberalization process. As courts come under attack and appear to be increasingly politicized, an examination of their behavior helps us to understand how they may find ways to survive and perhaps even to advance human rights in politically difficult times.

My focus in this project is on the subset of states that enacted court reform or otherwise underwent democratic transitions as the Cold War ended, precisely because it is in these states that the institutional role of courts is less entrenched and there is no deep well of legitimacy on which to draw. Just as importantly, these transitioning states are where human rights concerns are greatest. I focus in particular on top (or "apex") courts, because it is these courts whose mandates most frequently call on them to enforce international human rights law and, in doing so, risk putting them in direct conflict with political actors. For the purposes of this project, I examine the broad sweep of international legal obligations. In addition to the traditional focus on treaties, I include what is sometimes referred to as "soft" international law.[1] I take this to encompass a wide array of international law instruments, from customary international law (often incorporated by reference in domestic law), to aspirational declarations that have been agreed to by individual states, to international organizations' resolutions purporting to constrain their members. It is this broad panoply of instruments that make up legalized international human rights regimes, and the broad panoply is thus relevant to the inquiry at hand.

This book explains why some apex courts in transitional regimes have succeeded in not just protecting but at times advancing the cause of human rights—and why others have faltered. The book does not seek to explain when regime liberalization fails or succeeds full stop; rather, it elucidates the role of courts as protectors of human rights in less than auspicious circumstances. In particular, I examine apex courts in three transitional democracies: Colombia, South Africa, and Mexico. I analyze how each court's relationship with international law, political actors, and society at large explains the court's willingness and ability to entrench international human rights at the domestic level. My explanation focuses on three key contextual factors that I argue apply broadly to courts in democratizing regimes.

First, the court must be invested in international law. Courts vary in the degree to which they perceive international law to be part of their mandate, and thus whether they perceive it to be in their own strategic best interest to invoke international law when building institutional legitimacy. Second, even when courts have an interest in enforcing international human rights, they will only be able to do so to the extent they can resist or forestall backlash from the political branches. The courts best positioned in this regard are those that can rely on—and perhaps even cultivate in an iterative, dynamic process—an engaged public as a counterweight to political elites. Third, and most critically, the most successful apex courts are those able to control not just substantive rulings but also the arcane procedural and institutional rules governing access, adjudication, and remedies. These courts are the best positioned to pick and choose the cases most likely to enhance their legitimacy while strategically avoiding costly battles with political actors. Paradoxically, the courts that are most successful in the long run are those that sometimes choose to disappoint human rights activists in the short term.

The rest of this chapter situates my question in two broad areas of inquiry. First, scholars of international relations and international law have articulated numerous theories that seek to explain the relationship between legalized international human rights regimes and domestic rights outcomes. These theories explain not just varied outcomes but also a multiplicity of pathways, both instrumental and ideational, through which international human rights may take hold domestically. I examine the extent to which domestic courts play a role in these various theories and under what circumstances we may expect to see domestic courts making a meaningful difference in binding states to their international human rights obligations. Second, I am interested in the role of a specific institution in a specific type of regime: apex courts in young democracies. For this reason, I also briefly detail the extent to which the late twentieth-century democratic transitions provided fertile ground for a potential flourishing of domestic human rights litigation. In particular, I examine which states underwent democratic transitions and why they incorporated international law alongside court reform. This exercise paints, in broad strokes, an image of the increasingly democratic, human rights–oriented world that we now associate with the final decades of the twentieth century and which is now under an ongoing threat of retrenchment.

This global description, however, obscures the diversity of state-level experiences within the broad democratizing trend. It is this diversity that I seek to leverage in explaining the behavior of courts when they are faced with human rights claims. Therefore, in the final section of this chapter, I return to the domestic level to explain the potential problems domestic courts confront in their varied institutional environments. I sketch my answer to the questions raised throughout this chapter, setting the scene for a fuller exploration of my theory in Chapter 2. In that chapter, I lay out my complete theory of domestic courts as a "transmission belt" between international law and domestic politics, and I explain my case selection: the apex courts of Colombia, South Africa, and Mexico. Each of these three states experienced domestic transformation in line with the broad international trends outlined in this chapter. Each, however, did so in a manner that was true to its domestic imperatives, both societal and political. Consequently, the apex courts of these three democratizing states have operated within markedly different institutional environments. This variation in the courts' institutional settings is the focus of the remaining chapters of the book.

Before exploring domestic-level variation, though, it is important to understand why we might have a prima facie expectation that international human rights regimes could bind domestic actors. The theory explored in these pages, after all, makes certain demands of domestic courts. In particular, there is an underlying expectation throughout this book that domestic courts should, regardless of domestic social and political exigencies, tack toward compliance with the demands of international human rights law. Why might we expect this, based on our current understanding of international human rights regimes? It is to this question that I now turn.

International Regimes, Domestic Outcomes

What is the relationship between legalized international human rights regimes and domestic rights outcomes? Scholars have found that rights regimes produce understandably varied compliance results and that it is difficult to generalize across treaties (Cope & Creamer, 2016). Links between treaty ratification and domestic outcomes are highly contingent on the domestic environment (Cope et al., 2019; Hafner-Burton, 2012), and when rights regimes do have a positive effect, they tend to have this meliorating effect in partially free or transitional regimes (Simmons, 2009). The various theories that explain this international-domestic interplay can be organized into two broad categories. The first focuses on the attributes of liberal or liberalizing states and the use of international human rights regimes as explicit compliance mechanisms. The second category suggests a more subtle pattern of socialization and norms promulgation. Each of these two approaches offers the possibility that domestic courts help entrench international human rights.

The first set of mechanisms focuses on treaty law as an explicit mechanism by which states bind themselves to human rights obligations. This can occur either intentionally in the case of democratic states or inadvertently for nondemocratic states. Moravcsik (1995) argues that international human rights regimes emerge among states that already enjoy robust human rights protections. These well-functioning democratic states seek to maintain and perfect human rights protections domestically. In doing so, they build on a solid foundation of robust civil society and strong institutions, suggesting that human rights regimes are better at protecting rights than extending them to new regions. Indeed, a state's choice to join international regimes and to delegate legal decision-making power to an international tribunal can be explained as a way of locking in the preferences of currently dominant social actors (Moravcsik, 2000). Others have extended this logic to states beyond the core of established democracies.

Ginsburg (2006) argues that newly democratized and democratizing states both use international law as a hand-tying strategy. This lock-in logic extends even to insincere treaty ratifiers. When a nondemocratic state ratifies a treaty in bad faith, a later transition may allow activists to use domestic institutions to enforce what were once empty commitments (von Stein, 2016).

Here, domestic courts play an important role to the extent that they offer a venue for legalized activism. Transnational activists may push a state toward the ratification of an international treaty; those same activists or newly empowered activists may then leverage domestic institutions to ensure compliance (Hathaway, 2007). Indeed, the existence of an independent domestic judiciary may allow domestic enforcement of international human rights laws even in the face of majority opposition (Hathaway, 2005). Simmons (2009) provides the most comprehensive theory along these lines. She argues that international law can change the relative strength of individuals and groups within a state, giving the newly empowered the ability to seek enforcement of rights through a strong, independent domestic judiciary. The key to court relevance in all of these theories is treaty ratification coupled with a strong domestic court system.

The interplay of courts and human rights is, however, more variegated than simple incorporation followed by judicial enforcement, and research has begun to unpack this phenomenon. Domestic compliance with international human rights obligations is not an all-or-nothing proposition; states may simultaneously improve in one area while increasing abuses in an area less prone to scrutiny. For example, courts' usefulness in enforcing human rights obligations may be limited to issue areas with relatively low costs of evidentiary production (Lupu, 2013). Courts provide a place for information to become public; advocacy on the part of NGOs may thereby lead to shifts in patterns of abuse (Hafner-Burton, 2008). Even where they fail to prevent abuses, however, courts seem to play an important role in changing government behavior. In situations in which states derogate from human rights treaty obligations, courts may be unable to prevent derogation but may nonetheless encourage executives to disclose information explaining the derogation (Hafner-Burton et al., 2011). All of these theories demonstrate the important role that domestic courts can play as part of the broader international human rights regime, but the primary mechanism requires treaty ratification alongside a strong judiciary.

A second set of theories shifts the focus from treaty ratification to the diffusion of norms. These norm-based theories are often consistent with, yet run parallel to, theories that focus on adherence to international treaty law.

Here, authors argue that the nature of compliance with international legal obligations is the result of value shifts, either in terms of beliefs about what is appropriate behavior for states, or in terms of the understandings of what is appropriate for domestic actors.[2] Many of these explanations for state behavior rely on the possibility of social interactions to redefine actors' interests. In the classic formulation, international organizations may encourage specific behavior among their members through processes such as back-patting or opprobrium (Johnston, 2001). These organizations provide reassurance for elites or help socialize them to adopt new behavioral modes (Pevehouse, 2002). Over time, this socialization process may redefine the interests of states themselves, and the process of a norm cascade helps explain the role of substate actors in both the promulgation and internalization of these normative shifts. Such processes have the ability to change standards of appropriate behavior, not only for states but for their leaders as well (Finnemore, 1996; Finnemore & Sikkink, 1998; Risse et al., 1999; Sikkink, 2011).

Domestic courts can play a role in this process of norms promulgation by providing an institutional site for the norm to be articulated and adopted. According to Koh (1997), states comply with international law when transnational actors provoke an interaction that requires interpretation and eventual internalization of the norm; domestic courts act as one site for this "transnational legal process."[3] Even in states that do not ratify binding treaties, active, independent courts may be willing to incorporate international law into their jurisprudence by adopting a monist approach (Waters, 2007). As such, these theories see domestic courts as part of a larger, multifaceted process of legal convergence across the international system.

This ideational convergence goes hand in hand with other professional activity across national boundaries, resulting in the formation of judicial networks across the legal profession. This allows courts to engage in collegial discourse leading to legal harmonization through broad doctrinal debates. The historical timing of this discourse may simply be explained by increased globalization and communication among key actors. According to Slaughter (2004), resistance to a single global authority does not obviate the need for collective decision-making; instead, government agencies and decision-makers engage in transnational networks as an alternative form of decentralized global governance. Courts are no different from other government actors in that their sphere of competence inevitably impinges on analogous actors in foreign jurisdictions. Members of the judiciary engage in transnational communication to manage cases that from a purely practical standpoint raise transnational issues, such as corporate bankruptcy proceedings. This transjudicial dialogue has gone much farther than functional needs would suggest, however, with judges routinely citing one another's reasoning in cases dealing with human rights violations, privacy rights, and the death penalty (Slaughter, 2004, p. 101).

Beyond any doctrinal influence such dialogues may have on judicial decisions, the very act of engaging in transnational communication may influence judges at a personal and professional level. Multiple mechanisms may be at play in this convergence toward a common professional identity. Practical elements of professional education may be key, such as training in foreign law or expertise in foreign languages (Law & Chang, 2011). Institutionalized, face-to-face meetings among members of national judiciaries might also play an important role (Slaughter, 2004). Elite participation in transnational tribunals provides one possibility for this elite socialization (Borgen, 2007). Scholars analyzing this process highlight parallel patterns of convergence in judicial actors' understandings of the law, as well as in their sense of professional identity. The heightened level of judicial interaction may reinforce the idea among judges that they perform a particular constitutional role with a separate professional identity (Slaughter, 2004, pp. 101–102) and that this special role empowers courts vis-à-vis other domestic actors (Benvenisti & Downs, 2009). Others have followed a similar sociological tradition to explain that a crucial element of domestic court behavior is the way judges view their role in the constitutional system (Landau, 2005; Scheppele, 2002). This suggests that the transnational legal process goes beyond doctrine to encompass judicial actors and the institutions they occupy. Throughout this process, courts increasingly become sites where international concerns are able to take root within the domestic system.

The (Domestic) Rule of (International) Law

These two clusters of theories—the first focused on treaty ratification and the second on norm internalization—both take seriously an idea first articulated by Slaughter and Alvarez (2000) and reiterated by Slaughter and Burke-White (2006): the future of international law is domestic. As such, domestic courts play a special role in all of the theories, acting as a "transmission belt" between international human rights regimes and domestic rights articulation. While international courts proliferated in the final decades of the twentieth century (Alter, 2013), the flourishing of domestic courts was even greater.

The expansion of domestic judicial power during this period was global in scope (Gauri & Brinks, 2008; Ginsburg, 2003; Hirschl, 2007; Shapiro & Stone Sweet, 2002; Tate & Vallinder, 1995). Even in states following the civil law tradition, the trend toward written constitutions strengthened the hand of the judiciary vis-à-vis legislatures (Merryman & Pérez-Perdomo, 2007).

Constitutional reformers at the domestic level have placed their bets on the ability of courts to entrench democracy and human rights. The creation of a constitutional court has been one important hedging tactic against societal backsliding (Ackerman, 1997). These courts would be the forum, and international law the medium: new democracies incorporated international law into their founding documents at an increasing rate in the post-WWII era (Elkins et al., 2013; Ginsburg et al., 2008). Transitional democracies were more likely than other governments to undertake this incorporation of international law (Ginsburg, 2006).[4] At the same time that political reformers were incorporating international law, they elevated it in the hierarchy of norms, often granting treaty and even customary law supremacy over local legislation (Ginsburg, 2006; Ginsburg et al., 2008). In short, the turn to international human rights regimes and the strengthening of domestic judiciaries followed a similar logic: adherence to a set of institutions could help prevent a return to a darker past. Figure 1 shows the incredible geographic diversity of these states considered to have "transitional regimes" during the last quarter of the twentieth century.[5]

But why courts? After all, domestic courts are but one small piece in a complex array of political, institutional, and ideational forces—it would be

Figure 1. States with Transitional Regimes, 1975–2000.

unrealistic to consider them the sole reason regime liberalization succeeds or fails. Courts are, however, an important and unique piece of this puzzle. Courts represent the fulcrum between an international idea and a domestic material outcome. Importantly, they provide a unique point of access for citizens to leverage human rights law. Unlike international courts, domestic courts are embedded in the domestic political and administrative apparatus. Unlike other domestic political institutions, domestic courts are simultaneously awash in legal normativity that, in the case of international human rights law, is outside the unilateral determination of domestic political actors. They are the one place where international law, domestic institutions, and the public meet, not as part of the political process of campaigns and horse trading but in a self-consciously nonpolitical venue that nonetheless promises a tangible outcome.

This unique institutional setting presents domestic courts with important advantages in the fight to advance human rights. First, domestic courts are directly accessible by their citizens in ways that international courts are not. This is true not just in terms of legal standing but also in terms of pragmatic considerations. A claimant faces fewer practical barriers when dealing with a local court as compared with an international court that is potentially a continent away and operating in a different language. Second, as part of the domestic constitutional structure, courts can issue binding rulings, including injunctions that apply to specific governmental departments or actors, in ways that international courts generally do not. Embeddedness in the domestic system breeds familiarity, and it promises immediate legal effect.

At the same time, domestic courts' unique institutional setting places them in a correspondingly unique peril when adjudicating human rights cases. Many of the potential advantages are also potential risk factors. Take again domestic courts' local embeddedness. Shapiro's (1986) classic formulation of the court describes it as a triad in which two actors seek a neutral third to adjudicate their dispute. One of the main arguments against the efficacy of international tribunals is that they can fulfill the adjudicative function but lack direct enforcement power over state actors. Although at first blush this seems like a meaningful distinction between international and domestic courts, it ignores the fact that domestic courts themselves lack the kind of enforcement power over state institutions that they exercise over private actors. In a dispute between two private actors, the court can be reasonably sure that government actors will enforce rulings. As Staton and Moore (2011) rightly point out, however, the lack of a third party to enforce an international court's decision applies equally to domestic courts when the state itself is a party to the dispute (p. 560). Holding neither the legislature's power of the purse nor the executive's power to compel, domestic courts have long held the reputation of being the least dangerous branch (Bickel, 1986; Hamilton, 2008). But least dangerous in turn means most vulnerable. They are similarly situated to international courts in that enforcement of their rulings is outside their power.

Having its rulings ignored, however, is only one of the challenges a domestic court faces. Consider by way of contrast an international court adjudicating a human rights issue. A state may balk at the international court's ruling; the government may refuse to implement the judgment. Ultimately, the state may repudiate the court's jurisdiction or withdraw from the court's institutional apparatus altogether. Unless the aggrieved state finds other like-minded states, however, at the end of the day an international court will survive the recalcitrant state's ire. In contrast, a domestic court cannot assume such a happy ending. Just like the international court, the domestic court may see its ruling ignored or its reasoning dismissed as unworkable. Unlike the international court, however, a domestic court that offends its government may find itself facing a significantly shortened life span, government-imposed institutional retrenchment, or a court-packing scheme that tames the court by transforming its personnel. Given this predicament, how does a court ever assert itself as a meaningful policy space?

This quandary is a recurring theme in these pages, as it begs the broader question of whether domestic courts can ever act as effective enforcers of international human rights law. Once international law has developed in an issue area, once a state has chosen to ratify a treaty, once domestic political winds have shifted, once human rights aspiration is translated into much less ideal government practice, how do courts respond? Do courts cleave tightly to the demands of international law, thus protecting their claim to be faithful interpreters of the hopeful but often rarified language of "the law"? Or do courts instead pledge allegiance to domestic governmental prerogatives, protecting their institutional longevity at the expense of individual human rights? In short, when do courts matter?

Domestic Courts: Between Possibility and Peril

The answer, it turns out, is surprisingly elusive. Indeed, the ability to elude is at the heart of my argument: courts are at their most effective when they are adept at selectively evading and engaging the attention of two groups:

politicians and the public. Courts face a potential trade-off between immediate enforcement and long-term effectiveness. If a domestic court is able to selectively engage human rights issues on a case-by-case basis—if it can pick its battles—it stands the best chance of acting as an ongoing enforcement mechanism over the long term.

Studies of court enforcement of human rights generally assume that courts do one of two things: rule in favor of a claimant or rule in favor of the government. This intellectual starting point has focused attention on specific types of questions: How do courts gain the institutional strength to rule against governments, and when do governments comply with adverse rulings? Why do courts cite international or foreign law in their rulings? Do courts rule in accordance with their understanding of the law, in pursuit of their sincere policy preferences, or in strategic consideration of politicians' likely response? Are civil law or common law courts more likely to rule against the government? With all of these questions, the inquiry begins where court activity is presumed to end: with the ruling.

My argument arises from the insight that, when deciding cases, courts often have a third option: they can change the outcome not through substantive rulings but through the manipulation of rules governing access, adjudication, and remedies. This recognition that courts generate more than a binary output variable (the ruling) expands our understanding of the factors governing their effectiveness. Courts face a clear dilemma when they are asked to rule against a unified government. Ruling against the government invites backlash; and in such a situation, we might expect the court to capitulate and rule in favor of government actors. Court acquiescence in a substantive ruling, however, may negatively affect the court's legitimacy as a "rule of law" actor and thereby undermine the basis of its claim to exist as a countermajoritarian institution in an otherwise majoritarian democratic system. Courts vary in their ability to overcome this dilemma. Some courts may control procedural mechanisms that allow them to increase the public salience of an issue in hopes of forestalling a backlash. Alternatively, they may reformulate institutional access rules to remove the court from the dispute altogether, in effect retreating to fight another day. Only when such options are not available must a court risk an unpopular ruling that invites backlash or risks its legitimacy.

Whether or not courts are able and willing to accomplish this depends on institutional factors: whether or not international law is embedded in the domestic legal framework, whether the high court develops a public support structure independent of elected branches, and whether or not the court itself controls procedural mechanisms governing access, adjudication, and remedies. The theory developed in the next chapter predicts that courts are most likely to emerge as successful, long-term enforcers of human rights when they occupy institutional settings characterized by high marks in all three of these areas. A high level of embedded internationalism, an orientation toward the public, and a system in which arcane rules are within the court's control all suggest an ability to selectively engage human rights issues. This comes with a trade-off, however. The ability to avoid overly contentious issue areas allows the court to avoid backlash, but it does so at the expense of any immediate ruling. The result is paradoxical: courts that are successful over the long term are unlikely in the short term to consistently offer a hospitable forum to support human rights across the full panoply of potential issue areas.

Given this troubling paradox, how can we define success, and which courts achieve success? I turn to these questions in Chapter 2. There, I first lay out a theory of domestic courts as strategic, legitimacy-seeking enforcers of international human rights law. I draw on the judicial politics literature to elucidate the strategic approach to court activity on which I base my theory. I expand on this foundation by demonstrating how, for courts, strategic behavior depends on the ability to provide legally legitimate rulings. The court's strategic, legitimacy-seeking calculus is conditioned by several institutional factors. First, does international law constitute an embedded feature of the domestic legal landscape? Second, does the court enjoy broad links to societal actors beyond the political elite? Lastly, and most important, does the court's institutional development allow for creative articulations of procedural law? Where the answer to each question is yes, I argue, a domestic court has the highest likelihood of maintaining relevance in the sphere of human rights policy. For a court in a new democracy, it is this ability to maintain relevance that serves as the mark of success.

CHAPTER 2

Three-Dimensional Decision-Making in the Domestic Judiciary

Consequences

Under what conditions do apex courts in democratizing regimes entrench international human rights protections? Scholars of comparative judicial politics increasingly talk about courts being "consequential" (Kapiszewski et al., 2013). Courts may act as veto players, incentivize activists to mobilize, directly oversee policy implementation, or act as public fora for debate, thereby heightening awareness of an issue. In any of these situations, the court has a meaningful impact on government policy. Those who bring a case may not get exactly what they want, but the judicial process changes the outcome from what it might otherwise have been. Judicialization has consequences.

As discussed in Chapter 1, several theories of human rights regimes expect domestic courts to play this consequential role in policy formulation by linking the world of international law to a domestic legal outcome. This heavy burden takes many forms. Domestic courts may act as translators of international norms, aiding a norm cascade by reformulating its provisions in ways that make sense for the domestic constitutional settlement. Courts may provide an institutional focal point, providing an alternative forum for individuals or groups to directly invoke the rights guaranteed in treaties. Courts may act as lock-in mechanisms, acting as veto players that prevent rights retrenchment following treaty ratification. The myriad theories constitute multiple formulations of a single promise: courts will protect human rights. To understand how and when domestic courts will rise to such lofty expectations, it is necessary to treat them as more than legal conduits. The focus by necessity turns to the operation of those courts within the domestic political environment and how these courts balance the demands of international law with the many other political demands any domestic institution must face.

Courts as Political Actors

A belief in law's independent force lies at the heart of international human rights regimes. And yet today few if any social scientists would assert that legal decision-making exists independently of social and political forces. The approach taken in this project threads this needle by recognizing that courts are strategic actors but that the strategy they pursue depends necessarily on their treating the law as an independent force. Treating the law *as if* it were independent of political concerns is itself a political strategy, one which courts follow as a means of accruing legitimacy in a democratic system.

The extent to which courts hand down legal rulings without concern for political factors is a foundational issue. The assumption that law acts as its own, insulated force—legal formalism—is a claim that most commentators today reject on its face. This was not always the case. At the start of the twentieth century, legal interpretations were undergirded by classical legal assumptions of formalism and autonomy. Legal questions were seen as consisting of doctrinal puzzles that could be solved through logic, or at times by reference to the moral reasoning of natural law. The law was understood to act as an autonomous field of human inquiry, and as such was not seen to answer to political strategy or instrumentalism (Bodansky, 2015). Legal realism successfully challenged these notions, asserting not just the political nature of legal reasoning but also the political utility of law: the law itself could be a means to an end. The idea that courts provide an apolitical institutional output informed solely by legal formalism has never recovered from the challenge put forth by the legal realist school in the 1920s and 1930s. Social scientists today are the heirs to this empirical approach to the law.

As a result, the debate in recent years has focused on the relative balance among judges' own political preferences, the strategic constraints imposed by external political institutions, and the limiting effects (if any) of legal doctrine on institutional decision-making. Academics, practitioners, and judges themselves have not, however, fully jettisoned the legal approach. Fealty to law-based decision-making remains an at times dubious but nevertheless relevant consideration. The concepts of precedent and stare decisis affirm the ongoing influence of past judicial decisions. The concern with legislative intent similarly represents an assertion of law's autonomy, with legal text and the motives behind it serving as a real constraint on judicial decision-making (Segal, 2010). It must also be recognized, of course, that members of the judiciary still regularly claim that the law has an independent force. Many judges would dispute any accusation of partisanship, arguing that the law, not political affiliation, guides their decision-making.

This conception of law as a force independent of politics achieved its purest theoretical form in Kelsen's formulation of an apex court as guarantor of the constitutional order (1961). Playing this guardian role would require a strict adherence to legal norms. Any devolution into politics—into power seeking on the court's own behalf—would compromise the unique role of the court, calling into question the reasons for its very existence. Of course, there is a gulf between this theory and actual practice. A constitution, after all, is nothing if not a map of power relations within a society. *Pace* Kelsen, any attempt to control the workings of those power relationships—even if only to maintain balance across its moving parts—inherently involves an assertion of political power. A nonpolitical court that maintains the political order is, at its most fundamental level, a contradiction in terms.

Scholars of judicial politics attempt to right this conceptual paradox. Three approaches dominate this discussion: the attitudinal approach, the strategic approach, and historical institutionalism (Whittington et al., 2010). Both the attitudinal and strategic approaches start with an assumption that judging is one more way in which actors promote personal policy preferences. Historical institutionalism complicates this by recognizing the possibility that law informs any strategic calculation. All three approaches have emerged out of the American context, but their assumptions and methods are increasingly reflected in accounts of comparative and international law and politics, and their insights provide guidance to the analysis of court activity undertaken in this book.

The first two approaches, the attitudinal and the strategic, offer clear rejections of the idea that law, in and of itself, binds judicial decision-making. Judges, like all other societal actors, have policy preferences. It is not surprising, these approaches assume, for judges to decide the cases before them in line with those preferences, seeing as courts are just another arena for public policy formulation. According to the attitudinal approach, judicial preferences are all that matter. In contrast, the strategic approach recognizes that other institutions constrain the ability of judicial actors to achieve outcomes that align perfectly with sincerely held preferences. Of particular concern are those political institutions that constitute the balance-of-power framework. The executive and the legislature are the institutions most capable and likely to check a high court, so it is with regard to these political institutions that the court must tailor its decisions.

Although the attitudinal and strategic models of judicial behavior often appear in tension, they are, in many respects, compatible approaches with differing emphases. For example, when Segal and Spaeth (2002) argue that judges decide cases in line with their sincere preferences, they acknowledge that institutional constraints theoretically could limit these decisions. They note, however, that these constraints tend to be absent when dealing with an institution such as the U.S. Supreme Court. Likewise, strategic models do not disagree with the assumption of sincerely held judicial preferences but rather predict that the articulation of these preferences will be limited by prospective interactions with other branches of government. The latitude for sincere policy proclamations by judges will vary according to the institutional configuration in which the court operates.

Attitudinal and strategic models have in common their treatment of institutions as platforms for the articulation of preexisting policy choices. Actors are rational, and as such they are able to use institutions to further their policy goals. Institutions do not, however, define actor interests themselves. In this telling, the maxim that where one sits determines where one stands is misguided, if not entirely incorrect. Where one sits instead determines how one goes about achieving the goals for which one already stood. This shared basis clearly distinguishes attitudinal and strategic approaches from pure legal approaches; the latter instead assume that logic and formalism determine the outcome of cases, not an individual's policy preferences. In the latter approach, the judge serves merely as a conduit through which the spirit of the law is animated. To be sure, a judge may hold policy views independent of the law, but those views constitute variables extrinsic to the legal process. A judicial actor seeking to impose sincere policy preferences of her own (no matter how institutionally constrained) is, in the law-centric worldview, yet another contradiction in terms.

Here, the third approach to studying judicial politics, historical institutionalism, provides guidance by helping to bridge the law and politics dilemma. In particular, and in contrast to adherents of attitudinal or strategic models, historical institutionalism accepts that norms, rules, and accepted patterns of behavior can inform the preferences of actors within those institutions. Institutions, then, are not merely the playground on which strategic choice occurs; institutions also inform the preferences that strategic actors pursue (Smith, 2010). The recognition that institutions can inform, and not merely constrain, preferences opens up important avenues for exploring the role of legal doctrine within an otherwise strategic analytic framework. For courts, legal doctrine is an important aspect of institutional makeup, and as such can be analyzed as an influence on actors' preference formation, as well as a constraint on the ability of actors to achieve their policy goals once those preferences have formed. Judicial actors do not have to behave cynically in seeking the court's institutional legitimacy in a democratic system; those in the court do not even have to behave in a self-consciously strategic manner. The institution itself already reflects and informs the preferences of those who operate within its walls. They act strategically by acting sincerely, with law as their guiding institutional framework.

This is the approach adopted here. For courts, strategic behavior and legalism are bound up with one another. The court's legitimacy depends at least in part on other actors having faith in the court's legal expertise and ability to operate from a position of political neutrality. In short, to act strategically, a court must (appear to) provide legally sound rulings. It builds its legitimacy—and political power—by acting in an avowedly apolitical manner. Law *is* the court's strategy. This is how an undemocratic institution is sold to a democratic populace.

Building Legitimacy

This is particularly important when considering the multiple sources of institutional support on which courts rely when constructing their authority. In states undergoing democratization, all branches of government are tasked with building their authority, distancing themselves from the previous regime's unpopular policies, and securing the buy-in of a newly empowered citizenry. A court—whether newly established or newly reformed—must build its authority from the ground up. For newly empowered judiciaries, every decision either contributes to or draws upon a relatively shallow reserve of societal good will. These young courts cannot simply assume compliance with a ruling, as could a long-established court in a mature democracy. In this one respect, at least, apex courts have more in common with other local institutions than with their older, foreign, judicial brethren.

Gibson (2012) notes the challenges courts have in establishing legitimacy in democratic societies, where elections and accountability serve as the primary sources of legitimacy (p. 88). Although theoretically elections could be a source of court legitimacy, popular judicial elections are exceedingly rare globally. Even in the United States, a country regularly seen as an outlier due to its practice of electing judges, the ultimate determiners of legality—Supreme Court justices—are subject to only the most attenuated form of electoral accountability through the appointment process. As for accountability following their appointment, these justices are constitutionally guaranteed *not* to be accountable to the public. This lack of pre- or post-appointment public accountability is indeed the norm globally. Given this, how do courts establish legitimacy in the face of the so-called "countermajoritarian difficulty"? This is actually a two-part question. First, in this context what is meant by legitimacy? Second, how do domestic courts go about developing that legitimacy?

The term "legitimacy," with its close etymological link to "law," is particularly relevant when analyzing courts. On its face, the term invokes a sense of institutional authority, acceptance, and appropriateness. Such a capacious term, however, lends itself to multiple uses and thus to significant ambiguity. Fallon's (2005) study of legitimacy examines the multitude of meanings this term bears and is informative for the present discussion. Although he wrote of the American constitutional context, his treatment provides guidance when analyzing judicial legitimacy around the globe. He explains that discussions of legitimacy simultaneously draw on distinct but interwoven understandings. Two of these understandings, legal and sociological legitimacy, are particularly important to the consideration of courts in young democracies.

Legal legitimacy implies simply that a court has acted in a way that reflects the law. A court acts in a legally legitimate manner when its ruling is in line with a correct or reasonable interpretation of the law. It does not mean that no alternative reading of the law is possible, but merely that the court has offered what could be described as a reasonably plausible interpretation according to the standards of the relevant legal community (Roux, 2009, p. 109). The plausibility of a ruling is what matters. If every legal dispute had a simple answer, there would be no role for lawyers, judges, or courts. To claim that a ruling is legally legitimate, then, is not the same as saying that it was the only correct reading. Another court may have concluded differently. Indeed, this is the premise upon which courts of appeal operate, overturning rulings as incorrect without dismissing the judges who issued the original rulings as corrupt or incompetent. Legal legitimacy encompasses rulings that are later determined to be incorrect, so long as they do not reflect an abuse of discretion.[1] It is this sense of legal legitimacy to which I refer throughout the rest of this project when speaking of the "legitimacy" of a specific court ruling.

Sociological legitimacy, on the other hand, refers not to the legal community's acceptance of a ruling's interpretive plausibility but to the broader public's acceptance of the relevant institution's claim of authority. This sense of authority, importantly, should not come from a fear of punishment or hope for material gain but rather from a belief in the appropriateness of obedience to the authority in question. This aligns closely with the rational-legal form of legitimate domination described by Weber (1978, pp. 212–226). This sociological legitimacy in turn encompasses several different forms of public regard, including authoritative, substantive, and institutional legitimacy.

The first two forms, authoritative and substantive legitimacy, color the public reception of particular acts. In the case of courts, this means individual judicial rulings. When the court possesses authoritative legitimacy, the public believes it ought to obey a ruling, whether or not that particular ruling was correctly decided. Substantive legitimacy must surpass a higher hurdle. To claim substantive legitimacy the public must believe that the content of the individual ruling was the correct outcome. Hence, this type of legitimacy is also referred to as "content legitimacy." What distinguishes substantive legitimacy from the legal variety is in large part the audience. Substantive legitimacy, like other forms of sociological legitimacy, concerns the general public. Legal legitimacy, meanwhile, is less concerned with public opinion than with the judgment of the relevant legal audience. Obviously, this legal legitimacy often overlaps with the other forms of legitimacy. Indeed, the broader sociological legitimacy of the court, as an institution, is bound up with and draws upon the legal legitimacy of its rulings.[2]

Institutional legitimacy is the one form of sociological legitimacy that takes as its object the court as a whole, rather than individual decisions. It is particularly important as a buttress for the court's institutional longevity, as it reflects public support. This form of legitimacy is located in the general public's belief that the institution in question is fair and competent and produces rulings that are worthy of respect and compliance, even if at times individual rulings are not in line with one's individual preferences. A young court's institutional legitimacy begins with the legal plausibility of its rulings. In constructing this reputation of legal legitimacy, of an authoritative interpreter of the law, the court secures its role in the institutional apparatus of government. In other words, over time the legal legitimacy of individual rulings may accrete into a broader sociological legitimacy for the court as a whole. When a court (or other institution) holds this type of institutional legitimacy, social scientists would consider it as having "diffuse support" among the public (Gibson et al., 1998; Gibson & Caldeira, 1995).

Social scientists measure diffuse support through the use of opinion polls. This serves as a useful proxy, but it is an imperfect proxy for the broader question animating this project: does a court play a meaningful role in protecting human rights. Public support for a judicial institution does not directly result in the court's rulings being implemented. Rather, public support acts indirectly by alleviating the threat that political actors—who themselves *are* directly responsible to the public—will challenge the court. This real threat of electoral loss is one mechanism by which politicians are convinced to grant the court its ongoing role in the political system (Vanberg, 2005).

This is not, of course, the only incentive shaping political actors' treatment of courts. Diffuse support acts as a buttress against political actors who might otherwise seek retribution when the court rules against them, to be sure. But just as elites can attack an apex court, so too can they support it when doing so furthers elite interests—regardless of whether or not the public has much faith in the judicial institution in question. In other words, a court may benefit from elite support not mediated by public concern. Elites may find a court useful for enforcing legal bargains (Landes & Posner, 1975), for example, or political actors in transitional regimes may support a court because they fear future electoral losses (Finkel, 2005; Ginsburg, 2003; Hirschl, 2000). Of course, even here the future shadow of legal legitimacy should not be discounted too greatly. After all, present politicians have little reason to support the court today if they have no faith that the court will, in the future, be able or willing to interpret the law faithfully as the politicians have written it. Even among these strategic political actors, a kernel of faith in legal interpretation undergirds their calculations. Legally legitimate rulings are the currency with which courts purchase their institutional legitimacy, whether directly from self-interested politicians or through the middleman of diffuse public support.

To summarize, there are many paths by which a court may find itself playing a meaningful role in the political system. The legal legitimacy of particular rulings may lead to a broader institutional legitimacy, which in turn incentivizes compliance by elected officials who fear voter punishment. Alternatively, elected officials may have incentives for supporting a court regardless of voter attention, providing further space for a court to act as a meaningful policy space. Institutional legitimacy, once acquired, may provide a court with room to maneuver in the domestic institutional environment, and help ensure the longevity of a young court. How this plays out in the context of international human rights law is the focus of the next section.

A Theory of Legally Constrained Strategic Behavior

Courts are rightly concerned about their institutional legitimacy, and they face challenges to this legitimacy from political actors as well as the broader public, who are tolerant of nonmajoritarian institutions only to the degree that those institutions are not hostile to broadly accepted policy goals. At the same time, the public may at times become a source of support, providing a court with a buttress against political backlash. In the realm of international human rights law, the process of building legitimacy is complicated further by the fact that the court may have to engage international law in addition to the domestic legal framework it is already expected to oversee.

Returning to the traditional strategic account of judicial decision-making provides a useful entry point for this discussion. This approach provides a unidimensional account of judicial politics that highlights the court's interactions with elected officials. This classic balance-of-power framework begins with a consideration of the attitudinal and strategic decision-making accounts of judicial behavior. Consider the simplified policy space in Figure 2, adapted from Epstein, Knight, and Martin's (2001) familiar framework. The horizontal line represents a domestic policy space, with points representing various institutions' respective policy preferences: from left to right, C represents the ideal point of the court; L represents the preferred policy of the median legislator; and E represents the ideal point of the executive. To give meaning to these points in the context of international human rights law, we could imagine that points to the left are more in line with the demands of international human rights commitments, and those to the right are increasingly in conflict with those rights. One could imagine, for example, points farther to the right representing policy positions that are restrictive of free speech, and points to the left representing policies more protective of speech. Alternatively, points to the right could indicate policies that refuse to acknowledge informed consent of indigenous groups to development on their lands, and points to the left could indicate policies that fully incorporate indigenous groups into decision-making practices. And so on.

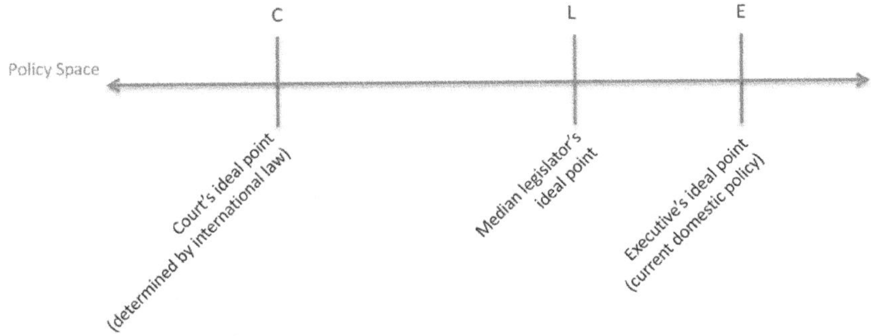

Figure 2. Law-Based Decision-Making. Adapted from Epstein, Knight, and Martin (2001).

A current domestic policy, representing the executive's ideal policy point, is represented along the continuum by point E. In a state with an independent judiciary that is tasked with enforcing legal commitments, the court's policy preference is indicated farther to the left, at point C, representing a policy in compliance with international law. (The assumption at this stage is the same one that is often made in the literature on legalized international human rights regimes—namely, that a duly ratified treaty will be enforced sincerely by an independent court.) The median legislator's ideal policy position is represented by point L. A domestic claimant then brings a legal challenge, arguing that international law requires overturning the domestic policy in favor of the international legal commitment (point C). According to this simplified approach to analyzing decision-making by the court, one would expect the court to rule in favor of the claimant, overturning the domestic policy in favor of one in line with commitments to international law.

The strategic court model predicts a different outcome, as depicted in Figure 3. Although a court might prefer to set the domestic policy at its ideal point, it is also aware of institutional constraints. In particular, it is aware that legislative actors have an ideal policy position at point L. As such, the indifference point for the political actors between the current policy and an unacceptably "international" court ruling would be represented by point I. (Points I and E are equidistant from the median legislator's ideal point, L. Because current policy has not provoked a legislative response, presumably neither would a policy at point I.) Knowing this, the court is also aware that any ruling to the left of point I would invite backlash, which could take the form of a new law at point L and also possibly undermine the court's institutional

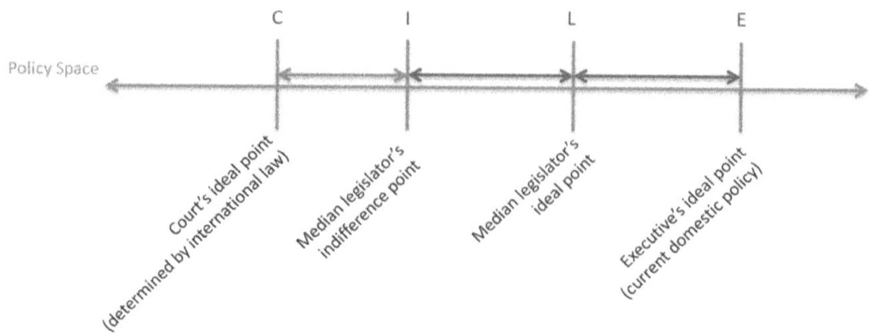

Figure 3. Strategic Decision-Making. Adapted from Epstein, Knight, and Martin (2001).

power. As such, a strategic court should rule at point I—closer to incorporated international law (and thus the court's ideal point) but not so far outside the legislative actors' acceptable policy preferences so as to invite a response.

Most strategic accounts, therefore, conclude that the court in these situations can be expected to rule in favor of a policy position at point I, since it represents the policy closest to the court's preferred outcome that is still able to avoid legislative backlash. This strategic account provides important insights owing to its concern with a single dimension of judicial politics: the interaction between the court and the elected political branches. This balance-of-power consideration is, for purposes of my theory, the "first dimension" of consideration. In the sections that follow, I build on this model by adding two more dimensions. The second dimension accounts for the court's relationship with international law. The third concerns the court's relationship with the public. The second and third dimensions taken together help account for a crucial element of judicial decision-making that is often left out of strategic models: legitimacy.

Internationalism: Superficial versus Embedded

A court's first dimension of consideration is interbranch relations—the classic balance-of-power consideration at the heart of traditional accounts of judicial politics. This suggests, however, that elected officials are the only audience for judicial policy output. This is a difficult assumption to sustain. Once we jettison the idea that a court is interested only in espousing "true" readings of "the law," with no accounting for politics, we must in fairness consider other potential audiences that could influence the strategic calculus. If courts prospectively tailor their rulings to take into account the reactions of elected officials, it seems reasonable to assume court actors may also take into account other audiences of concern to international human rights law: namely, the international-human-rights legal community and the domestic public. These, respectively, constitute the second and third dimensions of consideration for the theory presented in this chapter.

The litigants in the opening pages of this book had an expectation that a domestic court would enforce international human rights law. Academic theorists and constitutional reformers in transitional states place similar expectations on these young institutions. In the model I have outlined, the court's ideal point (point C) is taken to reflect international legal norms—hence the possibility of tension with elected political leaders when actual policy deviates from the demands of international law. For any of this to hold true, the court must be invested in international law. It must perceive international law to be part of its legal mandate and of concern to its audiences; otherwise, enforcing international law would play no role in the court's strategic quest to build institutional legitimacy over time by issuing legally legitimate rulings. I refer to variation along this dimension as "international embeddedness"—the degree to which the domestic system incentivizes a court's consideration of international human rights norms.

When analyzing such variation, one traditional approach has been to categorize a state as either "monist" or "dualist" in terms of its legal system's relationship with international law. States following the monist tradition treat domestic and international law as a single body of law, with international law directly incorporated into the state's legal system. The dualist approach conceives of domestic and international law as two distinct, independent fields; for states following this tradition, international law would be seen as having no binding force until domestic political incorporation through legislation. Unfortunately, this legal formalism is less helpful in predicting how states actually function across a wide variety of issue areas (D. L. Sloss, 2020). South Africa and the United States, for example, have often been considered monist, given their constitutional elevation of international law, yet both states have adopted doctrines that allow only some treaties to be self-executing or that allow for the legislature to disregard international law. For purposes of this project, therefore, I eschew a strictly formalistic approach in favor of a bifurcated understanding of the domestic legal system's relationship to international law. Instead, I examine international embeddedness as a variable operating at two levels, the first institutional and the second professional. The first concerns the degree to which international human rights law is formally incorporated, either through treaty ratifications or constitutional elevation of international law. The second focuses on the degree to which members of the court are themselves ensconced in a professional network dedicated to international human rights such that we might reasonably expect them to factor international law into their rulings.

The first level considers whether or not international law is embedded in formal domestic legal institutions, as represented by the constitution's treatment of international law and the government's ratification of treaties. As outlined in Chapter 1, a hallmark of the third wave of democratization was not just the establishment and strengthening of independent judiciaries alongside human rights commitments. This wave of democratization occurred at a period when liberal internationalism's human rights rhetoric was at its zenith. As such, constitutional reforms were carried out as part of a "plugging in" to international human rights regimes, often explicitly linking international human rights with a guarantee of protections against democratic backsliding. Some states incorporated the language of international human rights treaties without ratifying the treaties themselves; others have done the reverse. Some states' constitutions require laws to conform with international law; others put treaty law on the same level as national law. The most ambitious require court consideration of international law, empowering courts to reject laws that do not pass muster. Whether a state ratifies treaties and the degree to which the constitution elevates international law are indicators of a court's institutional prerogatives. The failure of a court to take international law into consideration under these circumstances would call into question a decision's legal legitimacy.

Constitutions and treaty ratifications do more than provide binding legal source material, however; they also provide meaningful rhetorical guidance. (It is here that I part ways with the formal legalism of the monist-dualist approach.) In addition to providing formal legal guidance to courts, constitutions offer a meaningful signal as to what goals a society considers to be important and valid, both in terms of the society's aspirations for the future and as a rejection of past mistakes not to be repeated (Scheppele, 2003). A court seeking to build its legitimacy with various domestic constituencies can look to the constitution—and to the number of human rights treaties that were or were not ratified at the time of democratization—as an indication of a society's constitutional settlement. Certain courts have proven to be adept, after all, at modulating the balance of domestic and international legal source material. They may avoid known international precedent in favor of domestic sources of law; similarly, they may cite foreign and international law to bolster the legitimacy of rulings that respond to domestic contingencies (Roy, 2004; Smithey, 2001). Constitutional elevation of international law and multiple treaty ratifications, therefore, suggest a court would have strategic—as well as legal—reasons to make appeals to international human rights law.

In addition to this institutional element, a court's international embeddedness is reflected in the professional and reputational concerns of justices themselves. As discussed in Chapter 1, professional identities are bound up to greater or lesser degrees in professional networks that cross borders. These may begin with common educational backgrounds, face-to-face meetings at conferences, or intellectual cross-pollination that occurs in case citations or law journals. In any event, this transjudicial dialogue has the potential to enmesh formerly domestic actors in increasingly international exchanges that both inform their intellectual outlook and guide their professional considerations. When a judge's educational background has provided grounding in international human rights law, that judge is, ceteris paribus, more likely to be able to draw on these resources. When the justice herself considers participation in international forums, overseas teaching, or work in foreign venues to be part of her professional identity, this likewise indicates a heightened personal sensitivity to international considerations. These indicators, both educational and professional, can be examined for individual judges to determine the extent to which they participate in increasingly internationalized conceptions of the judiciary. The more justices share this international perspective, the more likely a court is to exhibit a concern for international human rights law in its judicial calculations. This could be either because international law informs the sincerely held preferences of those on the court or because international networks form a part of the professional audience for rulings. In either case, the degree of international embeddedness in the form of professional networks should influence court output.

These factors—institutional and professional—determine the degree to which a court's institutional environment is characterized by embedded internationalism and thus the degree to which international law will act as a constraint on court rulings. In this theory and in the case studies, I examine the extent to which the constitution and professional networks reflect this international embeddedness. When the constitution calls on the court to enforce international human rights law and the justices are predisposed to do so due to professional considerations, the court's institutional environment is characterized by fully embedded internationalism. When only one of these factors is present (formal legal context or professional formation), the court's institutional environment is deemed moderately embedded. When both factors are absent, the court's environment reflects, at best, superficially embedded internationalism. The greater the degree of embedded internationalism, the more likely a court will be to consider this second dimension of legitimacy-seeking alongside the first dimension of balance-of-power concerns. The third and final audience that a court must consider is the domestic public. Like political actors and the international legal community, this audience provides a third dimension of consideration as the court builds its legitimacy.

Support Orientation: Public versus Elite

The public provides an alternative means of institutional support for the judiciary. Courts in transitional regimes may begin with very little diffuse support from the public, either because they are entirely new or because they are, like other governmental institutions, starting from a place of reform. In either case, a strategy that seeks to build institutional legitimacy by proactively accommodating government rights violations is unlikely to succeed. The court may survive, but it will not build a public base of support in the process. Yet locking in rights protections—and presumably constraining the elected political branches when they violate rights—is one of the primary reasons these courts are created or strengthened during times of transition. Building public support allows courts to serve this function. Young courts can slowly build their legitimacy by ruling against government actors only to the extent that the overall population gains (Carrubba, 2009). When society is more aware of legal issues, it raises the electoral stakes for political actors' noncompliance with judicial rulings (Vanberg, 2005). Courts are also apparently less passive than generally acknowledged in this process; they actively attempt to publicize important cases (Staton, 2006). In effect, under certain circumstances courts are able to balance the public against political actors.

Of course, building this reservoir of institutional legitimacy takes time. It also requires, obviously, an engaged public. Under what conditions can a court cultivate the public such that the court can balance the public against political actors? As a practical concern, different elements of the court system matter. First, can the public access the courts to protect their rights, or is access instead restricted to a small portion of societal actors? Second, does the legal system empower courts throughout the judicial system to hear and rule on cases challenging government actions, or is this important oversight limited to a single court? The first reflects the ability of societal actors to seek judicial review; the second represents the court system's capacity to provide this review. Together, these two factors determine whether a court system—and its provision of rights enforcement—is open only to elites or offers a resource to the population more generally. When, in turn, the court looks for institutional support, does it rely exclusively on the elite, or does it also turn to the public? I term this dimension of consideration the "support orientation." Is the court system oriented toward the public or toward elites?

To determine this, we must first know how broadly accessible the court system is. Domestic political incentives often provide the impetus for judicial reform, and a stronger, more independent court system is often the result. Access to this court, however, varies significantly. In some states, only political actors may bring claims that a law is unconstitutional. In others, the standing to challenge legislation is dispersed more widely. In some systems, court review of legislation can only happen after the legislation has passed; in others, it can happen before. When access is limited, the court system is unlikely to become a meaningful part of most citizen's lives. In such situations, the court is restricted to an elite support orientation; the public simply does not provide a latent resource for the court to engage and cultivate, and the court has to concern itself primarily with balance-of-power considerations (the first dimension). In contrast, court systems in which citizens enjoy broad access should provide more fertile ground for the court to develop a public support orientation that allows for the eventual balancing of the public (the third dimension) against political actors.

In addition to access, the possibility of a public support orientation depends on whether courts other than the apex court are empowered to engage in constitutional review. This is in some ways the flip side of access. Whereas "access" refers to the public's ability to enter the court, the "locus of constitutional review" refers to the ability of a court to entertain public claims. In diffuse review systems, such as those in the United States or Argentina, the power of judicial review exists throughout the court system—all courts of general jurisdiction are empowered to review government actions, providing numerous points of entry to check government behavior. In concentrated review systems, meanwhile, this review power is centralized in a single apex court, as envisioned by Kelsen. A concentrated locus of review is theoretically appealing in the Kelsenian framework, as it conveys the illusion of an apolitical body separate and apart from the political system and broader judicial system; the apex court is engaged solely in the protection of the constitutional structure. The reality tends to be more problematic. In concentrated systems, the single apex court risks becoming highly politicized due to the nature of its mandate (Epstein, Knight, & Shvetsova, 2001; Ginsburg, 2003). In addition, because these politicized judicial actors are located in a single institutional site, political actors themselves are more readily able to shape the court's membership. As Dahl (1957) noted more than half a century ago in the United States, a court's ideal policy point will only deviate from political actors until political actors have had the opportunity to appoint new judges—even in independent court systems. Indeed, constitutional courts in newly democratized states are often the embodiment of "judicialization from above"—the attempt to ensure that relevant judicial decisions are made by individuals whose policy preferences approximate those of politicians, be they members of the outgoing regime or the newly empowered (Hirschl, 2008; Roux, 2018).

Diffuse systems of review disrupt this process; they provide less efficient principal-agent monitoring by politicians (Stone Sweet, 2000, p. 134). In addition to making monitoring more difficult, a diffuse review system also makes retroactive control harder: replacing all judges throughout a court system is simply not as easy as replacing those sitting in a single apex court. The conservative project to reshape the American judiciary in the late twentieth century, for example, was a generational project that had as its target not just the Supreme Court but also the broader judiciary and its legal support structure (Teles, 2012).

Diffusion offers yet another advantage: the judicial system has the potential to become publicly relevant across society, not only to those at the top of the political system. A court system in which citizens have broad access to the system and can use it to challenge government rights violations increases the salience of legal issues in the public mind. This, in turn, increases the likelihood that the public will see the court system as a resource to be protected against political attack. Moreover, broad linkages between the public and the court system mean that the apex court is able to draw on a much broader base of information when selecting and ruling on cases. In systems in which courts throughout a state hear claims against the government, the apex court is better positioned to gauge the relative importance of issues and to determine the degree to which general consensus has or has not emerged. In short, a system of diffuse review allows the judiciary to work as a learning system, and the apex court benefits from this elucidation of societal demand.[3] A corollary effect is that the apex court may be better positioned to shape its interactions with the general population. When litigants attempt to bring claims that are politically toxic, a diffuse system may provide the high court with the ability to abstain from interceding against the government through procedural tools such as declining to certify an appeal.

A public support orientation, then, points to two latent resources for the court. First, it provides an alternative base of support for the court, potentially freeing it over time to balance the public against political actors. This complicates the strategic analysis in any single case, but in such a way as to potentially shield a rights-affirming court from backlash. Second, a court with an institutional orientation that provides broad access to the public benefits from these increased societal linkages. On the one hand, broad access means increased legal salience for the public. On the other hand, it means the court system as a whole is a learning system with the potential to pick and choose cases, avoiding the most difficult and embracing those that allow it to accrue further legitimacy. A public support orientation guarantees that a legitimacy-seeking court has a third dimension of consideration. The result is a court whose legitimacy-seeking strategic calculus is informed by balance-of-power issues with the elected political branches (the first dimension), its legal legitimacy under international law (the second dimension), and its diffuse support among the public (the third dimension). How a court orients itself among these three dimensions is, finally, constrained by its procedural environment.

Procedural Environment: Constrained versus Flexible

Most current theories of international relations discount the important distinction between substantive and procedural law at the domestic level. Scholars of international relations and international law have a keen awareness of the important interplay of the substance of domestic and international law, as represented by the large literature on transnational judicial process and dialogue. Few scholars have looked at the flip side of the coin: the procedural rules governing domestic hearings about legal obligations. In general, this concern with procedure has been left to comparative and Americanist scholars. Tushnet (2009) examines macro-level procedural norms, such as the judicial review of statutes and the horizontal effect of constitutional rights.[4] Ginsburg (2003) discusses the effect on constitutional court jurisprudence of restricting court access to political institutions. Staszak's research on retrenchment highlights the importance of procedural rules in determining the contours of the American judiciary (Staszak, 2010).

When the international human rights literature enters this discussion, it remains primarily focused on international or regional courts. Keohane et al. (2000) provide the theoretical framework that outlines the importance of court access in the context of international legal disputes. For the two decades before and after their article, empirical work maintained a focus on international or regional courts, and it continues to do so. One of the most important examinations of procedural rules remains Stein's (1981) examination of the role of direct effect in the constitutionalization of the European court system. Similarly, Burley and Mattli (1993) demonstrate how the reference mechanism of Article 177 of the Rome Treaty (the treaty establishing the European Economic Community) empowered the Court of Justice of the European Union by procedurally linking it to domestic courts.[5] Alter and Helfer (2009) explore an analogous relationship between domestic court reference mechanisms to the Andean court. Along similar lines, Cichowski (2006) finds an important role for the European Court of Human Rights in assisting European citizens in gaining access to supranational and national courts. These regional approaches, however, focus on procedural mechanisms linking domestic court systems, judicial actors, and legal claimants to international institutions, not on the links between citizens and their own courts. It is as if domestic variation in procedural laws were of little consequence in effectuating international human rights regimes.

Overall, then, the role of procedural rules in international human rights regimes has concentrated on two distinct arenas: procedural rules at the regional court level and procedural rules linking the domestic system to the international regime. This neglects the important, distinct procedural environment within the domestic judicial system. These purely domestic mechanisms influence the development and enforcement of international laws within domestic courts, and they vary greatly across domestic judicial regimes. As such, the focus has begun to shift, but only slowly. We see the importance of domestic procedural variation in more recent studies that have examined the link between domestic procedures and international substance. Lupu (2013) emphasizes the important role of evidentiary standards in prosecuting human rights violations. He finds that treaty ratification only improves rights outcomes when the cost of producing justiciable evidence is relatively low. Michel (2018) demonstrates the importance of a victim's right to private prosecution under procedural law in Latin America; the ability of a court to review a prosecutor's decision *not* to prosecute a crime increases the likelihood that a victim can seek justice. As Lupu and Michel demonstrate, this variation matters for domestic enforcement—yet there is much more variation to uncover.

By focusing on domestic procedural rules, we gain significant explanatory leverage. First, it allows a discussion of court enforcement to go beyond the well-worn territories of the European Union, where a much stronger history of institutional integration exists among member states and supranational institutions. The sui generis nature of the European system counsels against easy transference of the theories developed there to other regional systems, or to the international system generally, where institutional mechanisms linking local courts to international courts are less well developed or simply nonexistent. Second, and perhaps more importantly, a focus on domestic procedural mechanisms allows an examination of the ways in which courts are able to operate covertly. In particular, this elucidates court behavior even when rulings are not made and the court thereby avoids political backlash or public criticism. Laws prohibiting torture, protecting privacy, guaranteeing health care, and other core protections—these all comprise important legal regimes that are likely to be not only substantively rich but also relatively well known and debated in society. They form the focal points around which activists coalesce and political pressure builds. The law itself consists, however, both of these primary rules that govern society and what Hart (1997) calls secondary rules: the rules that govern primary rules. Rules governing access to courts, the ability to bring claims, the right to challenge a ruling, the determination of precedent, the oversight of remedial measures—these secondary rules shape the ability to create and enforce primary rules, but because of their technical and at times opaque nature, they are much less likely to attract broad-based public attention. The groups among whom these secondary rules do attract attention are invariably lawyers and judges, as it is they who are trained in the use of these elite tools.

Rules governing access vary according to legal family and local custom, and they include the rules that govern standing, private prosecutions, joinder and intervention, pleadings, class actions, and so on (Chayes, 1976; Cichowski & Stone Sweet, 2006; Sikkink, 2011). The specific configuration of access rules varies widely across legal systems and within systems across time and issue area. Furthermore, there is no clear logic linking different procedural norms to specific substantive areas of law. (For example, broad standing is not necessarily a hallmark of environmental regulatory regimes; the restrictiveness of class action certification does not covary with fair-wage regulations; and not all court systems engage in structural oversight of educational rights remedies.) International treaties, as well as non–treaty-based legal norms, often aim to provide rights to individuals or to impose obligations on the part of states. When these substantive norms are applied to individual domestic court systems, however, they encounter widely divergent procedural filters. In some states, access mechanisms may align with the actors or interests most likely to make a legal claim; in other states, individuals seeking to enforce the same treaty right may find that they lack appropriate standing in the domestic court system. In both systems, the level of judicial independence, traditionally defined, may be nominally identical. The ability of strategic actors to engage with that system, however, will inevitably vary.

In a single time period, these institutional rules will constitute relatively static frameworks reflecting the history of interplay between the judiciary and the political branches. This results in differential local articulations of international legal norms. Take, for example, the ability of individuals to maintain a criminal cause of action against elected officials. Norm-diffusion accounts of political leaders' criminal liability argue that conceptions of official accountability may change a victim's willingness or ability, from a cognitive standpoint, to frame an injury as a human rights violation (Sikkink, 2011). Recognizing a harm and framing it as a potential legal claim is, however, only the first, tentative step in enforcing a legal right against government persecution (Felstiner et al., 1980). What form a claim against the government takes depends on the procedural mechanisms available, as Michel (2018) demonstrates. Where domestic procedures allow only government officials to pursue criminal complaints, victims find themselves foreclosed from independently seeking court action and instead have no choice but to rely on the willingness of political actors to pursue a claim on their behalf. The exact same injury may provoke a different response, however, if individuals are able to take advantage of private prosecution procedures. In such systems, victims are able to pursue their claim through the courts, notwithstanding political hesitancy. Indeed, in such cases, the victim is able to proceed unless and until the political branches mobilize to engage the judicial branch directly through intervention in the individual case or through systemic restriction of judicial access—effectively reversing the veto structure.

It is clear that procedural rules vary across legal systems. Complicating this picture, however, is the fact that procedural rules vary within any individual state's court system. A domestic system may, for example, provide group standing for enforcement of a labor claim but not for an environmental claim. Moreover, these procedures vary not just across issue area but also across time. To be sure, each potential litigant faces what appears to be a set procedural environment. These procedural rules, however, are less "sticky" as time proceeds. Sometimes they evolve organically during litigation as nuance develops; at other times, political actors engage in targeted reform. What matters for the purposes of this project is who sets those procedural rules. When these rules have been isolated from the political sphere, either as a result of unchallenged historical legacy or because court reform has implicitly or explicitly delegated rulemaking to the judiciary, courts are better able to exercise discretion and control litigants' access to the legal system.

Here, I examine the extent to which this "procedural environment" is *constrained* or *flexible*. In short, how much control does the court have over its own operations? This takes into consideration such aspects as how free the court is to alter its procedures, whether it is able to expand or contract its docket, whether it can determine what types of claims it hears, how much leeway it has to bring external actors into the court system to augment its own capacities, and whether it is able to implement oversight of its remedies.

It should be noted that although this is related to the concept of judicial independence, it is conceptually distinct. "Judicial independence" is a catch-all phrase used to describe several related traits relating to a court's ability to make unbiased rulings. Commentators have identified at least three potential sources of interference with the judicial process; each is, appropriately, related to a specific attribute of judicial independence. "Party detachment" refers to a judge's lack of a stake in the current proceedings or direct relationship with the parties to a dispute. "Individual autonomy" refers to the judge's ability to decide a case without being subject to oversight from other members of the judiciary, other than oversight that results from respect for precedent or regular appellate means. Lastly, judicial independence only exists if the court system exhibits "political insularity"—an institutional distinctiveness from other governmental organs and a separation from the concerns and control of these other institutions (Fiss, 1993). Procedural flexibility is a conceptual cousin to this third form of independence, but the two are nevertheless distinct. Judicial independence, for example, primarily focuses on more easily quantifiable system-wide measures, such as the length of judicial appointment terms and the existence of salary protections (Cameron, 2002; Cross, 2010; Ríos-Figueroa & Staton, 2009). Procedural flexibility, as conceptualized here, is concerned not with these institutional markers but with the ability of the court itself to control the "secondary rules" previously outlined.

A flexible procedural environment is important in that it indicates the court's ability to control its interactions, not just with other *political* actors but also with other *societal* actors. With regard to political actors, courts face an important choice when deciding cases against the government: uphold the law as they perceive it, or defer to the policy preferences of the government. Either course of action offers the court risks and rewards, with questions of legitimacy being balanced against the potential for political backlash. At the same time, a court's ability to control access allows it to manage this risk through an alternative mechanism: modulating the court's relationship with the public and screening cases that provide the potential for conflict with powerful government officials. When courts exercise control over procedural rules, they have a greater capacity to avoid altogether cases that invite political retribution, giving them breathing room to avoid conflict while focusing on those cases that build legitimacy over time.

This allows courts to engage in what Bickel (1986) termed the "passive virtues." Bickel argued that courts should avoid reaching a decision when deciding a case would have negative consequences for the nation; the court could do this by denying certiorari, finding an issue not ripe for decision, or declaring an issue to be a nonjusticiable political question. Courts around the world have expanded well beyond this repertoire. In addition to the prospective methods outlined by Bickel, courts also exercise restraint during and after the adjudicative process by carefully choosing which law to apply or by returning issues to the political branches for further consideration (Delaney, 2016). Courts engage in this behavior not only to improve policy outcomes but also in pursuit of their institutional interests. Dixon and Issacharoff (2016) divide this behavior into two types, first-order (explicit) deferrals and second-order (implicit) deferrals, with the latter often couching claims of judicial authority in dicta as part of an otherwise restrained ruling. These second-order deferrals allow a young court to avoid political confrontation while making a bid for a more expansive future, analogous to the U.S. Supreme Court's decision in *Marbury v Madison*.[6] Ultimately, control over arcane procedural rules expands the range of options for a court to engage in this type of strategic avoidance of conflict.

These previous analysis have been primarily concerned with the court's interbranch relations—the first dimension of consideration. Controlling procedural mechanisms, however, also allows the court to alter the rules in ways that may be legitimacy-enhancing across both the second (international law) and third (public) dimensions. Along the second dimension, a court in a flexible environment can selectively draw on a broad array of international law resources, highlighting its role as a forum for human rights concerns. Alternatively, the court could restrict direct application of treaty provisions as necessary to reduce the salience of international law in individual cases. Lastly, along the third dimension, courts in flexible procedural environments can proactively engage the public. As demonstrated by Epp (1998), courts rely on broad societal support structures to enhance rights outcomes. Landau (2018) has shown that this support structure consists of a heterogenous mix of actors, and that a court may at times strengthen supporters of a civil society in ways that redound to the court's benefit. This suggests that support structures are themselves dynamic and, at least in part, responsive to the initiative of the court. By manipulating the rules that govern friends of the court briefs, the joining of cases, or the certification of class actions, for example, courts may broaden the field of stakeholders in cases, thereby providing further capacity to avoid deferring to the government.

Procedural flexibility, then, is the fulcrum atop which the three-dimensional court pivots. Rather than being locked into a one-dimensional strategic interaction with political institutions, the court can modulate the salience of international law or pivot toward the public in individual cases. In doing so, the court can vary its level of conflict with elected branches in such a way as to support the court's own institutional legitimacy. Importantly, this process works across time periods in a dynamic, iterative fashion. A court that limits a claimant's ability to directly invoke treaty language will subsequently see the supply of litigation decline—and with it the opportunity for political conflict. A court that permits class action suits potentially increases the societal reserve of activist litigation but also the societal bulwark against political backlash. This dynamism suggests that a court acting strategically in a flexible procedural environment will be able to shape the degree and form of judicial involvement in international human rights entrenchment. When this procedural flexibility is constrained, so too is the court's room for maneuver.

Implications

Figure 4 combines these concepts and builds on the simplified policy space introduced in Figure 3. This last version complicates the initial policy-space diagram by including the potential for varying levels of domestic court "self-censoring" through the strategic use of procedural rules. A court's ability to engage in this dynamic behavior is determined by whether its procedural environment is flexible or constrained (i.e., whether it controls the procedures governing the selection of appeals, whether it is free to alter standing rules, and so on). Courts in a flexible environment can modulate their engagement with international law, at times invoking it and at other times attenuating its relevance through such doctrines as the self-executing treaty doctrine. Of course, the ability of the court to make use of this resource is further conditioned on the judicial system's public or elite orientation. A system with a greater public orientation suggests a less restricted menu from which the court can choose: there are more potential litigants seeking to enforce international legal norms and more civil-society actors that view the court as a resource worth protecting at the ballot box. It also indicates a greater opportunity for the court in question to determine when it might balance public opinion against the threat of political backlash, as the court will have more information on the salience of any particular issue in society and a greater ability to cultivate potential court allies. Whether or not the court grants these potential allies access to the court is determined by the court itself in a flexible procedural environment—hence, the lines between societal actors and the domestic court in the figure. Opening the doors, so to speak, allows a court to balance public concerns against the political branches. Closing the doors allows it to avoid controversial cases, preventing in advance any legitimacy gap that might arise from a problematic substantive ruling.

Rulings to the left of the indifference point (point I) again suggest situations in which the court's ideal ruling might invite backlash from political actors. The question, of course, is will the court's ideal point fall to the left of point I, and if so, by how much? The long tradition in the American politics literature started by Dahl would indicate that, over time, we should see convergence between the court's ideal point and that of political actors who appoint judges to the court. Authors such as Teles (2012) complicate this story by explaining that convergence is a slow, painstaking process, and not the quick result of electoral outcomes. A three-dimensional theory of court behavior complicates this process even further. It does so by recognizing that

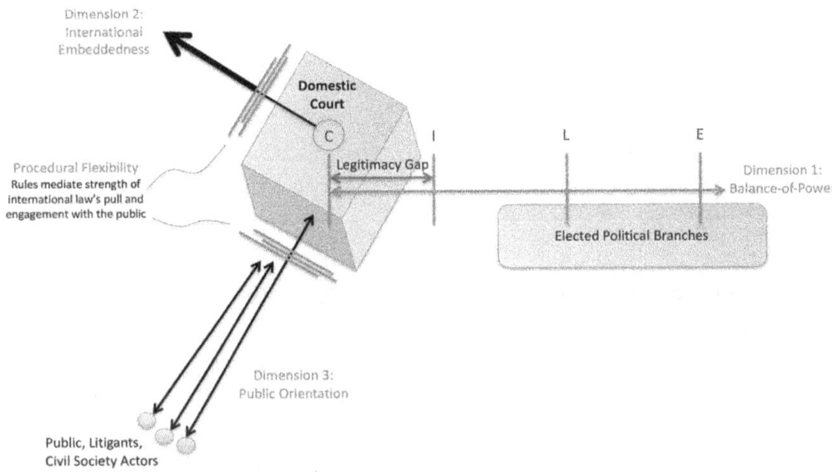

Figure 4. The Three-Dimensional Court.

rules of international law, unlike rules of domestic law, do not arise exclusively in the domestic institutional framework. This operates on two levels, first by *reducing* court constraint vis-à-vis political actors and second by *increasing* court constraint in terms of the potential legitimacy costs of siding with the government. The overall effect is to more tightly bind the court to the demands of international human rights law in a given case.

First, the entire point of a "lock-in" mechanism such as a human rights treaty is to remove the law in question from the purview of elected officials. The degree to which lock-in mechanisms are institutionalized is indicated by the degree of embedded internationalism. In short, is international law elevated in status above normal legislation? In states with deeply embedded internationalism, international law attains the rank of constitutional or quasi-constitutional status, and this has a direct effect on interbranch politics. Namely, this means that the legislator of concern for a court acting strategically is not the median legislator but rather the legislator occupying the tipping point for treaty override.

In states where international law is superior to normal law, this implies that the distance in policy space between points C and L (and therefore points C and I) shrinks. The real-world effect is that, at an institutional level, the court is freer to enforce international law without the threat of legislative override—more legislators have to agree in order to rebuke the court's conformity with the demands of international law. The degree to which the legislative ideal and indifference point shifts will vary across polities according to the legislative process, but in all instances the direction is the same: toward the court. After all, no constitution makes it easier to amend the constitution than to pass simple legislation. In short, constitutionalization matters for international law. It increases the likelihood that a court will consider international law binding, but it also increases the court's freedom to rule in line with international law without the fear of legislative override.

Second, embedded internationalism acts directly on the court by acting as a pull on the court's ideal point, altering the legitimacy calculus. It does so by increasing the costs the institution and its members would entail were they to ignore international law and rule in favor of the government. Whereas the U.S. Supreme Court may be the "final arbiter" of domestic law, such as whether the Obamacare (Affordable Care Act) mandate is a "tax," domestic courts are only one of many competing final arbiters of international legal issues. As such, failure to rule consistently with the holdings of other courts (or with hierarchically superior courts in the case of supranational institutions) may invite accusations that the court has pandered to political branches more readily than in the purely domestic law situation. An environment of embedded internationalism, then, heightens the legitimacy threat for capitulating to the government. In effect, in these internationally embedded systems, the location of point C is determined by international actors as much as it is by domestic actors.

In such situations, the court may no longer be able to mask a ruling at point I as nevertheless comporting with international law (point C). Point C is neither purely within the control of the domestic court, nor is it hidden from view. In legal jargon, point C is simply the "law" or "precedent." In political science terminology, it is technically the "revealed preference" of the court, and what is revealed is also subject to scrutiny. As a result, any ruling to the right of point C in policy space produces a quandary for the court. On the one hand, rulings farther from point C are likely to call into question the court's "nonpolitical" status, the source of its institutional legitimacy. On the other hand, rulings closer to point C are more likely to invite political backlash that directly undermine the court's strength. The potential legitimacy gap when ruling *for* the government as well as the likelihood of political backlash when ruling *against* the government both increase as the distance between C and I increases.

It is precisely in these situations that we should expect a flexible court to engage in procedural legerdemain. As the distance between C and I increases, a court operating in a flexible procedural environment has the option of engaging the public to the extent that it has indications that public support is greater than government opposition. Alternatively, when no such public or civil society support is available, it should seek to filter the case (and similar cases) out of the system by manipulating procedures. This could take several forms: tightening standing requirements, reducing the applicability of a ruling, or even ceding jurisdictional turf to another institution. In short, the court should use institutional mechanisms to reduce the supply of judicial activity in ways that over the long term reduce the harm to the court's legitimacy in the face of both domestic and international audiences. Only where the court is both unable to engage in procedural manipulation and lacks public support should it risk a ruling that either invites backlash or damages its legitimacy as a rule-of-law actor.

In total, this provides a three-dimensional view of court behavior. The first dimension is the traditional interbranch policy space that by now is familiar to those studying judicial politics. The second dimension is the degree to which the apex court is tied into international human rights regimes, described here as embedded internationalism. The third dimension is the degree to which the court has links not just to political actors but also to the public at large. The flexibility of the procedural environment represents the fulcrum. Apex courts exist in a delicate equipoise, balancing the often-competing demands of politicians, the public, and the international human rights legal community. Some courts feel the strong pull of international law. Others are subject to the pull of a public enjoying broad access to judicial review. All but the most unsophisticated of courts are aware of the demands of political actors.

Whether or not a court is able to address those political concerns often depends on whether or not it has the flexibility to modulate the strength of its ties to the domestic public and to the international realm. A court with no broad public access or no links to international law undoubtedly offers few prospects for enforcing international human rights. At the same time, a court constrained to hear every case and to render every opinion in line with the strictest international human rights law may ultimately find itself unable to avoid political backlash. The courts most capable of enforcing international human rights—not just in the instant case but over the long term—should be those that are able to modulate their links to the international and to the public, dialing up and down the supply of human rights litigation in response to what it perceives as the manageable demands of the public. By doing so, these courts shield themselves from the most politically contentious cases while offering a forum for human rights adjudication that provides the best opportunity to increase legal legitimacy without provoking political backlash.

Having put forth this theory, I make the following claims to be tested in this project:

Claim 1: *The supply of rights adjudication is not directly reflective of the potential demand for litigation.* In procedurally constrained systems, the legislature may change access procedures or court jurisdiction to prevent the court from enforcing international human rights law. In flexible systems, the court itself may restrict access when seeking to avoid political backlash. In either case, the occurrence of human rights violations does not translate directly into legal claims, even when statutory or constitutional provisions might otherwise suggest broad access. This is intrinsically related to claim 2.

Claim 2: *When a court enjoys a flexible procedural environment, procedural rules will be epiphenomena of the court's strategic legitimacy concerns.* Procedures governing access, adjudication, and remedies are often seen by scholars as predictive of the likelihood of rights enforcement. To be sure, this is true in situations in which political actors have established these procedures and the procedures are governed by inflexible institutional arrangements. In contrast, courts that enjoy a flexible procedural environment are able to control access, adjudication, and remedies so as to further the court's own concerns over institutional strength and legitimacy. In such situations, procedures are more appropriately interpreted as intervening variables, subject to manipulation by the court.

Claim 3: *A flexible procedural environment increases the likelihood that a court will successfully maintain or expand its enforcement role over time.* A court that lacks procedural flexibility is unable to screen the most contentious cases out of the system or to offer rulings that move in the direction of human rights compliance without being openly antagonistic to political actors. A court that possesses greater procedural flexibility should, in contrast, be able to use that flexibility to limit rulings while setting favorable precedent or to expand institutional capacity to oversee rights enforcement efforts. Flexibility may also allow courts to limit exposure to backlash in the face of unified political opposition to court interference. This leads to a paradoxical result: a court is more likely to increase compliance with international human rights law over the long term when it is able to do so selectively across issue areas in the short term.

Claim 4: *A public support orientation will provide greater opportunities for the high court to avoid political backlash by balancing public concerns against political considerations.* Any court acting strategically should attempt to avoid overt political confrontations. If a court serves as the apex institution in a system with relatively diffuse connections to the public, it gains information and can build a constituency from across society. It can use this information to determine under what circumstances the court's ruling will be in line with the public's preferences. In such situations, the court will be empowered to issue rulings against the government with diminished concern for political backlash, because political actors would in that scenario be operating against the public. In elite-oriented environments, this is less likely, because the court lacks information on which legal issues are salient to the broader public and is unable to build an independent support base among the public.

Claim 5: *A high degree of embedded internationalism is more predictive of judicial enforcement of international human rights law than is state ratification of treaty law.* This is particularly true of courts that enjoy a flexible procedural environment. Internationally embedded courts are likely to enforce human rights norms even if the treaties containing these rights have not been ratified or incorporated by the state. Conversely, a court that is only superficially embedded internationally is likely to eschew international law considerations in favor of domestic contingencies. Of course, at early points of constitutional transformation, these two factors might be linked (because ratification of human rights and reform of the court may occur as dual prongs of an attempted rights lock-in). Over the long run, however, an internationally embedded court should continue to draw on international law—even if a particular treaty has not been ratified—when opportunities present themselves.

Case Studies and Methodology

I test these claims across three case studies. Each case study focuses on an individual state and the willingness and ability of the highest court to engage in the enforcement of human rights obligations under international law. The first case study examines the Colombian Constitutional Court (CCC) during the 20 years following its creation in 1991. The second study examines the South African Constitutional Court (SACC) in the 20 years following that court's establishment during the transition from Apartheid in 1993. The third and final case study examines the Mexican Supreme Court of Justice of the Nation (SCJN) for the 20 years following major court-strengthening reforms in 1994.

I chose these courts because they exhibit a high degree of variation in their enforcement of international human rights law over the 20-year study period, as well as variation on the key independent variables outlined in Table 1. In addition, the case studies were selected for their potential to shed light on my theory's validity vis-à-vis other political science theories that seek to explain court enforcement patterns. The CCC was chosen as a least-likely case. The CCC and its justices have enjoyed reputations as strong international human rights enforcers, and the Colombian constitution allows for (indeed, requires) a high degree of court referencing of international and foreign law. Attitudinal theories that predict that courts act in line with sincerely held preferences, as well as theories that predict that sincere legal readings will guide court rulings, would thus both predict a court that consistently rules in favor of international human rights law. Legitimacy-seeking strategic behavior of the type predicted by my theory should be extremely unlikely. The South African case, meanwhile, allows for testing of the theory alongside those explanations of court behavior that suggest a court's ability to rule is conditioned by the occurrence of fractured government or veto points, in particular given that court's orientation toward elites as opposed to the broader public. The SACC's reputation as a relatively reliable enforcer of international human rights law during a 20-year period of one-party dominance suggests greater nuance than current theories can easily explain. Lastly, the Mexican SCJN serves as a negative case for the majority of years under consideration. Despite a court reform that greatly strengthened that court's independence from political actors, the SCJN has, until relatively recently, failed to emerge as a venue for meaningful international human rights enforcement. It also represents a case with internal variation on the independent variable of international embeddedness, beginning rather low and increasing in later years. Unlike the other two courts under examination, however, the SCJN exists in a highly constrained procedural environment. The case study demonstrates how this aspect limits the ability of the SCJN to adapt to fill a changing role over time. Lastly, the spread of cases allows for the control of other potentially important factors. Both Colombia and Mexico are Latin American states operating within the robust legal normative and procedural framework of the inter-American system; the outcome in each case varies, however, suggesting that cultural, linguistic, or other regional factors are not determinative. At the same time, the inclusion of the South African case enhances the robustness of any findings; the importance of institutional flexibility, for example, is not limited to the Latin American experience.

Table 1. Independent Variables

Court	*International Embeddedness*	*Support Orientation*	*Procedural Environment*
Colombian Constitutional Court	High	Public	Flexible
South African Constitutional Court	Moderate	Elite	Flexible
Mexican Supreme Court of Justice of the Nation	Low → moderate	Limited public	Constrained

The theory claims that a domestic court's docket does not necessarily reflect the underlying societal potential for judicial protection of human rights abuses. Put differently, the supply of adjudication does not necessarily reflect the demand for adjudication. For example, if a court successfully restricts access in one area of the law, litigation attempts will be thwarted without the court offering a ruling either for or against the government. As a result, any meaningful inquiry into the domestic court's institutional output cannot consist merely of a review of decisions. Instead, I proceed so as to test the claim that the court may hear and decide cases in certain issue areas, avoid hearings in other areas, and encourage increased litigation in yet other areas of the law.

In this analysis, I follow what George and Bennett (2005) call the "method of structured, focused comparison" (p. 67). In this method, questions reflective of the research objective guide data collection so that the researcher can conduct systematic comparisons of disparate cases. For this project, methodology must address the claim that a court's "supply" of adjudication is not necessarily reflective of litigant "demand." To account for this potential incongruence, I begin each case study by determining areas of international human rights law where a state's compliance is lacking. It is in these areas—where the elected political branches are failing in their obligations to international law—that we would expect litigants to be more likely to turn to the courts for relief. These areas represent the raw material that might lead activists to pursue claims. I determine which areas are most relevant by systematically reviewing human rights reports by governmental, nongovernmental, and international organizations to determine a baseline level of human rights violations and, thus, potential areas for court intervention during the 20-year period of study.[7] The reviews consist of annual human rights reports from the U.S. Department of State, reports by UN treaty-based and charter-based bodies, state reports that are required under the human rights treaty system, and annual country reports by the organizations Human Rights Watch and Amnesty International for a two-decade period following court reform in each state.

Using the findings of this systematic review, I select for each state two broad issue areas to examine based on their sustained relevance to human rights observers. In Colombia, the conditions faced by internally displaced persons (IDPs) and extrajudicial killings by the Colombian military establishment are recurrent themes. In South Africa, the most consistent areas of concern are civil and political rights in the criminal justice field and socioeconomic rights in the area of the right to health. In Mexico, the first subcase covers impunity for grave human rights violations in the overlapping areas of extrajudicial killings, torture, and disappearances of civilians; the second subcase examines the rights of indigenous communities. Interestingly, the examination of each state results in one subcase from an area of law that could be considered a first-generation human right (civil and political) and one from an area that is more properly categorized as a second- or third-generation right (socioeconomic or group identity). This is an outcome of the methodology described in the preceding paragraph, as opposed to an intentional restriction on subcase selection. Nevertheless, this results in even greater variation within each case study and greater ease of cross-country comparison. The entire process yields a complete set of six country–issue-area subcases for comparison, which are listed in Table 2.

For each subcase for each state, I then examine the same 20-year period to determine areas of congruence between expected and actual litigation patterns in the two areas of human rights law. I explore whether and to what extent the courts become engaged in each area of the law—that is, the extent to which they supply adjudication to meet the demand. This second stage

Table 2. Subcases

Court	*First-Generation Right*	*Second- or Third-Generation Right*
Colombian Constitutional Court	Extrajudicial killings	Displaced persons
South African Constitutional Court	Criminal proceedings	HIV treatment
Mexican Supreme Court of Justice of the Nation	Impunity	Indigenous peoples

of data collection includes a review of primary and secondary literature on court rulings and human rights compliance in English (as well as in Spanish for Colombia and Mexico) to determine relevant court cases and trends within each subcase.[8] I rely extensively on academic writing, as well as governmental and nongovernmental reports. I then expand my research to include news articles, government gazettes, and legal documents in order to trace the development of the human rights situation on the ground, court intervention (or lack thereof) in each issue area, and the governmental response. The diversity of sources is intended to capture a broad range of opinions on the activities of each court, rather than rely exclusively on the court's own articulation of its role and operations as reflected in court rulings. For each subcase, I use these materials to test my theory by examining the degree to which international embeddedness, public support orientation, and procedural flexibility account for the court's willingness and ability to improve compliance with international human rights law.

The Colombian case highlights the important role that a public support orientation and institutional flexibility can play in enabling a court to selectively enforce human rights, even when that court is highly sensitive to considerations of international law. The degree of institutional flexibility is relatively high for Colombia; it is clear that where this flexibility exists, the CCC has been able to use it either to avoid issues or to extend its capacities. The CCC's effectiveness is greatly enhanced by a public support orientation that provides constant feedback on the relative importance of issue areas but also empowers the court, vis-à-vis political actors, by increasing the role of the judiciary in everyday citizens' political calculus.

In South Africa, the SACC exhibits a distinct pattern of rights enforcement. The lack of broad access has prevented the SACC from nurturing any extensive public engagement with the judiciary, depriving the court of the sort of public support structures seen in Colombia and that might otherwise inoculate the court against political attack. Despite the relative exclusion of the public from the constitutional realm and the existence of a single, easily monitored apex court, the SACC has nonetheless been able to make use of an extremely flexible procedural environment to reduce the number of confrontations with the overwhelmingly dominant African National Congress. This has likewise been tempered by the relatively moderate international embeddedness of the court system, which allows the SACC to weave international law into its decisions alongside domestic concerns arising out of the country's difficult history, but to do so on the SACC's own terms.

The Mexican SCJN has trod the most difficult path. At first glance, this court's limited role in enforcing international human rights law might seem to be a result of its relatively low level of international embeddedness. A deeper investigation, however, reveals that even when the SCJN has signaled a willingness to enforce human rights, it has struggled to do so. Ultimately, the moderate level of public access coupled with an extremely rigid procedural environment has prevented the high court from escaping political monitoring or effectively engaging the public.

These three courts demonstrate the complex interplay of the variables under consideration in this project. At the same time, the project undoubtedly begs the question of how one defines a successful domestic court. Indeed, it is reasonable to question whether a domestic court that eschews its enforcement role in select areas of international human rights norms is, in fact, playing a meaningful rights-protecting role at all. After all, when a court fails to give immediate effect to a right, it risks disempowering those who looked to the judiciary for vindication (Young, 2019). It is important to remember, however, that each court operates in a transitional regime, and often under circumstances that would test the institutional capacity of even the oldest, most well-respected courts. As such, I argue that even though these three courts have been constrained, they have over time increased the likelihood of outcomes that favor human rights by offering, in some situations, an additional venue for members of the public and activists to bring human rights issues to light. Courts' engagement with these issues has not been uniform, but nor should we expect uniformity given the nuance of each policy area and each political context.

Contributions of the Project

It is important to recognize what this study does not attempt. I make no claim to a full accounting of the myriad paths through which international law can effect change in a domestic system. As explained in Chapter 1, international human rights regimes have multiple routes through which they bind (or attempt to bind) actors within the state. The focus here is on domestic courts and their role in this complex ecosystem. The theory and case studies I present focus on the ability of courts to contract, expand, and morph the implementation of human rights under international law. I do not attempt a systematic accounting of civil society groups' use of those claims to influence public opinion or to shame governments. Nor do I examine local activists' use of courts to create and mobilize coalitions or alter bureaucratic agendas. Although these legal mobilizers undoubtedly play a part in the larger story of rights enforcement, here they are bit players; judges and politicians have the starring roles.

This study also limits itself to claims against governments. In various areas of law, courts may have their greatest impact when litigation targets private actors through the horizontal enforcement of laws and regulations.[9] Nevertheless, for two reasons I maintain my focus on litigation in which the government is a party. First, the present theory seeks to explain judicial behavior across various issue areas as part of a single theoretical framework. As such, it makes sense to rely uniformly on cases in which the government is a party, as this removes from consideration an unnecessary confounding variable and keeps comparative cases as structurally similar as possible. (Although certain types of rights cases—e.g., racial discrimination cases—might involve purely private actors, it is difficult to imagine a purely civilian-civilian case involving executive power or military abuses.) In addition, cases in which both parties are private actors do not present courts with the same power dynamics as cases involving the government. Where both parties to a suit are private actors, the court speaks for the state and can theoretically call on the police and military to enforce its decisions. Where one party is the government, however, the court cannot assume state actors will enforce a ruling. Such cases problematize the traditional triad approach to courts, as the court is no longer a truly neutral third party; rather, the court is part of the governmental apparatus it seeks to affect. It is not clear that the current theory would apply with equal force in the context of purely private disputes, and so I do not attempt theoretical shoehorning.

It is my hope that this project will contribute to several theoretical and empirical inquiries in international relations and international law. It addresses unexplained variation by leveraging comparative case studies more extensively, revealing variation both across and within states. The majority of judicial politics literature, meanwhile, refrains from either cross-national or within-country comparison. Kapiszewski and Taylor (2008) find, for example, that more than two-thirds of the judicial politics literature focusing on Latin America examines only one country. A more recent volume of comparative judicial politics contains a dozen case studies, nine of which "compare" one state only, with two more focusing on a single region of the globe (Asia and Central Europe, respectively) and the last focusing on politics within one issue area (religion) (Kapiszewski et al., 2013). Moreover, within the field generally, judges and judiciaries are seen as acting consistently across legal issues. As Huneeus (2010) notes, "Studies of foreign systems . . . have tended to emphasize a single, coherent judicial view on law and judging, with judges as passive recipients of that view" (p. 219).

This project addresses the first of these issues by conducting a comparative analysis across two regions and three states; it addresses the second issue through an examination of differing judicial enforcement patterns across issue areas within each of the three states. The project also addresses an even more surprising scholarly lacuna: the interaction of international human rights law and constitutional law. As Cope et al. (2019) note, "Although numerous studies explore the impact of constitutional rights and many others consider the effect of human rights treaties, no study has considered either their relative importance or how they complement, substitute, or generally interact" (p. 2). This project addresses this concern by explicitly integrating the analysis of courts' treatment of international and constitutional law.

I also increase our understanding of courts by treating judicial actors as entrepreneurs. Current theories focus on variations in ratification patterns, the nature of specific human rights, or the motivations and strategies of activists. In each account, courts are passive institutions that others use instrumentally. While it is true that courts are recipients of litigant claims, this is not the whole story. I show that courts also transform the claims they hear, both in terms of their treatment of individual cases and their use of those cases to shape legal and policy outcomes over the long term. Judges act in ways that create opportunities for themselves and for human rights enforcement by crafting procedures and forging new autonomies.

Lastly, my theory moves beyond the notion that the law is either purely nonpolitical or simply another field for politics. Courts act strategically, but they also take law seriously. Any court that fails to treat law as a unique field of inquiry will quickly find itself without a claim to legitimacy in a democratic system. This confluence of strategic behavior with legal normativity also means that political considerations ensconced in law at one point in time shape the likelihood that legal tools will be available in a later period. In this way, the law is inherently path dependent, focusing on legislative intent, the development of rules, and the importance of precedent. By taking into account the hybrid nature of law and legal action, my theory is better able to address variation in state compliance with human rights obligations by recognizing that courts are both bound by the law and potentially able to manipulate its articulation at key moments of doctrinal and institutional development.

For scholars and advocates of international human rights law, the assumption is often that better doctrine leads to better outcomes. My research sheds light on when this is true for international law that enters the domestic system, and what institutional factors may improve the likelihood of normatively desirable outcomes. When exactly that occurs varies widely by state and by issue area, as will be seen in the case studies.

CHAPTER 3

Colombia: Balancing Act

Article 22: Peace is a right and a mandatory duty.
—Political Constitution of Colombia, 1991

Introduction

In 1990, in the midst of a national state of emergency that saw three presidential candidates assassinated, President César Gaviria called for the creation of a constituent assembly. The goal was clear: write a new constitution that would strengthen state institutions and provide a new framework for citizen-government relations. By 1991 the arduous task was completed, and representatives of the people of Colombia had inaugurated a new political settlement that transformed Colombia from an *estado de derecho* (a rule-of-law state) to an *estado social de derecho* (a *social* rule-of-law state). This new constitution incorporated a broad panoply of socioeconomic and political rights, bound the state to international human rights law, granted unprecedented citizen access to the court system, and created a new constitutional court—the Columbian Constitutional Court, or CCC—to enforce these new protections.

On paper.

Two decades later, Colombia was home to the planet's largest internally displaced population[1] and played host to human rights law violations resulting from decades of civil conflict. Yet Colombia had also made unquestionable progress since the adoption of the 1991 constitution. Some rebel and paramilitary groups had disarmed, the government was engaged in an ongoing peace process, and the country had seen a flourishing of judicial activity aimed at protecting many of the rights promised in the new constitution.

Much of this activity was due to the clear emphasis that the new constitution put on judicial review of legislation and executive decrees and on compliance with international human rights obligations. At the time of the new constitution's adoption, Colombia had spent 35 of the previous 42 years in a "state of exception." These states of exception, in which constitutional protections and international human rights were often suspended, were not subject to judicial oversight in the years leading up to 1991. On the contrary, the pre-1991 Supreme Court considered the review of states of exception to be a political matter for Congress and the executive.[2] This changed under the new constitution, with the new CCC exercising mandatory review of legislation and presidential decrees of states of exception. Unlike its predecessor court, the new court has often overruled states of exception as being unwarranted by facts on the ground (Uprimny, 2007, p. 51).

Alongside this mandatory review has come a massive increase in the use of the court system by citizens to protect their rights under the constitution. In terms of citizen access, the new *acción de tutela*[3] is arguably the most important of the new procedures inaugurated in 1991. This protective action allows any citizen to file a petition with any court in the country without need of an attorney when a fundamental constitutional right is threatened or violated. The petitioned judge is legally bound to prioritize the petition, rule on it within 10 days, and provide an order of relief where appropriate. The mandate is broad, with no clear restriction on what the judge may order to ensure that a citizen's enjoyment of the fundamental right is restored (Cepeda-Espinosa, 2009). These new powers have resulted in a constitutional court that commentators have described as "hyperactive" (Gloppen et al., 2010, p. 52).

In the pages that follow, I explore the theory proposed in Chapter 2 in the context of the Colombian court system, with a focus on the CCC. For the purposes of my research, Colombia serves as a least-likely case (George & Bennett, 2005, p. 121). The CCC and its justices all enjoy reputations as strong international human rights enforcers, and the Colombian constitution allows for a high degree of court referencing of international or foreign law. The Colombian judiciary, moreover, has historically enjoyed a reputation as a relatively independent actor compared to other Latin American states (Cifuentes Muñoz, 2002). The establishment of the CCC built on this tradition, creating an institution to protect international human rights that were broadly incorporated into the constitutional framework. The court's reputation as a strong rule-of-law actor with a history of judicial independence suggests a court that is able to rule without taking into account political considerations or public concerns.

In addition, the constituent assembly that drafted and adopted the constitution represented a diverse group of societal stakeholders,[4] indicating widespread support for this incorporation of human rights protections (Uprimny, 2007, p. 59). In other words, the court should not have to act strategically; enforcing human rights seems in line with a broad consensus. Indeed, the court's legitimacy has grown beyond reproach on the domestic scene, and members of the court should, therefore, feel institutionally secure. These factors all suggest that the CCC should be free to take an activist stance and consistently rule in favor of international human rights commitments. This prediction is the same under both attitudinal theories that predict courts will act in line with sincerely held preferences, as well as under those theories that predict that sincere legal readings will guide court rulings. Legitimacy-seeking strategic behavior of the type predicted by my theory should be extremely unlikely.

I will argue, however, that the CCC does engage in this strategic behavior. The court's legitimacy is highly sensitive to international human rights law issues, meaning that the court is predisposed to rule in line with these legal commitments. At the same time, the public orientation of the constitutional system and the relatively high degree of procedural flexibility condition the manner in which the court goes about crafting its decisions. This allows the CCC to take into consideration concerns of both political actors and the public and to engage selectively in the enforcement of international human rights law. It also explains variation in the disparate patterns of CCC enforcement of the two legal issue areas under consideration, internally displaced persons (IDPs) and extrajudicial executions. As will be explored throughout this chapter, different areas of the law in Colombia exhibit varying degrees of court-centered human rights enforcement, in terms of both the court's willingness to rule and the effectiveness of court-directed compliance measures. This variation allows for a richer understanding of the processes at work in determining outcomes across legal domains. It also makes Colombia an appropriate case for testing my theory because of the within-case variation on the dependent variable.

The Colombian Institutional Setting

Before proceeding to the subcases, I will position the Colombian case in the project's theory. The theory posits that a court's enforcement role will depend on the degree to which the high court operates in a system characterized by embedded internationalism, on whether or not the court enjoys the potential for a support structure oriented toward the public, and the court's overall level of procedural flexibility. The theory further posits that a high court is most likely to maintain or expand its ability to enforce international human rights law when it scores highly on each of the three variables. The following sections explore each variable as it applies to the CCC. In summary, the CCC is best characterized as operating in a system characterized by deeply embedded internationalism, as presiding over a court system with an orientation toward the public, and as possessing a relatively high degree of procedural flexibility. On the basis of these variables, the theory would predict that the CCC should be deeply concerned with the legitimacy concerns arising from human rights issues, and that the orientation toward the public should provide the court with information on public concern over human rights as well as a means of balancing the public against backlash from political elites. Furthermore, the flexible procedural environment should allow the CCC the opportunity to act selectively, controlling the flow of litigation to the high court in such a way as to enforce international human rights in publicly salient issue areas while avoiding litigation in more politically problematic areas of human rights.

Deeply Embedded Internationalism

The court's institutional legitimacy is tied directly to international human rights law. Indeed, Colombia may represent a high-water mark for embedded internationalism. Whether a court operates in a context of embedded internationalism entails both (1) the court's institutional setting, such as whether its stated function includes enforcing international human rights law, and (2) a consideration for individual justices' concern with upholding a reputation as a court that complies with international human rights law. Not all courts are empowered or expected by their politicians and publics to enforce international law obligations (Sloss, 2009). Likewise, some courts are much more eager to consider international law, whereas other courts are more willing to embrace their country's "exceptionalism" (Bradford & Posner, 2011). In both institutional design and the outlook of its justices, the CCC can only be considered extremely predisposed toward compliance with international human rights obligations.

From an institutional standpoint, the court is directly empowered in its role as interpreter of the 1991 constitution to enforce human rights law. This occurs along several legal routes. First, the constitution specifically guarantees human rights by requiring respect for international humanitarian law and requiring any law regulating "states of exception" to conform with international treaties.[5] Moreover, the government is required to submit declarations of states of exception to the CCC for immediate review.[6] Second, the rights protected by the tutela action and reviewed by the court are likewise interpreted in light of international human rights law.[7] Lastly, the CCC hears constitutional cases and cases relating to international human rights not only because of direct jurisdictional grants in the constitution but also because the constitution's incorporation of international law in effect bootstraps international law into the realm of Colombian constitutional law.

The justices of the CCC have even expanded this constitutional and statutory emphasis on international human rights law. The constitution includes a supremacy clause in Article 4 declaring the constitution to be the ultimate source of law. Interestingly, the court has clarified the relationship between the constitution and international law such that human rights law can overcome what otherwise appear to be constitutional lacunae. The court has done this through development of the concept of a constitutionality block (*bloque de constitucionalidad*).[8] This concept incorporates various extraconstitutional sources of human rights law into constitutional doctrine, specifically treaty law and decisions made by treaty-based international organizations. As such, even in areas of jurisprudence that do not directly invoke human rights law, the latter binds the former. This can go beyond lacunae to override direct constitutional grants of power to other institutional actors. Attempts to amend the constitution, for example, may be restricted if the court finds the amendment conflicts with human rights obligations (Dixon & Landau, 2015; Roznai, 2017). The result is a system of deep legal monism in which international law infuses every aspect of constitutional adjudication, with the CCC directly importing standards that no elected official has endorsed and that theoretically conflict with existing practice. International court rulings, doctrinal developments at UN bodies, development of customary law, and legal interpretations of peer courts in other states are all directly invokable by the court without intervening political processes. Of course, treaty law does remain a primary source of the legal obligations espoused by the CCC, and a complete list of these major human rights obligations is included in Appendix 2.

In addition to these institutional prerogatives, theories of transnational judicial dialogue (Slaughter, 2004) would predict that the justices have personal incentives to follow international law in their rulings. A review of justices' biographies indicates the degree to which each individual justice was trained at a foreign institution, worked in a foreign country, or regularly traveled abroad for conferences. The inclusion of this matter in their biographies indicates the personally subjective importance of this internationalized professional identity. Of 30 regularly appointed justices over the 20 years of this study, 18 can be categorized as having this heightened awareness of international influences and international reputational considerations. They are marked with an asterisk (*) in Figure 5.

This individual concern for international law can be translated to the institutional level. Because CCC judges are selected for periods of 8 years, commentators regularly refer to three distinct periods: the first court, from 1992 to 2000; the second court, from 2000 to 2008; and the third court, beginning in 2008 and continuing through the end of the period under consideration.[9] In each such court, a majority of justices had been trained overseas, worked overseas, or considered their international conference work important enough to include it in their professional profiles. In light of these institutional and professional considerations, international human rights law can be seen as playing a key part in determining the legitimacy of the court, and the ideal point of the CCC itself can be seen as predisposed to compliance with international human rights law. Embedded internationalism means the CCC, both as a result of its legal framework and as a collective of individuals, should see its institutional legitimacy as tied to its international law rulings.

A Public Support Orientation

In addition to being highly attuned to the demands of international law, the CCC benefits from its role as the apex court for a highly diffuse system of review with broad citizen access. The primary source of this wide accessibility is the tutela writ, and this provides two key advantages to the court. First, the tutela ensures that there is significant litigation on human rights claims before any politically challenging cases reach the apex court. Rather than proceeding directly to the highest courts, these claims are brought throughout the judiciary, preventing political actors from quashing human rights claims by attacks on a single apex court. Second, the tutela ensures a broad-based public

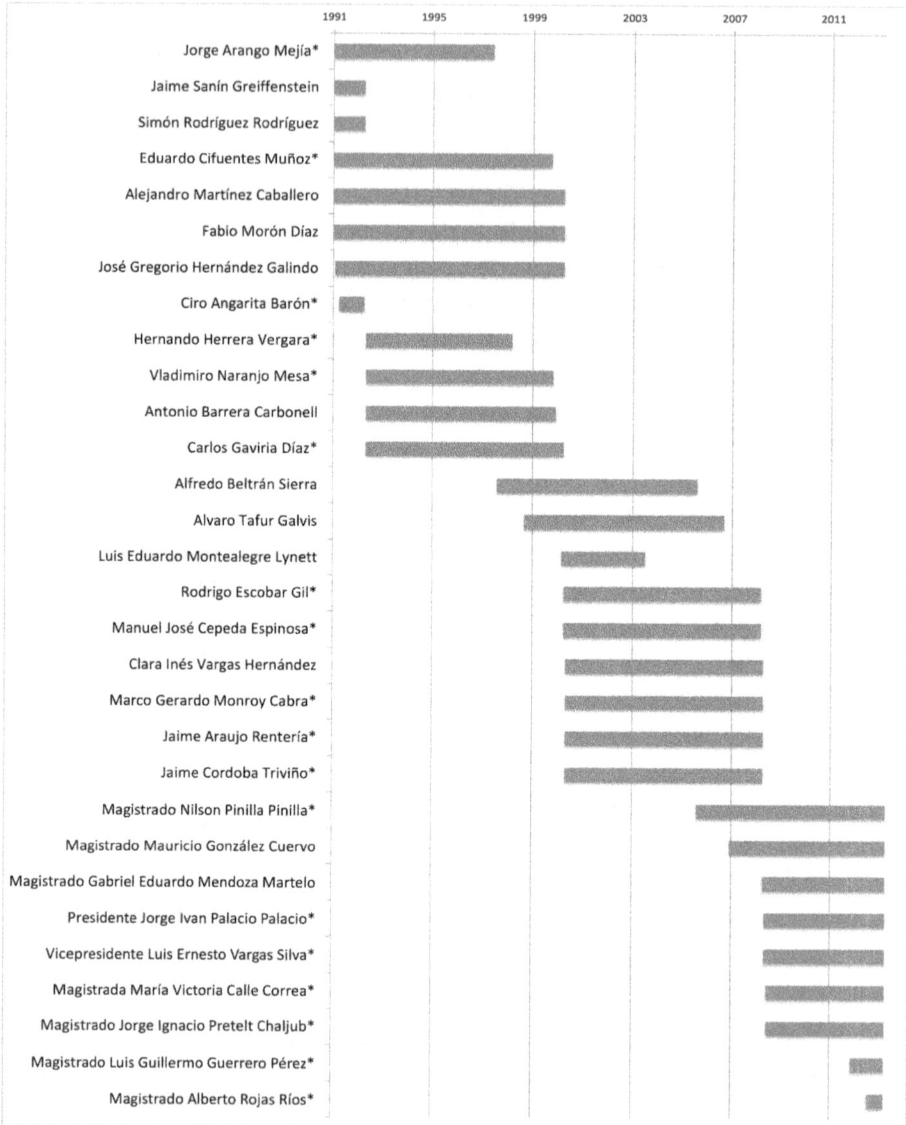

Figure 5. Justices of the Colombian Constitutional Court.

engagement with the judicial system. As a result, legal issues are incredibly salient in Colombian society, and attacks on the judiciary involve political risk. The wide base of litigation activity also provides the CCC with ongoing information from all segments of the population, allowing the court to gauge the relative importance of human rights issues. This provides the court with the ability to choose from an extremely wide array of issue areas in which to concentrate its limited institutional resources, and to determine when to engage otherwise politically risky human rights issues.[10]

To be sure, this public orientation does not blind the CCC to the concerns of political actors; the traditional first dimension of consideration is alive and well. Rather, the public orientation of the court system ensures that the court's base of institutional support is not limited to these elected political branches. The court looks both to the concerns of political actors and to the concerns of the broad public. Because of the court's wide base of public support, interactions with political actors have a less determinative effect than they would in a more concentrated system of review dominated by elites. Instead, in the Colombian system, interactions with political actors also serve as a means of ensuring that the court remains aware of political actors' ideal policy points and of the need to prevent potentially dangerous ideological divergence between the CCC and other institutions. This occurs in several ways. First and foremost, the 1991 constitution requires the court to review legislation and presidential declarations of "states of exception" to confirm their compliance with constitutional and international human rights law.[11] This provides a constant source of information on government policy agendas as the government submits briefs supporting or opposing legislation and decrees. In addition, the court receives information on governmental support for different policy pronouncements based on the reports of the national attorney general (*el Procurador General de la Nación*). Under the 1991 constitution, the national attorney general is required to provide an opinion on all such issues of constitutional control,[12] providing a further feedback mechanism for the court.

In addition, the court's appointment procedures limit the extent of ideological drift over time. A justice's relatively short term (8 years) lessens the likelihood of substantial policy drift between justices and the politicians who appointed them. The entire court is, in effect, renewed every 8 years. Also, the appointment procedure itself involves numerous actors across all three branches of government. The Senate is charged with electing justices to the CCC from lists presented to it by the president, the Supreme Court, and the Council of State.[13] This institutional attribute by design makes the CCC much more responsive to policy concerns than the other high courts in Colombia, the Supreme Court and the Council of State, both of which select their own replacements from Superior Judicial Council nomination lists. Lastly, research has found that justices who visited senators' offices during the selection process were more likely to be appointed. Interestingly, those who were considered moderate rather than ideologically extreme were more likely to be appointed, as this allowed them to garner more widespread support in the Senate (Montoya García, 2011). In short, those justices who demonstrated political awareness—as opposed to any particular political preference—ended up on the court.

This level of political engagement has not prevented the court from ruling against government actors. Instead, the high degree of access stemming from the tutela has allowed the CCC to take into consideration public concerns as well as those of politicians. It is difficult to overemphasize the importance of the tutela as a link between the people and the court system. In terms of process, an individual in Colombia can go to any local judge and request enforcement of a constitutional right. If the individual is not satisfied with the outcome, that person has the right to appeal the ruling. As a result, tutelas reach the CCC from all areas of the country and from members of all socioeconomic classes. The tutela provides an ongoing indication of which issue areas are important to the population at large.

Within a year of the new constitution's inauguration, the tutela was being widely discussed in Colombian society. Moreover, this "direct path between the constitution and the citizen," as one newspaper put it, was encountering resistance from established institutions like the Supreme Court as the citizens found a new institutional route to enforce rights: "From night to morning, everyone speaks of the tutela. The government defends it, lawyers discuss it, newspapers editorialize over it, citizens timidly begin to exercise it, and the Supreme Court refuses to apply it."[14] As time passed, entrenched institutions' resistance and ambiguity over the tutela's utility both quickly faded.[15]

Use of the tutela doubled by the end of its second year, and within two decades the number of writs filed grew by almost 4,000%. The phenomenal growth of the tutela can be seen in Figure 6. By the end of the second year of the constitution's being in force, the newspaper *La semana* was singing the new writ's praises: "The tutela has the virtue of protecting the people on the street, beggars, the illiterate, doctors, sick, workers, pensioners, prisoners, executives, the unemployed, housewives, children, elderly, students, professors, and dissidents. Everyone."[16] Strikingly, the CCC itself aided this expansion in the use

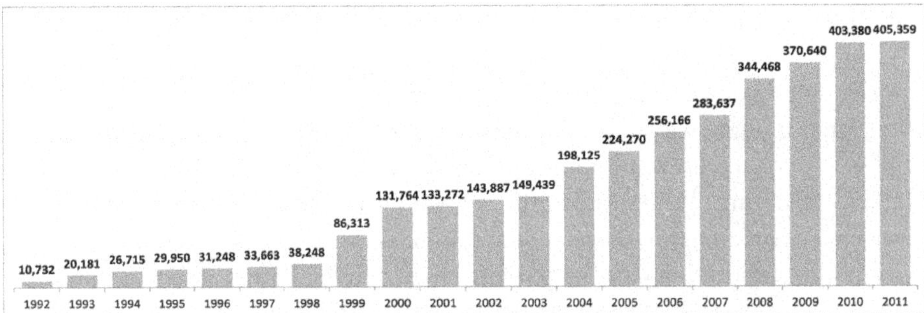

Figure 6. The Rise of the Tutela: Number of Writs Filed per Year, 1992–2011.

of the tutela over time, demonstrating the means through which courts can enhance their institutional strength by cultivating a public support structure. Although originally the tutela was intended to protect fundamental rights, the court ruled that ancillary rights could also be implicated when the failure to protect those ancillary rights would impinge on an underlying fundamental right. The result was a further expansion in the scope of issues the court could choose to oversee.[17]

The success of the tutela has allowed the judiciary to enjoy a rights-affirming role in the public consciousness. Just as the tutela has provided broad public understanding of the importance of law, so too has it provided the CCC with a broad understanding of public concerns. The diffuse review of government power has in effect created a capacious intake valve for the court to learn which policy areas are generating grievances among the citizenry. This has redounded to the court's benefit, enabling it to engage public policy development in international human rights law, an area that directly informs the court's strategic legitimacy calculus. Lastly, the court's highly flexible procedural environment means that it is able to pivot to those areas of greatest public concern, further enhancing its institutional legitimacy.

A Flexible Procedural Environment

Procedural flexibility has allowed the court to build its legitimacy by approaching different areas of law in a nuanced fashion. To be sure, there are areas where the court has less flexibility than in other areas, and under these circumstances the court has had more difficulty shielding itself from politically difficult cases. The majority of issue areas, however, have found the CCC able to employ institutional mechanisms either to expand or contract its engagement with litigants, enhancing the court's effectiveness over time.

First, though, it is important to recognize that even in an environment otherwise characterized by a high degree of flexibility, the CCC does face some constraints. Procedural flexibility is at its lowest in the Colombian context in the area of elite-driven constitutional controversies. As noted previously, the constitution requires the court to review legislation and presidential declarations of states of exception to confirm their compliance with constitutional and international human rights law.[18] Many of the court's most controversial cases have involved exactly these types of rulings that it is required to hear and rule on under the constitution; it simply cannot avoid these issues through procedural legerdemain. Indeed, under each of the first four post-reform presidents, the government responded to CCC rulings by proposing overriding constitutional amendments, two of which passed (Rodríguez-Raga, 2011; Uprimny, 2007). This demonstrates that even the well-respected CCC is not immune to political backlash. What is most impressive is that even in these instances, the court has found ways to use procedural flexibility to reduce political conflict. For example, it may defer a ruling, allowing a contested law to be in effect while the government proposes an alternative formulation (Cepeda-Espinosa, 2004).

In most instances, though, the CCC is able to employ the full panoply of procedural mechanisms. In an *actio popularis*, wherein a citizen can challenge the constitutionality of a law under abstract review, the court can reject the claim on procedural grounds. It is, therefore, able to avoid or minimize conflict not just in terms of the remedy (such as deferring a ruling for a year) but also through the forms of access and adjudication. The degree to which the CCC maintains control over its docket in this manner is clear from the variability in its acceptance of these claims. For example, in 1992 more than 90% petitions were rejected on procedural grounds; in 1993 just over 40% were rejected on procedural grounds (Cepeda-Espinosa, 2004). This flexibility ensures the court's ability to remove cases from the its docket without addressing the substance of claims and, therefore, before they become a source of political controversy.

The flexible procedural environment is extremely important in adjudicating tutela writs. The volume of writs filed throughout Colombia represent an incredible demand for adjudication, which the CCC can then supply on its own terms. This ensures that the court has a wide range of issues from

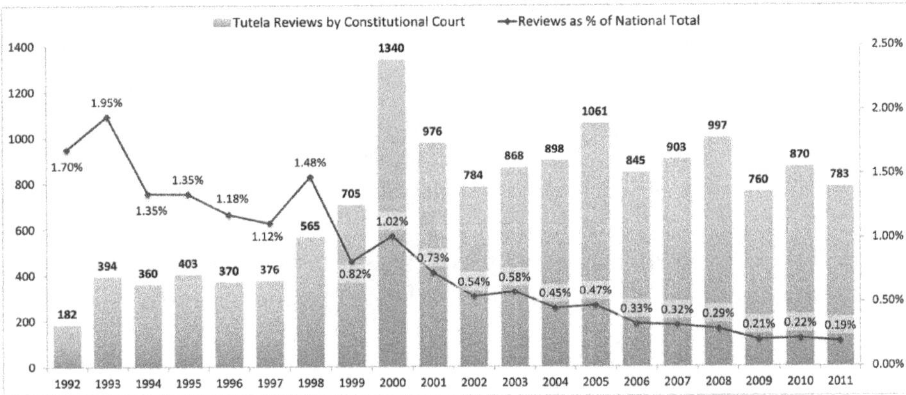

Figure 7. Docket Control in the Colombian Constitutional Court, 1992–2011.

which to select when determining how to focus its limited institutional resources. The court has unchecked discretion as to which tutela appeals it will review, and panels of justices make these determinations based on subjective criteria. As seen in the discussion of IDPs in the next section, the number of tutela revisions received at the CCC acts as a fire alarm to individuals in the court that a legal issue is a matter of serious public concern. Like any institution, however, the CCC must deploy its limited resources selectively, and the degree of selectivity is illustrated in Figure 7. Although the number of tutela appeals reviewed by the court increased fourfold in the court's first 20 years of operation, the percentage of cases reviewed has never gone above 2%. Indeed, by the early 2010s, it consistently fell to well below 0.25%, demonstrating the extreme selectivity the court employs. This selectivity is emblematic of the CCC's flexible procedural environment, and it helps to explain the differing responses to the two human rights issues explored in the subcases.

Subcase 1: Internally Displaced Persons

Armed civil conflict has been a fact of life in Colombia for decades, with ongoing violence between government forces, guerilla groups such as the FARC and ELN,[19] and paramilitary groups. One consequence of this ongoing violence has been a humanitarian crisis in the form of more than five million internally displaced persons over 25 years, and as many as 300,000 newly displaced persons annually (Vidal-López, 2012, p. 7). Internal displacement disproportionately affects vulnerable populations. The average age of members of the displaced population is 23 years, and half of the population is under the age of 15 years. Members of indigenous and Afro-Colombian communities represent 37% and 13% of the number of displaced, respectively.[20] This compares to their share of the overall Colombian population of just 3.4% and 10.6%, respectively.[21] Members of the internally displaced population have limited access to housing, employment, and basic services. As many as 98% live below the poverty line, with 79% living in extreme poverty.[22]

An "Unconstitutional State of Affairs"

In 2004, the CCC finally ruled that this situation had reached an "unconstitutional state of affairs." The magnitude of rights violations had grown to such an extent that further tutela actions with individualized claims against individual government agencies could not be considered effective. Rather, the violations collectively constituted a structural problem that could only be addressed by the court through the implementation of a new legal framework.

The ruling came on January 22, 2004, in the CCC decision known as T-025/04. In the ruling, one of the court's tutela review chambers consolidated 108 separate tutela filings.[23] These various filings represented 1,150 displaced families consisting overwhelmingly of women, children, the elderly, and members of the indigenous population—Colombian society's most marginalized members. The court noted that many of the individuals who were party to the action had already registered in the state's Unified Registry for the Displaced Population, or RUPD, but that problems clearly persisted.[24]

In its decision, the court relied on a combination of international human rights law and domestic constitutional and statutory law. As already noted, the Colombian constitutional system directly incorporates international law, so the international legal framework provides the outer bounds of what is permissible in the domestic context. The primary international law document cited by the court was the 1998 Guiding Principles on Internal Displacement. This UN-sponsored set of principles was an attempt to restate international human rights law and international humanitarian law as it applied to displaced persons, and it described the protections to be afforded to displaced persons, including freedom from discrimination, the right to assistance, and rights to dignity, life, and security, among other protections.[25]

Colombian Law 387 of 1997 provided the domestic framework.[26] It represented the first domestic Colombian law to attempt to treat the IDP issue in a systematic manner and offered the government's first recognition of state responsibility to address the problem. It also provided a definition of IDPs, set up a national registry system to track areas of expulsion and areas of reception of the displaced, and created the National System for Comprehensive Assistance to the Displaced Population (known by its Spanish-language acronym, SNAIPD).[27]

The court used the UN's Guiding Principles to interpret the substantive rights of the population, noting that this was one of the most important sources for determining the extent of rights to be enjoyed by displaced persons.[28] Of note, the court indicated that it considered many of these principles to be part of the *bloque de constitucionalidad*, indicating their peremptory status in the domestic legal system. This emphasis on international law is also noteworthy given that Law 387 provided an enumerated list of rights that itself endorsed the right of IDPs to seek and receive international assistance and to enjoy internationally recognized fundamental rights. The CCC made clear that international principles provided the substantive content for many of the broad statements of principle found in Law 387.

The ruling contained two distinct types of orders to the government. It ordered responses to the specific, concrete demands of individual tutela petitions in line with previous proceedings. In an important deviation from previous cases in this area, however, the court issued structural orders, requiring systemic changes in service provision to the displaced population as a class.[29] This was the first time the court made pronouncements applying to the class as a whole, rather than individual claims (Garavito & Franco, 2010, pp. 84–85).

At this first stage of engagement, however, the court primarily issued broad rulings that ordered the government to comply with its domestic and international legal requirements but left it up to the responsible bureaucratic agencies to determine budgets, establish appropriate mechanisms, and develop other administrative details. The court only provided deadlines for the completion of these initial changes. Only after the repeated failure of government agencies to achieve acceptable outcomes did the Court begin more direct oversight of the process, inviting further litigation, hearings, and involvement by civil society actors as a means of pressuring the government.

The overall result has been an ongoing process of CCC oversight, including more than 20 public hearings (Rodríguez-Garavito, 2011, p. 1694) and in excess of 300 follow-up orders, as the court has attempted to refine the initial order in line with evolving facts on the ground.[30] The court's orders have been wide-ranging. They have included orders establishing a schema for measuring governmental compliance levels,[31] reviewing government budgets and requiring institutional oversight to reduce waste,[32] ordering the government to undertake a national coordination plan to more effectively deliver services,[33] and ordering the use of "indicators" to measure the displaced population's effective enjoyment of rights.[34] In addition to these general orders, the court has issued orders indicating the need to create special commissions or oversight processes that protect the needs of special groups. These have been aimed at protecting leaders of the displaced populations,[35] women,[36] children and adolescents,[37] indigenous groups,[38] Afro-Colombian communities,[39] and persons with disabilities.[40]

The government has responded to many of these demands with new laws and decrees. Decree 250 of 2005 instituted a new national plan and renewed requirements for SNAIPD, including setting appropriate budgets for its various constituent agencies to deal with the displaced population and oversee implementation of national policies.[41] In 2008, the government passed Law 1190, which attempted to improve delivery of services by clarifying the obligations of Colombia's territories toward the displaced population.[42] Despite these governmental efforts, the CCC, in April of 2009, created a special chamber to continue overseeing implementation of T-025.[43] The chamber has, on more than one occasion, ruled that the unconstitutional state of affairs continues, thus extending the court's oversight in this area.

As it has broadened its oversight, the CCC has relied extensively on civil society and NGOs. This has occurred in several ways, all of which serve to increase the inclusiveness of policy development and oversight procedures. The court has depended on NGOs and other civil society actors to provide information on compliance.[44] Indeed, many of these actors joined forces to create a follow-up commission (the Comisión de Seguimiento) to monitor public policy in the area of forced displacement. The commission has been afforded a semiofficial role in the compliance process, being tasked by the court with providing data and policy feedback.[45] This judicial empowerment of outside actors has not been limited to domestic groups. When determining the adequacy of governmental budgetary outlays,[46] for example, the court relied on data provided by the Office of the United Nations High Commissioner for Refugees (UNHCR). As such, the court has buttressed its incorporation of international legal principles by using international qualitative and quantitative measures of compliance with those standards.

In addition to this civil society monitoring through the court, the rulings have promoted a higher level of civil society participation in the policy *formulation* process. In addition to providing data and reports on governmental compliance, these same domestic and international organizations have been tasked with providing feedback on proposed changes to government policy. The court has gone so far as to require that the government receive and review this feedback as part of the policy-making process. In addition, the presentation of this feedback often occurs in the public forums held by the court as information-gathering mechanisms. By inviting (and even requiring) the participation of these groups in public hearings, the court has made the forums serve the additional purpose of educating the public about the issue and shining public attention on the policy debate.

Outcome

Can the CCC's efforts to intervene in this policy area be considered successful? Measuring compliance with human rights obligations presents several difficult questions, but here I consider two. First, it is unclear to what extent human rights decisions should focus on rulings favoring individuals, as opposed to those requiring structural changes in a state's mistreatment of a group or in a government's provision of requisite services. In other words, must effective remedies focus on the individual or group? Second, how do we judge a successful outcome? Is a reduction in violations sufficient, or is complete amelioration of the situation necessary before we can say a court has provided an effective remedy to a human rights violation?

The CCC answered the first question itself: violations of displaced persons' rights could not be corrected through a series of remedies targeting particularized claims. Compliance with domestic commitments to international human rights law required a system-wide transformation. This was made clear both by the court's characterization of the problem and by the procedures it used to address that problem. By declaring the IDP problem an unconstitutional state of affairs, it sent a strong signal that the issue could not be resolved in piecemeal fashion but would instead require systemic changes. It oversaw these systemic changes through hundreds of individual orders that brought governmental representatives, members of Colombian civil society, and international organizations together to diagnose the problem, reform the system, and provide new means of delivering services. The result of this

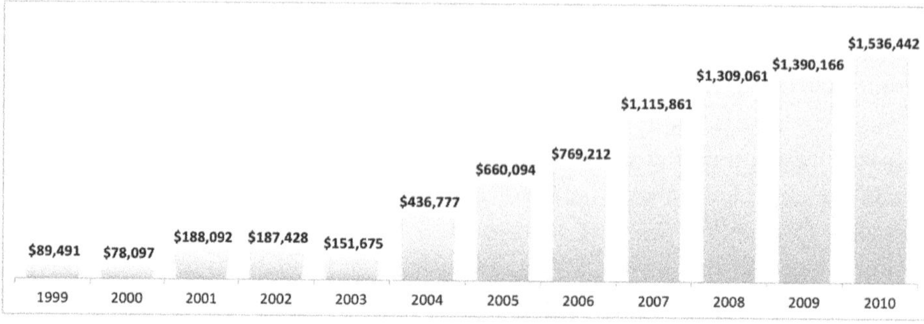

Figure 8. Government Expenditures on Internally Displaced Persons in Colombia, 1999–2010.

transformation can be seen in Figure 8. Governmental expenditures were dramatically increased following the ruling in 2004, and they continued to increase in later years.

This leaves the second question: Is amelioration enough or must the situation be completely remedied? Here the outcome has been much more ambiguous. Not only has the number of displaced persons failed to decline, but it may have increased. The numbers in Figure 9 relate this story. The official records track the number of individuals displaced both in terms of their declaration to the government (dashed line) as well as their reception into the state recovery system (dotted line). The solid line indicates nongovernmental estimates by the NGO Consultoría para los Derechos Humanos y el Desplazamiento (CODHES).[47] Several observations are possible. First, in early years of the crisis, the CODHES numbers are systematically higher than those produced by the government. For example, in the first half of 2011, CODHES estimated there were approximately 89,750 displaced persons in Colombia, compared to the official governmental estimate of 44,144. Second, the government figures actually increase after the timing of the ruling, whereas CODHES's numbers remain relatively flat, though they are given to yearly variation. This is important, as it indicates that the spike in government numbers does not *necessarily* indicate a rise in the number of displaced persons beyond that reported by NGOs, but perhaps merely an improvement in accounting. Indeed, part of the structural remedy ordered by the CCC was an improvement in the registration system. (As registration was required before receipt of government benefits, this was a priority area of reform.) In any event, the fact remains that an incredibly large population of displaced persons remained in an extremely precarious human rights situation, one that

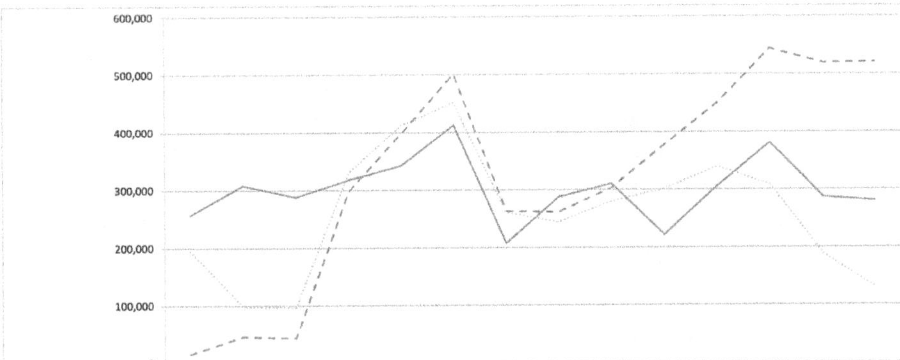

	1997	1998	1999	2000	2001	2002	2003	2004	2005	2006	2007	2008	2009	2010
Official (Receptions)	194,880	97,915	96,696	329,549	412,257	451,650	260,899	244,025	279,663	301,509	339,641	308,030	188,342	131,652
Official (Declarations)	16,323	46,090	43,654	297,410	397,444	501,244	262,945	261,437	302,536	377,241	449,859	543,917	519,356	520,409
NGO Estimates	257,000	308,000	288,127	317,375	342,243	412,553	207,607	287,581	310,237	221,638	305,966	380,863	286,389	280,041

Figure 9. Number of Internally Displaced Persons in Colombia, 1997–2010.

likely will not be totally eradicated until the government and insurgent groups resolve the larger conflict that has plagued Colombia for half a century.

For these reasons the CCC's treatment of the IDP issue must be deemed a qualified success. Despite the sustained difficulties faced by the displaced population, the structural changes to the registration system and the concomitant increase in public expenditures has benefited numerous groups and individuals. This is not to say that the humanitarian crisis has been averted, rather that the outcome should not be dismissed, given that it occurred during a period of extreme civil unrest and military insurgency.[48]

Linking Theory and Practice

The theory in this project postulates that in situations where an apex court is presented with a legal claim arguing that the current government policy is not in compliance with international human rights obligations, the considerations of a legitimacy-seeking strategic court will occur along three axes. The court will be concerned with prospectively anticipating the response of elected political actors and tailor its response accordingly. At the same time, tailoring will be informed by two other dimensions. First, the tailoring will be constrained to the extent that the court's legitimacy is bound up with international human rights law. Second, where a court enjoys a public orientation, it should be able to gauge the relative importance of the issue and consider balancing the public against political actors. Taking these factors into consideration, a court such as the CCC that enjoys high levels of procedural flexibility should be able to control court access, adjudication, and remedies such that the highly salient human rights issue is turned into a legitimacy-enhancing opportunity.

Evidence from both primary and secondary source materials reveals significant congruence between theoretical expectations and the CCC's activity when addressing the IDP issue. Was this an area where the court had a legitimacy concern? The court has an incentive to rule against government policy when failure to do so threatens the court's reputation as a rule-of-law actor. Here, this clearly seems to be the case; the CCC operates in a system of deeply embedded internationalism, so a ruling that ignored international human rights law would be highly unlikely. Not only did the CCC indicate the expansive nature of the human rights violation in its rulings, this situation was well documented by both domestic and international human rights organizations in the lead-up to the case. As such, the court had an incentive to rule against the government and risked paying a legitimacy cost if it failed to do so.

Did the relative weight of government opposition to a court intervention outweigh the potential of the court to leverage the public in support of compliance? Here, too, the facts seem to comport well with theoretical predictions. The government had already indicated a willingness to address the IDP issue with its passage of Law 387 of 1997, which acknowledged state responsibility in this area and set up a national registry system, albeit an ineffectual one. Along the first dimension of consideration, then, the CCC could anticipate only limited resistance to judicialization of the IDP issue. In addition, along the third dimension of concern—the public—the court had ample reason to believe it could leverage public support in this issue to pressure the government to comply. As the court noted in its ruling, the number of tutela proceedings on this issue area was large enough to raise serious concerns within the court. In this sense, the tutela "alarm system" worked quite well. In addition, the numerous organizations that offered reports and friend-of-the-court briefs demonstrated the ready availability of civil society actors to provide resources the court might not be able to manage on its own, further providing insurance against any potential government noncompliance.[49] Importantly, the court also used its flexible procedural environment to bolster its public support orientation, dynamically enhancing its institutional standing across time.

Lastly, although the court acted in line with theory, this subcase indicates the limits of any court's ability to address human rights concerns on its own.

As such, it further underscores the importance of procedural flexibility to a court's success. The CCC expressed a real concern for scarce judicial institutional resources when dealing with the IDP issue. It noted early on in the process that the structural failure to provide for the rights of the displaced population had resulted in the overcrowding of the courts and the excessive reliance on the tutela (Cepeda-Espinosa, 2004, pp. 32–33). Even following the initial ruling, the extent of oversight was taxing on the court. The monitoring process involved the generation of 1.5 million pages of judicial records, a number cited by the court itself as one reason it proceeded with the establishment of a special enforcement chamber to handle all related matters.[50] Here, the flexibility of the CCC's procedural environment provided additional maneuverability to address a situation that challenged not just government policy, but the court's institutional capacity itself.

Along all axes, the activity of the court demonstrates congruence with theoretical expectations. The government had previously failed to comply with what was framed as an international human rights obligation but simultaneously failed to demonstrate a strong unified opposition to compliance. The court had indications of public concern over the issue in the form of extensive use of the tutela in this issue area, and it was thus able to balance public concern against elected branches of government. The court further leveraged outside actors in an attempt to increase the likelihood of government compliance with the court's ruling. Lastly, it did this while being cognizant of the institutional cost to the judiciary itself, and it used its procedural flexibility to enhance the likelihood of a successful, legitimacy-enhancing outcome.

Subcase 2: Extrajudicial Executions

Like claims put forth by displaced indigenous persons, claims against the government and the military for human rights violations exhibit mixed success. What little success has been achieved follows a similar yet distinct pattern to that seen in the case of displaced persons: judicial manipulation of procedural rules in the nation's courts has allowed targeted judicial oversight. Here, however, the manipulation of procedural rules has had the opposite effect of that seen in the case of displaced persons: a restricting rather than expansion of the CCC's involvement in crafting a policy response. Faced with a lack of strong public support in the face of political opposition, the court has acquiesced and allowed disputes to unfold in other political and judicial venues. Two interacting dynamics have characterized this process. First, the combined resistance of the military and its political supporters threatened the institutional prerogatives of the court; second, the court reacted by limiting its direct involvement in this legal issue area, instead formulating procedural tools that allowed for the unfolding of these cases in other venues. The overall result has been the opposite of that witnessed in the area of IDPs: a closing off of litigation reaching the CCC and a lack of court-centered enforcement, despite this issue area's high level of legalization.

In this section, I consider the grave human rights violation of extrajudicial execution. In particular, I focus on a problem known in Colombia by the rather anodyne phrase *falsos positivos* (false positives). This type of extrajudicial killing follows a common pattern and has its roots in government programs. Under various government incentive programs, individuals are offered monetary rewards for assisting in the capture of criminal elements or participants in the armed insurgency that has plagued Colombia for decades. The military participates in these programs, offering incentives for the capture or killing of members of illegal armed groups. Pressure on military units also comes from the desire to increase the reported number of killed insurgents in the ongoing armed conflict. Military commanders have been provided with discretionary funds to assist with their operations, and these have been used to provide rewards to informers. It is under these circumstances that the problem arose. Victims are lured with false promises such as the offer of a job. Once a victim is in a remote location, members of the military murder the victim and arrange the scene to make it look as though the victim was a member of an armed subversive group or criminal organization. The victim is then included in counts of legitimate military targets (Alston, 2010).

The problem is widespread but imprecisely documented. Although the earliest allegations trace this phenomenon to the 1980s, the greatest number of *falsos positivos* are believed to have occurred beginning in 2004. The official figures of the Ministry of Defense, as reported by the Colombian government to the UN special rapporteur, are shown in Table 3. These numbers, however, reflect only the number of complaints of unlawful killings reported by Colombians to the government. Both Colombian and international NGOs claim a much higher number of killings. The highly respected Colombian Commission of Jurists reports significantly higher numbers over a comparable period; their accounting is also reported in Table 3.[51] The discrepancy is notable, and in fact other government actors report much higher levels of violations. By the early 2010s, the national Office of the Public Prosecutor

Table 3. Reporting of Extrajudicial Killings in Colombia

Reported by the Ministry of Defense		*Colombian Commission of Jurists*	
		July 1996–June 1997	155
		July 1997–June 1998	147
		July 1998–June 1999	120
2000	13	July 1999–June 2000	127
2001	8	July 2000–June 2001	105
2002	15	July 2001–June 2002	136
2003	30	July 2002–June 2003	187
2004	83	July 2003–June 2004	231
2005	125	July 2004–June 2005	218
2006	136	July 2005–June 2006	267
2007	96	July 2006–June 2007	287
2008	46	July 2007–June 2008	296
Total	**552**	**Total**	**2,276**

reported having 1,205 cases on its books; of these, 425 were in the stage of preliminary investigation, 641 were active cases, 68 were awaiting judgment, and 71 represented convictions.[52] As late as March 2013, various NGOs testified before the Inter-American Commission on Human Rights that extrajudicial executions had increased by 64% between 2002 and 2008,[53] with one organization estimating that the total number of executions had reached 3,347.[54] Despite the widespread pattern of this grave human rights violation, the court had only minimal involvement in crafting a solution. Instead, the CCC followed a reduced pattern of intervention in this policy area consistent with the theory's prediction that the court would limit intervention when faced with government opposition and little counterbalancing public support. The pattern has been the opposite of the court's treatment of IDPs: rather than expanding access, inviting litigation, and creating a structural approach to the problem, the court has limited access, avoided oversight opportunities, and addressed the situation in piecemeal fashion.

Resisting Oversight

Unlike the court's intervention in the issue of IDPs, its involvement in the area of extrajudicial executions does not revolve around a singular case. This is reflective of the court's failure to undertake a structural response to the problem. Instead, the relevant interactions between the court and the government have appeared only piecemeal in the decades since the inauguration of the 1991 constitution. Although, as Table 3 indicates, the problem of extrajudicial killings reached unprecedented levels in the mid-2000s, the problem had persisted for well over a decade. Indeed, the court's inability and unwillingness to intercede as the killings peaked can be seen as having their roots in that earlier period of military violations of international law.

The court had strong indications that the government would resist oversight in this area. Historically, jurisdiction over military prosecutions had been an area of contestation between the military and civilian courts. This unstable legal framework predates the 1991 political reforms and has extended well into the current constitutional era. As early as 1978, political violence prompted a decree by President Julio César Turbay that ceded jurisdiction over crimes related to political violence to military tribunals.[55] The military courts were also given the authority to determine whether they or civilian courts had jurisdiction over a matter. The Supreme Court (the highest court prior to the 1991 constitutional reforms) finally challenged this situation in 1987, when it ruled that the military courts were unconstitutional, that it had competence to decide jurisdictional disputes between civilian and military courts, and that the civilian courts should have jurisdiction over crimes alleged to have been committed outside the scope of military duties (Nagle, 1995, p. 73). This challenge was short-lived. Under the 1991 constitution, the military retained jurisdiction over crimes committed by the military,[56] and soldiers were granted a specific carve-out provision granting them immunity from prosecution for any constitutional rights violations committed under direct orders.[57]

Within the first few years of its operation, however, the CCC moved to assert its authority over military tribunals. Two key rulings, one in 1995 and another in 1997, helped define the contours of debate. In 1995, the CCC ruled that active members of the military could not serve as judges on military tribunals because of the clear conflict of interest and threat to judicial impartiality.[58] The political reaction was swift and proceeded through both government and public channels. An exchange of letters between the minister of defense and the president of the court appeared in the media, with each demanding the other respect his institution's autonomy (Rodríguez-Raga, 2011, p. 108). Political leaders called for the CCC's abolition, and a court-packing measure started to make its way through the legislature. Although these initiatives ultimately failed, a different constitutional amendment was passed that same year allowing military tribunals to be composed of retired *or sitting* military personnel, effectively overruling the court's decision (Kyle & Reiter, 2013).[59]

Two years later, in 1997, the court again asserted its control over military tribunals. This time, it focused not on the role of military personnel but on the nature of the claims going before these tribunals. The CCC ruled that grave human rights violations were, by definition, outside the scope of military service and, therefore, logically, could not be considered by military tribunals. The court also found that in situations in which the applicability of military jurisdiction was not clearly proven, the civilian courts would retain jurisdiction.[60] By the turn of the millennium the back-and-forth between the government and the court had resulted in what could be seen as a truce. Although the court had reasserted its right to assess jurisdictional issues, political leaders had demonstrated that they would not accept intervention in the nature or functioning of military courts when the latter *did* have jurisdiction.

At the same time, these rulings highlighted a rift between the CCC and the other civilian judicial institutions—one that could potentially be exploited by political actors and threaten the court's institutional standing. The 1991 constitution had taken a shortcut to judicial reform, creating a new court on top of a preexisting judiciary. This, perhaps unsurprisingly, led to a series of counter-rulings between the CCC, the Supreme Court, and the Superior Judicial Council as they negotiated the limits of their respective jurisdictions. Citizens made use of the tutela, for example, to challenge rulings of the Supreme Court and the Superior Judicial Council, arguing that the latter institutions did not apply constitutional law correctly. The CCC's 1997 ruling on military jurisdiction joined this stream of jurisdictional disputes, as it purported to regulate for all courts the limits of jurisdiction. Within a year, the Superior Judicial Council announced it was not bound by the CCC's determination of jurisdiction and remanded a case to the military courts.[61]

According to one later analysis, these types of disputes between the courts had the effect of "delegitimizing the judicial branch and giving an opportunity to the executive to take sides as it sees fit, despite the executive's claim that it's leaving an eventual accord in the hands of the judicial organs."[62] This executive interference was in fact realized in the year 2000, when President Andrés Pastrana issued decree 1382, which purported to regulate which judges in the country could hear which tutela cases.[63] Political interest in these jurisdictional issues even spread to the Senate's selection process for new CCC justices. According to one study, a judicial candidate's position on this issue is more important to senators than the candidate's ideological views on substantive matters (Montoya García, 2011).

By the early 2000s, then, it was clear that involvement in military prosecutions could pose a risk to the court's institutional prerogatives. The threat of political involvement extended even to constitutional procedural law in the form of the tutela, an area in which the CCC had from its founding exercised significant autonomy. The court nevertheless found itself at the center of these issues as the decade continued. Constitutional reforms in 2002 aimed to transition the Colombian criminal justice system from a mixed inquisitorial system to a primarily accusatorial system of criminal prosecutions. Although the reforms did not primarily target military crimes such as the *falsos positivos*, the rights of victims would invariably be implicated because of the interplay between the criminal procedure code, victims' rights, and the question of jurisdiction. The CCC's earlier jurisprudence had already asserted that cases involving violations of human rights should go to the civilian court system, as such violations fell outside the scope of legitimate military duties.[64] In addition, the court, in a landmark 2002 decision, had found that victims had a right to participate in criminal trials and also to seek truth and justice—not just economic damages. Justice in this sense meant overcoming impunity.[65] The constitutional reforms, then, would shape how the judicial system dealt with cases involving victims' rights when and if members of the military ended up in civilian courts.

How precisely an accusatorial system, premised on the dueling viewpoints of prosecution and defense, could incorporate a third viewpoint—the victim's—was unclear. Although Colombia abolished private (citizen-initiated) prosecutions in 1938, the right of victims to participate in prosecutions so as to advance a civil claim alongside the criminal prosecution still existed. How this civil participation would function in the new model was unclear. Some in the preparatory commission that drafted the new language had argued for a strictly limited role for the victim as passive bystander, as the government and defendant engaged in a traditional adversarial proceeding overseen by the neutral third-party judge; others argued for a model more in line with restorative justice processes, wherein the victim is an active protagonist in proceedings. As is often the case, the constitutional reform language was intentionally vague in order to accommodate negotiators' differing and at times irreconcilable demands (Sánchez-Mejía, 2017). In particular, although the new constitutional language indicated that victims could participate in criminal proceedings under the new accusatorial model, it did not specify how or under what circumstances.[66] Instead, these issues were left up to Congress in subsequent legislation and, of course, by the CCC when it inevitably heard constitutional challenges to the new constitutional and statutory language.

Congress passed the new Criminal Procedure Code in 2004.[67] The law set out a series of protections for victims, ranging from humane treatment to reparation for damages to the receipt of information relating to the proceeding.[68] A claim of unconstitutionality was brought to the court in 2006, however, claiming that the new code failed to provide for effective enforcement of the rights to truth, justice, and reparation guaranteed by the constitution. The claim argued that these rights could only be effectuated by treating victims as equal parties in criminal proceedings, something the code failed to do.[69]

The court took this opportunity to reaffirm and even expand its earlier jurisprudence dealing with victims' rights. Its ruling in case C-454/06 followed the precedent it had set 4 years earlier in C-228/02, adopting a broad understanding of victims' rights beyond mere compensation. Rather, the court stated that, in line with constitutional guarantees and evolving international law standards, victims were entitled to effective judicial remedies. These included not just financial compensation but also truth and justice in the form of protections against impunity. The court located these rights not just in the Colombian constitution but in the constitution as informed by the Universal Declaration of Human Rights, the American Convention on Human Rights, the statutes of the International Criminal Tribunal for Rwanda and the International Criminal Tribunal for the Former Yugoslavia, the Rome Statute of the International Criminal Court, and emerging legal norms in the UN system.[70]

Beyond these broad statements, the court articulated specific procedural rights held by victims under Colombia's newly revised criminal code. A victim would enjoy the right to communication from the moment of interaction with authorities, rather than from the beginning of trial proceedings, as information relevant to the right to know could occur before formal intervention in proceedings.[71] Similarly, because the right to justice encompasses the victim's right to provide evidence and to prove a case, the victim must be permitted under the code to participate in preparatory hearings in a manner equivalent to the prosecution and defense.[72] In short, the rights of victims require involvement in the criminal proceedings that could not be easily substituted for by the prosecutor, given the latter's differing interests. These were real wins for victims of human rights violations. They went beyond symbolic gestures in support of victims' rights and instead indicated the court's willingness to craft procedural tools that promoted substantive rights.

The articulation of procedural tools to empower victims, it should be noted, primarily dealt with procedures that would be put to use in *other* courts. This is telling, as it parallels the CCC's response to another pair of questions resurfaced by the 2004 Criminal Procedure Law: the question of intercourt tutelas and who had the authority to regulate them. Specifically, Article 185 of the new code included language preventing the use of the tutela action to challenge a criminal conviction. The court rejected this limitation in case C-591/05, noting that it would create an institutional space where fundamental rights guaranteed by the constitution were not subject to protection using the tutela. Accordingly, the CCC declared that language of the statute to be inoperative and even stated that the tutela was beyond regulation by the legislature.[73] It buttressed this decision by referencing international treaty law binding on the Colombian state. In particular, the court noted that Article 2 of the International Covenant on Civil and Political Rights and Article 25 of the American Convention on Human Rights protected the individual's right to a "simple, effective, and short means of effective protection of fundamental rights"[74] and that allowing limitations of the tutela would, therefore, violate Colombia's obligations under international law.[75] In doing so, the court protected the integrity of the tutela—and reaffirmed the court's institutional prerogative to regulate this unique constitutional action while burnishing its reputation as guardian of constitutional and international human rights protections.

In the same case, however, the court reaffirmed case law that limited the practical use of the tutela. The CCC restated what essentially amounted to a domestic "exhaustion" requirement for intercourt disputes. These types of disputes had raised controversy before, both because of institutional competition between the judicial branches and because of a desire to respect the principle of res judicata. As such, the CCC stated that in intercourt disputes, all other judicial tools should be used prior to employing the tutela action, except when such a limitation would result in irreparable harm.[76] The court specifically stated that these other tools should include both ordinary and *extraordinary* judicial means, and only after all such means were exhausted would the use of the tutela be proper. The CCC also noted that, in addition to raising res judicata concerns, any other approach would potentially overwhelm the court system.[77] Capacity is, undoubtedly, a reasonable concern for any institution—but it must also be recognized as shifting the burden to those whose rights are at risk. The court also suggested that, like in its dispute with elected officials over military jurisdiction, it was willing to accept a truce with other judicial institutions to avoid unnecessary conflict.

These seemingly technical issues—despite their procedural nature—have the potential to significantly affect the enforcement of substantive rights, and indeed they have. Overall, extrajudicial executions have reflected mixed progress as a result of limited court intervention. On the one hand, the CCC has been receptive to cases that allowed it to fulfill its role as interlocutor between international law and domestic law, and to ensure that victims could claim more than mere financial compensation during criminal proceedings. On the other hand, the court used these cases to reassert its institutional oversight of critical areas, such as tutela procedures, but without assuming direct oversight of the underlying substantive violations themselves or the government's policy response. Instead, the initiation of suits was left to prosecutors (although, of course, victims were permitted to participate once suits reached the trial stage). Similarly, tutelas were prevented from becoming a conduit for diverting like cases into a systematic oversight proceeding by the CCC. In effect, the court deployed a rearguard strategy—safeguarding its institutional role as interpreter of international law and overseer of the tutela, but without making the CCC the primary player in adjudication of substantive cases that infringed upon constitutional and international human rights law. The result was an ongoing decentering of the court from any inquiry into the *falsos positivos* cases, unlike the court's prominent role in the IDP issue. Given the extensive backlog of cases, this constellation of procedural limitations left the vast majority of cases unresolved.

To the extent that improvements in rights enforcement have occurred, they have been attributed to the improvements instituted by the government itself following unfavorable press coverage of a specific episode in the ongoing *falsos positivos* series of killings. This particular episode involved the extrajudicial execution of at least 23 civilians lured from the city of Soacha near Bogotá. News of the killings became public in 2008 and led to President Álvaro Uribe's firing of more than 20 officers and soldiers, including 3 generals.[78] In addition to disciplining members of the military, the government undertook changes such as increasing monitoring of incentive programs and enhancing cooperation with international organizations (Alston, 2010, p. 11). The CCC, meanwhile, was not an active participant in crafting or overseeing the policy response.

Unfortunately, there is much more that could be done. It is clear that the court has not acted as aggressively as it could, given the example of its intervention and ongoing oversight of reform of the treatment of IDPs. For example, the UN special rapporteur recommended that all cases of extrajudicial execution be held in civilian courts, that more resources be provided to investigate allegations of extrajudicial executions, and that stated government policies on human rights and humanitarian law standards be effectively put into practice (Alston, 2010, p. 28). These are the types of systemic changes that the court has overseen through its structural ruling in the area of internal displacement, yet the court has avoided a similar role in the case of extrajudicial executions. Expanding individual victims' rights is undoubtedly an important piece of the puzzle, and the court should be lauded for its ability to bring those rights in line with international standards; but, nevertheless, it fails to address the systemic nature of the crimes.

Coda: Building on a Foundation of Retrenchment

The CCC thus constructed a foundational approach to dealing with these types of rights violations: simultaneously asserting the importance of international human rights law while retreating from ongoing systematic oversight of remedial efforts. It has built on this foundation with more recent case law dealing with the ongoing peace process between the Colombian government and the FARC. The *falsos positivos* cases are theoretically well within the scope of the peace agreement, but again the CCC has engaged in what could be called permissive retrenchment—CCC approval of a legal framework that will effectively remove the court from this policy area in favor of an alternative, ad hoc judicial structure. This result has occurred despite several years of the court's interaction with the peace process itself, through numerous public hearings, constitutional rulings, and episodes of judicial dialogue between the CCC and the International Criminal Court.[79]

The Colombian government under President Juan Manuel Santos spent nearly 4 years negotiating with the FARC in hopes of securing an end to the state's long period of civil unrest. These negotiations bore fruit, with the two sides reaching a tentative peace agreement in August 2016.[80] The government submitted this peace agreement to a national "plebiscite for peace" in October of the same year, hoping to strengthen the government's mandate in implementing the agreement. The plebiscite, however, had the opposite effect. It revealed the nation's deeply divided attitude toward the peace agreement: 50.2% against the agreement; 49.8% in favor.[81] Following this defeat, Santos abandoned the electoral route and implemented a slightly revised peace agreement through a fast-track legislative process.[82]

The revised "Final Agreement," signed in November 2016, included numerous provisions that caused consternation among human rights advocates. In particular, sections of the agreement dealing with prosecution for past crimes were to be dealt with under a Special Jurisdiction for Peace (SJP).[83] This SJP would operate separately from the permanent civilian court system, in effect creating a parallel justice system for crimes related to the conflict—including those allegedly committed by members of the military.[84] In a series of rulings, the CCC consistently ruled in favor of the peace process. In two of the most important rulings, claimants argued that the SJP prevented victims from exercising their rights under international law to seek prosecution for past human rights violations. They argued in particular that this violation would undermine the structure of the Colombian constitution, given its reliance on international human rights law. As such, the claimants urged the court to reject the SJP using the *bloque de constitucionalidad* doctrine. The CCC refused. Instead, the court reaffirmed its commitment to international human rights law, but did so by reframing international law as supportive of the Colombian constitution's Article 22, which guarantees the "right to peace." The CCC claimed that by furthering peace, the SJP and other aspects of the Final Agreement comported with both the Colombian constitution and the Colombian state's international human rights law obligations.[85]

This process shows the CCC's continued desire to avoid entering a prolonged conflict with the government on such a politically divisive issue. One aspect of the SJP framework is particularly telling: the treatment of the tutela, and by extension the role of the CCC in ensuring that future SJP rulings comport with international human rights law. With regard to the tutela, the SJP represents an unfortunate curtailing of that powerful procedural mechanism, not unlike the exhaustion requirement that the court permitted following the 2004 Criminal Procedure Law. However, whereas in that earlier episode the court asserted its final control over this procedural mechanism, here the court seems to have ceded ultimate control. Namely, the Final Agreement specifically requires that any tutela challenge of an SJP ruling occur within the SJP framework, not in the regular civilian courts. Only after all appeals have been satisfied within the SJP—and even then only with the approval of a sufficient number of SJP justices—can a claimant use the tutela to seek constitutional review.[86] This represents an astounding and unprecedented retrenchment of the CCC's control of the tutela. It also suggests that the SJP framework effectively allows for the curtailing of CCC oversight of human rights violations that occurred during Colombia's long civil conflict. A decade after the Soacha scandal, the court continues to avoid direct conflict with the government on this troubling issue.

Instead, the court has allowed the government to equivocate on this issue. Rather than conducting trials in the normal civilian courts, to the extent that any take place, they will happen within the SJP. While this outcome avoids the use of military courts, this alternative court system falls short of the spirit of the UN special rapporteur's report on extrajudicial, summary, or arbitrary executions (Alston, 2010), which argues in favor of the preexisting civilian system as required by the relevant human rights regimes. Instead, the civilian court system—in particular the CCC—is limited in its ability to assert final authority over the outcome of trials under the SJP. Notably, the CCC has affirmed its central role in the judicial system and its fealty to international law through numerous court rulings, but the practical effect is a quiet ceding of jurisdiction to an alternative venue when it comes to the most politically explosive cases.

Linking Theory and Practice

My theory postulates that when the CCC is presented with a claim that a government policy is not in compliance with international human rights obligations, the court will react in accordance with the relative strengths of organized government opposition to and public support for judicial enforcement. If government opposition is high and public support is low, it will not be possible for the court to balance the public against elite political actors. The prediction, instead, is that we will witness low levels of court engagement with the issue area, with the CCC going so far as to constrict public access mechanisms so that the court is less exposed to legitimacy-threatening legal activity. Evidence from both primary and secondary source materials reveals significant congruence between theoretical expectations and the court's activity in the area of extrajudicial executions.

Was this an area where the court had a legitimacy concern? The theory predicts specific forms of court behavior in those situations when government policy is in conflict with the obligations of international law, as this discrepancy between government policy and international legal requirements presents a legitimacy challenge to the court. This situation obtains in the area of extrajudicial killings. Not only did the killing of civilians clearly contradict well-established instruments of humanitarian law to which Colombia was a party, the situation garnered the attention of numerous NGOs and international organizations, including the United Nations.

Did the relative weight of government opposition to a court intervention outweigh the potential of the court to leverage the public in support of compliance? The empirical record again suggests support for the theory. The history of jurisdictional disputes between the court and political actors made clear that the government would not hesitate to side with military courts in a dispute, if necessary overturning CCC decisions through constitutional amendment. At the same time, the government enacted criminal and military justice reforms that subsequently transformed the prosecution system into an adversarial system while altering the traditional rights of victims under the Colombian constitution. More recently, the government has concluded a peace agreement that creates a special jurisdiction to try human rights abuses, despite the dubious legality of the mechanisms involved. The CCC has offered opinions on these matters and reasserted its ability to weigh the balance of rights under the constitution, but it has done so while generally permitting the changes made by the government.

The activity of the court demonstrates congruence with theoretical expectations. The government had previously failed to comply with what was framed as an international human rights obligation, and it simultaneously demonstrated strong unified opposition to compliance. The court had indications that the government's response would outweigh the ability to invoke public support to protect the court from noncompliance. As a result, the court restricted access and failed to provide oversight when given the opportunity. It has, in addition, allowed jurisdictional changes under the Final Agreement that will allow it to avoid hearing related cases in the future.

Linking the Theory to the Subcases

Why was the court more willing and better able to address the needs of displaced persons than those of victims of military violations of human rights? In both situations, the court did rule in favor of claimants and against the government. In the case of displaced persons, however, the court took on a much more activist role and required greater ongoing changes from the government. Interestingly, the court was more effective in an area of policy that required structural changes on the part of numerous government agencies, cost the government trillions of pesos, and was in a much less well-defined area of human rights law.

The difference between the court's treatment of IDP claims and its treatment of extrajudicial executions makes it clear that the CCC was far more willing to engage political actors and the public in the IDP cases. The different outcomes result from two factors. First, government opposition in the IDP cases was of a different magnitude from its opposition in the extrajudicial-killing cases, with government actors being far more willing to at least attempt to comply with the IDP rulings. Second, in the face of greater governmental reluctance in the extrajudicial killing cases, the CCC would have had to rely on a much stronger public counterbalancing to resist political retaliation. As I will explain, this was unlikely to occur.

Differing Levels of Political Resistance

The IDP rulings faced little concerted political opposition. Indeed, politicians conceded the normative importance of this issue by passing Law 387 in 1997. Of course, while Law 387 defined IDPs, it did little to address the costly material needs of this population in an effective manner. To the extent the court ordered changes, it was able to engage a public concerned about the issue in a way that increased political pressure and required government agencies to comply with the government's own stated policy goals.

In the military cases, on the contrary, politicians were quick to unite against CCC intervention, resisting or overriding court decisions. In such a situation, the court would have had to rely on extremely favorable public opinion in order to effectively pressure the government to comply with any decision against the military. It otherwise would face a choice of two negative outcomes: (1) rule in support of the government and accept accusations of capitulation, or (2) rule against the government and face ongoing threat of political retaliation. Faced with this situation, the court limited its exposure by ceding jurisdictional oversight to other institutions and failing to enact a larger juridical framework like the continuing chamber used in the IDP case.

Another factor making court intervention more palatable to the government in the IDP cases was the characterization of the problem being addressed. In the case of extrajudicial executions, the military (and thus the government) was the clear perpetrator. This contrasts with the situation of IDPs, where the problem has been framed not just as a government failure to deliver services but also as deriving from the illegal actions of third parties. According to records of the state registration system, IDPs in the year 2010, for example, blamed their displacement on the activities of guerrillas (32%), paramilitary groups (15%), other groups (15%), the national army (0.5%), and criminal gangs (0.1%) (Vidal-López, 2012). In this framing, the role of the government in creating the situation can be seen as negligible. This framing is also supported by accounts that suggest the incidence of forced displacement has increased during electoral cycles, the reasoning being that displacement is related to efforts by irregular armed groups to maintain control of local offices.[87] As such, the court's intervention furthered government interests in consolidating control and providing services in contested regions. The lack of government opposition to the ruling is, in this sense, consistent with Shapiro's argument that "a major function of courts in many societies is to assist in holding the countryside" (Shapiro, 1986, p. 23). Although the CCC ruled against the government, it did so in a way that furthered broader government interests.

Differing Levels of Public Concern

The theory presented here argues for the importance of public opinion precisely because a public support orientation provides the CCC with a potential source of political support independent of the government. In contentious cases, the court is unlikely to risk backlash if it does not have public support that might allow it to employ its array of procedural tools—such as increasing access to new claims or creating public hearings to further educate the public—in such a way as to increase pressure on the government and protect itself from backlash.

The court and other actors are well aware of this constraint. As already mentioned, the CCC regularly holds public forums, not only to gather information but also to educate the public. The court has also resorted to public appeals through news releases in an attempt to shore up its argument against political actors, and it has circumvented traditional news outlets and conducted direct outreach to the public through the use of social media. Of course, the court is not the only institution aware of this public opinion constraint; the military is also well aware of the need for public support, and it produces printed and online materials describing its outreach efforts and improvements in relations with the public. Indeed, it has gone so far as to remind the public

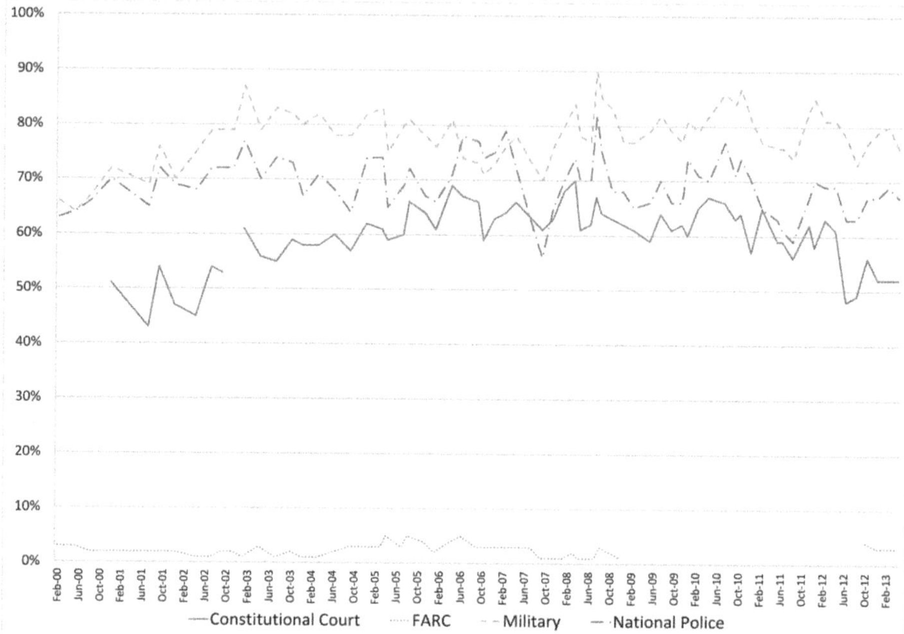

Figure 10. Public Support for National Institutions in Colombia, 2000–2013.

just how much the public supports the military. In 2009, for example, as part of National Human Rights Day, the Ministry of National Defense published a special report, in both Spanish and English, on its efforts to support human rights through security, noting that the "favorability rating for the Armed Forces and the National Police among Colombians" had reached, according to Gallup, "'82% and 70%, respectively.'"[88]

While there is no clear poll asking the Colombian populace their views on the issues of IDPs and extrajudicial killings, there are indicators of the likelihood of support for CCC intervention in these issue areas. Gallup polls can provide a general sense of the relative strength of public support for the court, as well as for the perceived targets of court intervention in each of the two cases. Figure 10 shows that the court's approval rating has consistently hovered around 60%, indicating the high regard in which the public holds the institution. Nevertheless, both the army and the national police regularly outperform the court in public opinion surveys, with the national police consistently receiving scores in the 70% range, and the army achieving public approval levels in the range of 80% or even 90%. Compare this with the public approval rating of the FARC, which seldom exceeds 5%. As mentioned earlier, armed groups such as the FARC are much more closely associated with displacement than are the army or national police. This makes the court's reliance on public pressure much easier in IDP cases than in cases of extrajudicial execution, because in the latter the court can be seen as attacking a set of extremely popular national institutions. And, of course, President Santos's 2016 plebiscite revealed the stark divide among the Colombian people on the issue of military conflict. In short, whereas in IDP cases the court can balance the public against politicians, in military cases no such balancing act is feasible.

Conclusion

Despite its propitious origins and stated dedication to international law, the Colombian Constitutional Court has only partially lived up to the perhaps unrealistic expectations placed on it from its founding. It has been relatively successful in addressing the crisis of internal displacement because it has been able to focus its efforts on requiring the government to provide services that, though expensive, were generally supported by large segments of the population and not systematically opposed by the political establishment. In contrast, the court's unwillingness to intercede in a systematic way in the area of extrajudicial killings points to the limits of any court-based strategy to enforce international human rights law. When government opposition is strong and there is little opportunity to engage the public, even an institutionally well-positioned court such as the CCC has shown it will not risk political backlash. Instead, the court has focused its scarce resources on areas of law where it can make a meaningful difference without risking its own institutional legitimacy.

Perhaps what is most striking is the area of human rights in which the court has been at least somewhat effective: IDPs. In contradiction to theories that would posit better outcomes based on legalistic rulings or on the importance of treaty ratification, the court has been more rigorous in supporting human rights law that is less codified. Extrajudicial killings are covered by numerous binding treaties to which Colombia is a party, including the International Covenant on Civil and Political Rights, the American Convention on Human Rights, and the Geneva conventions and their additional protocols, to name but a few. In addition, these obligations are directly imported and theoretically enforceable in the domestic legal system through Article 93 of the Colombian constitution. The Inter-American Court of Human Rights and the Inter-American Commission on Human Rights have likewise been active in their condemnation of rights violations in this area. All the predictors of an effective judicial role under traditional legal incorporation theories are present, and yet the CCC has failed to act according to expectations in this area.

The reason for this is the selective enforcement pattern of the CCC. The legal system's public support orientation allows the court to determine which areas of international human rights law are most likely to receive support from the population. Its flexible procedural environment then allows it to further bolster its public support apparatus, engaging civil society actors and increasing public awareness of the issues. The flexible procedural environment also allows the court to shape the flow of litigation on which it must rule. This has allowed the court to maintain or expand follow-up litigation in the area of IDPs; in contrast, this flexibility has allowed the court to avoid the heavily legalized area of extrajudicial killings, which threatened to invite a political backlash. An opening for judicial enforcement was much more evident in the much *less* internationally codified area of IDPs. The primary international law document dealing with this issue is the nonbinding Guiding Principles on Internal Displacement. Moreover, the very nature of the problem suggests the difficulty in subjecting this issue to international standards: the population of concern is defined as *internal* to the sovereign state.

Yet, it is in this issue area that the court has made the most forceful push to secure individuals' and groups' rights under international human rights legal principles. It has done this not just by reference to the Guiding Principles but by incorporating international measures of compliance and oversight by international bodies directly into its enforcement process. It was able to do this by changing and sometimes creating out of whole cloth procedures by which litigants, international organizations, NGOs, and even the public had a much greater role in the court system. The court was able to balance outside actors against government reluctance and bureaucratic foot-dragging using tools that it was not willing to risk employing in the area of extrajudicial executions. In doing so, the court strengthened its role in the domestic political system and maintained its institutional legitimacy as a rule-of-law actor.

The future of domestic judicial enforcement of human rights law in Colombia is likely to continue to reflect this pattern of selective enforcement and judicial balancing of political and public interests. Unlike the question of displaced persons, the question of grave military violations of human rights is one in which the court continues to avoid asserting a dynamic ownership role, as evidenced by the more recent peace talks with the FARC. This outcome is not ideal for those hoping to see courts act as effective enforcement mechanisms for all areas of international human rights law. It does, however, allow the CCC to continue to act in some policy areas, and it limits the ability of politicians to attack the court or claim that it is overreaching. Given the still transitional state of democracy and rights enforcement in Colombia, this outcome perhaps represents the outer limits of any court's ability to entrench international human rights protections domestically.

CHAPTER 4

South Africa: Majoritarian Difficulties

There are circumstances of transition where a certain measure of incongruity and even injustice is inevitable. In the present case, however, the incongruity flows not from the nature of the process itself, as contemplated by the framers, but from the mode of interpretation, as adopted by sections of the judiciary.

—*S v Mhlungu and Others*, 1995

Introduction

From April 26 to 29, 1994, South Africa held its first national elections open to all racial groups. On the first day of elections, a new constitution came into force,[1] marking the official transition from the former Apartheid regime and the dissolution of the racially constructed "homeland" system. A newly established constitutional court began enforcing the country's first Bill of Rights. President Nelson Mandela traveled to the United Nations and signed the International Covenant on Civil and Political Rights and the International Covenant on Economic, Social and Cultural Rights, signaling the end of the country's long isolation from the international community and its former rejection of international human rights legal norms (Thompson, 2001).

The adoption of a new constitution created a clear chicken-and-egg problem: how could the Apartheid legislature, illegitimate in the eyes of the vast majority of the population, be entrusted with the drafting and adoption of a legitimate constitution governing an inclusive multiracial state? The answer was to create a two-stage process. Multiparty negotiations would lead to an interim constitution that would include a schedule of 34 constitutional principles, covering topics ranging from intrastate fiscal relations to the role of indigenous law.[2] The Apartheid legislature passed this interim constitution as Act 200 of 1993. The Interim Constitution provided for the election of a new, bicameral legislature acting as a constitutional assembly that would, in turn, draft a final constitution for the new republic in line with the 34 principles. It was during this radical transformation in institutional structures that the South African Constitutional Court (SACC) came into being. Adoption of the final constitution would be contingent upon the SACC's certification that the new governing document was consistent with the agreed principles.

The new court would have a decisive role in the new regime, as it would be responsible for ensuring compliance with human rights embedded in the constitution and in international human rights law. Among those demanding an independent court was a newly disestablished racial minority eager to protect its rights against a newly empowered majority. Theories of court power would suggest, however, that the extreme electoral dominance of the majority's preferred party, the African National Congress (ANC), should lead to a compliant court. Yet this has not occurred, at least not in any clear systematic manner. On the contrary, the SACC has gained much of its reputation at home and abroad not just by enforcing international human rights law, but by enforcing rights in the face of government opposition.

My argument here is that the SACC has been able to walk this tight line between human rights enforcement and backlash from a dominant party by limiting its agenda and shaping the outcome of its rights-affirming cases in ways that leave wide discretion to government actors. The court has affirmed the role of international human rights in the domestic sphere and incorporated human rights principles into the common law. Unlike the Colombian Constitutional Court (Chapter 3), however, the SACC has not relied on any broad public support when pursuing its goals. Created as an elite institution, the court has continued to engage primarily along the balance-of-power axis, with little public engagement. Instead, it has also guarded its institutional legitimacy by establishing precedent that affirms its central role in the constitutional structure yet reaffirms the separation of powers and thus avoids antagonizing political actors. Most importantly, it has done this by manipulating access, interpretive standards, and remedies to ensure a constricted docket that asserts international human rights but limits the SACC's role in determining governmental implementation of its rulings.

The South African Institutional Setting

Before proceeding to the subcases, I position the South African case study in this project's overall theory. In Chapter 2, I developed this theory with an emphasis on the three variables that explain a court's ability to maintain or expand over time its enforcement of international human rights law obligations: a court's international embeddedness, a court system's public support orientation, and procedural flexibility. The theory posits that a court is more likely to enforce standards of international human rights law when it scores highly in all three variables. In the coming pages, I explore these variables with regard to the SACC. In summary, the court is best categorized as presiding over a system with a moderate degree of international embeddedness, an elite support orientation, and high levels of procedural flexibility. On this basis, the theory predicts a court that is inclined to enforce international human rights law but is simultaneously very easily monitored by political actors and, as a result, seeks to limit the judicialization of policy disputes.

Moderately Embedded Internationalism

For a court to act as a domestic enforcer of international human rights law, it must be institutionally and legally empowered to do so. After all, the legitimacy of individual rulings—and thus the development of broader institutional legitimacy—only depends on international law to the extent it is a relevant point of reference. From this perspective, the SACC is moderately well positioned to play an enforcement role, with strong constitutional law enabling the use of international law but with sufficient ambiguity to allow the SACC room to interpret, develop, and selectively apply the law. Much of the language in the Final Constitution reveals an intent to make South African law comport with international standards.[3] International human rights law was the source of much of the rights language found in the Final Constitution's Chapter 2 (the Bill of Rights),[4] and the text specifically incorporates international human rights law as a constraint on government action (or inaction) when applying these protections. All courts are also required to consider international law when interpreting the Bill of Rights,[5] and they are empowered to consider foreign law that is not directly binding on South Africa, such as regional court decisions and the jurisprudence of foreign domestic courts.[6]

Despite this, the language in the Final Constitution lacks clarity on the directly binding nature of international law. The members of the Interim Constitution Negotiating Council agreed early in the process that international law should play a much stronger role in domestic law as a means of protecting against backsliding. To accomplish this, they looked to the recently adopted constitution of Namibia, which in 1990 incorporated international law directly and accepted all ratified treaties as binding directly under national law (Killander, 2010, p. 387). This language was ultimately loosened, however, to require parliamentary action similar in spirit to the transformation principle that had long governed application of international law domestically—international law would only be binding if "transformed" into domestic law by the legislature. What accounted for this change?

The answer lies with the incoming majority's concern that minority parties would abuse international law provisions in the new constitutional structure as a way of either maintaining their Apartheid-era privileges or undermining national consensus. In particular, the Afrikaner Volksunie, a right-wing white secessionist group that had split from the Conservative Party, had advocated in favor of incorporating reference to the UN declaration on minority rights (Olivier, 1993, p. 7). In the face of these concerns and in a desire to maintain national unity, the direct domestic incorporation of international law was dropped in the text of the Interim Constitution. Instead, the state law advisers adopted language requiring both ratification and transformation into local law (Killander, 2010, p. 387). The final text of the Interim Constitution accordingly reads: "Where Parliament agrees to the ratification of or accession to an international agreement under subsection (2), such international agreement shall be binding on the Republic and shall form part of the law of the Republic, provided Parliament expressly so provides and such agreement is not inconsistent with this Constitution."[7] The Final Constitution adopts a substantially similar approach, again requiring both parliamentary ratification and legal transformation before international treaty law becomes binding domestically. Although, theoretically, this prevents direct judicial appeals to international treaties absent legislative action, the waters were muddied further when the Constitutional Assembly adopted language allowing for self-executing treaty provisions. The draft including this language was adopted in the final week of negotiations and, as such, received little attention (Killander, 2010, p. 388). The Final Constitution's language reads: "Any international agreement becomes law in the Republic when it is enacted into law by national legislation; but a self-executing provision of an agreement that has been approved by Parliament is law in the Republic unless it is inconsistent with the Constitution or an Act of Parliament."[8]

What exactly constitutes a "self-executing" treaty provision has proven as contentious in South African jurisprudence as it has in the United States. To date, the SACC has not clarified what is required for a provision to be directly applicable by the courts without enabling legislation, and this remains an area open to manipulation by judicial actors. This would prove to be a consequential opening for the court, as will be explored further in the second subcase study dealing with rights under the criminal law.

As a result of these textual changes, the role of international human rights law in South Africa's current legal system represents less of a radical shift from prior national practice than originally anticipated. For example, during and before the Apartheid era, South African legal practice considered international law under most circumstances to be part of domestic law. Customary international law in particular was considered to be an actionable part of municipal law; this was reinforced by the state's multiple interwoven legal traditions, including roots in both Roman-Dutch law and English common law (Dugard, 2011, pp. 43–46).

During the Apartheid era, domestic applicability of international law was severely restricted. Customary international law was considered subordinate to legislative action, although in such cases an affirmative act of Parliament was required to overcome the presumption of domestic applicability. Treaties likewise could be considered part of the domestic legal framework, but only following passage of separate legislation. An outgrowth of this rule was that acts and declarations of treaty-based organizations such as the UN Security Council were only accepted as domestically binding following separate legislation. Most importantly, the Apartheid government abstained from all of the major human rights treaties (Dugard, 2011, pp. 47–48). This is hardly surprising, given the state's at-times near-pariah status and the fact that treaties such as the UN-sponsored International Convention on the Suppression and Punishment of the Crime of Apartheid specifically targeted South African state practice.

On a textual basis, then, the current constitution still includes important textual restrictions requiring incorporation of international law and allowing for parliamentary override. These restrictions, however, create a permissive environment—the SACC can make use of international law, but it is not required to do so absent political actors' incorporation of international law into the domestic legal sphere. The more radical post-Apartheid change came not from changes in what was constitutionally required but rather in the attitude of politicians toward the use of international law as a benchmark for domestic policies. In particular, constitutional reform was accompanied by the signing of numerous human rights treaties. Thus, although doctrines governing incorporation of treaty law are in many ways a continuation of the Apartheid-era stance, the courts now have a much wider range of options from which to draw on when it is politically acceptable to do so. In the years following the 1993 transition, South Africa signed and ratified the majority of international human rights instruments, including the Convention on the Rights of the Child (June 16, 1995), the Convention on the Elimination of All Forms of Discrimination Against Women (CEDAW; December 15, 1995), the Rome Statute of the International Criminal Court (July 17, 1998), the International Covenant on Civil and Political Rights (ICCPR; December 10, 1998), the International Convention on the Elimination of All Forms of Racial Discrimination (December 10, 1998), the Convention on the Prevention and Punishment of the Crime of Genocide (December 10, 1998), and the Convention Against Torture and Other Cruel, Inhuman or Degrading Treatment or Punishment (December 10, 1998). The state has also ratified a number of regional human rights treaties, including the African Charter on Human and Peoples' Rights (July 9, 1996). A complete list of major international human rights instruments to which South Africa is a party is included in Appendix 2.

In line with this changed political posture, international human rights law has enjoyed a relatively robust role in the courts. Indeed, the SACC even considered international human rights law as a benchmark when certifying the Final Constitution.[9] It also made clear in its early jurisprudence that when deciding Bill of Rights cases, the courts should interpret rights provisions in line with otherwise nonbinding international legal instruments, including decisions of international judicial bodies and reports of specialized agencies.[10] Once treaties have been ratified and undergone domestic implementation, courts are enjoined to apply any reasonable interpretation of legislation that is consistent with them.[11] Courts are also required to apply customary international law absent contrary legislation or constitutional amendment,[12] and it is up to the courts to decide what customary law is binding on the republic (Olivier, 1993, p. 11). Where no legislation speaks to an issue, judicial opinions—and thus the common law—must be brought into line with customary international law. As a result, the principle of stare decisis can no longer be used by the courts to prevent application of a new, contrary rule under customary international law (Dugard, 2011, p. 50). The legal framework for a robust domestic implementation of international human rights law is clearly present.

This has left the SACC with a high degree of discretion in its application of international law. There are clear indications of the constitution's drafters' intent that human rights law be binding on the courts and government actors. At the same time, although the constitution provides ample support for an expansive use of international human rights law, much ambiguity remains: courts are required to "consider" international law but not necessarily apply it; what constitutes a self-executing treaty is undefined. As a result, the role of international law in domestic jurisprudence is dependent not just on the constitutional text or on treaty ratification but, more importantly, also on the degree to which the justices individually and collectively are concerned with enforcing international law.

To determine whether individual justices are sensitive to international human rights law, I conducted a review of each justice's personal biography to determine whether the justice was educated in a foreign institution, worked in a foreign country, or regularly traveled abroad for conferences and presentations. The review relied on information available on the SACC's website, namely the individual biographies of each justice and transcripts of the justices' responses during their appointment interviews with the Judicial Service Commission. Although not determinative of an individual justice's attitude toward international law, overseas training and work do indicate exposure to legal traditions beyond the domestic system and a willingness to engage with a legal community conceptualized internationally. These internationally oriented justices are indicated with an asterisk (*) in Figure 11.

Overall, a majority of justices have experiences that provide them with this heightened sensitivity to international law concerns. Of the 24 justices who have served on the SACC, 19 report having some educational or work experience abroad. This individual exposure translates to the institutional level as well; justices with exposure to international law influences have constituted a majority of the justices at all periods of the SACC's operation.

It should also be noted that this exposure to international law influences is not restricted to SACC justices. On the contrary, all new members of the South African legal community are exposed to international law doctrines through the legal education system; the vast majority of universities require international human rights law as part of their legal training (Heyns & Viljoen, 2001, p. 489). As such, practicing attorneys are increasingly able to avail

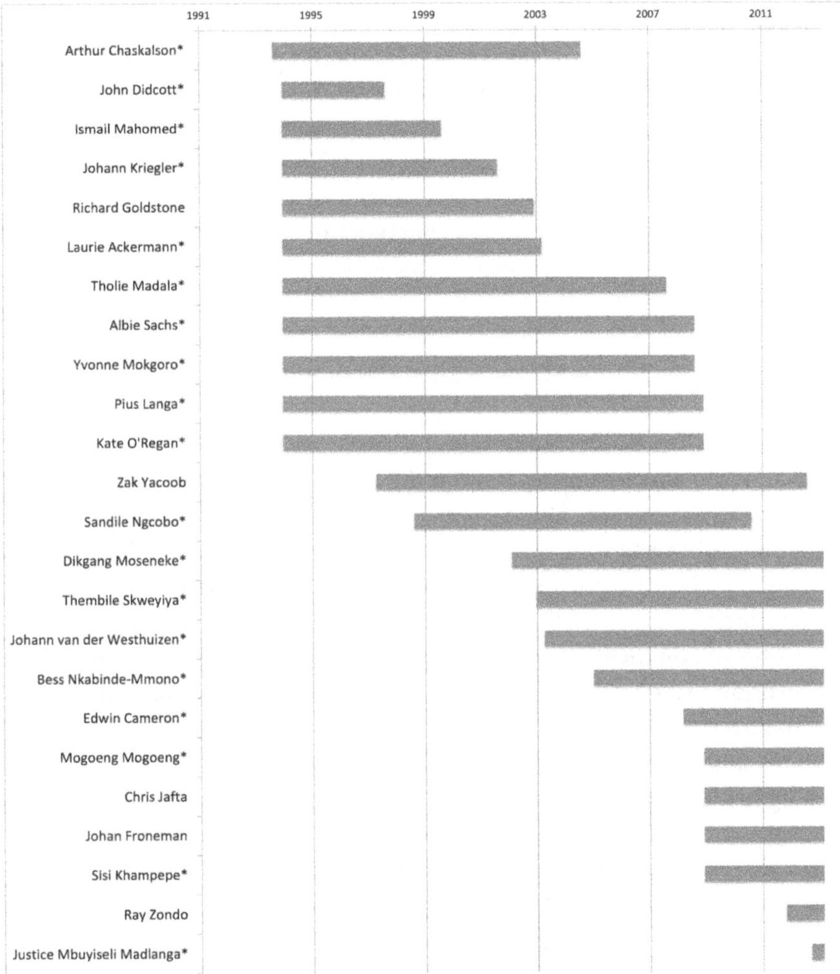

Figure 11. Justices of the South African Constitutional Court.

themselves of international human rights doctrines that may find purchase in the SACC's jurisprudence. This also translates into increased awareness by judges in the High Courts and other courts as increasing numbers of lawyers trained in the post-1994 system enter practice (Heyns & Viljoen, 2002a, p. 66). In the viewpoints of judges, then, the SACC can be seen as inclined toward compliance with international human rights law. This general inclination is tempered, however, by the Final Constitution's ambiguity toward international law's directly binding nature. As such, the SACC can be considered to operate in an environment in which international law is moderately embedded in the legal system. While international law exists as a potential resource, the constitution does not, in all instances, require compliance—only consideration. This moderate level of embedded internationalism has allowed the court to dial up and down its reliance on international law while building legitimacy. Meanwhile, the court's action along the third dimension has trended in a single direction: less engagement with the public.

An Elite Support Orientation

The South African court system is overwhelmingly oriented toward the elite. As such, it remains unable to draw on the broader public as a source of support to counter concerns about political backlash. This is true both in terms of the locus of constitutional review power and in the level of public access to the court. To begin with, structurally, South Africa's rights review system is concentrated in a politically relevant, easily monitored apex court. This concentration of adjudicatory power developed over the nation's 4-year period of transition to a post-Apartheid regime. The transition to a politically inclusive multiracial society was accompanied by a radical restructuring in the relations among the legislative, executive, and judicial branches. The most striking institutional change was the creation of the new constitutional court entrusted with powers of judicial review. Although the Interim Constitution originally limited the SACC's jurisdiction to constitutional issues, later constitutional revisions and SACC legal interpretations resulted in an apex court with powers to review all legislative and executive acts in the country.

Under Apartheid, South Africa followed the tradition of parliamentary supremacy found in many common law states. This situation no longer obtains. Both the 1993 Interim Constitution and the 1996 Final Constitution explicitly provide for constitutional supremacy; legislative and executive acts inconsistent with the constitution are to be considered null and void.[13] Under the Final Constitution, this judicial review of governmental activity was expanded to include review of governmental *inactivity*, where such inactivity could be seen to infringe on a right under the constitution.[14] This submission of legislative and executive activity to judicial review was accompanied by a restructuring of the court system, with the new SACC for the first time exercising exclusive review of constitutional law questions, including legislative certification, constitutional amendments, and compliance with binding international human rights law.

The requirement to submit legislative activity to judicial review began at the earliest moments of the new state's founding, with the constitution itself subject to certification by the SACC. Adoption of the Final Constitution would be contingent upon the SACC's certification that the new governing document was consistent with the 34 agreed principles in the Interim Constitution. The SACC, despite being a young institution, did not hesitate to exercise this veto power. In its first major ruling, the court rejected the Final Constitution,[15] sending it back to the Constitutional Assembly to address areas not in compliance with the constitutional principles. This was seen as an extraordinary assertion of judicial power for the new institution, not least because 86% of the delegates to the assembly had voted in favor of the Final Constitution's adoption (Woolman & Swanepoel, 2008). The SACC also took this opportunity to ensure its future institutional standing, finding as grounds for noncertification the inclusion of constitutional provisions that allowed for ordinary statutes exempt from judicial review.[16] The Constitutional Assembly remedied these faults, and the SACC certified the revised version on December 4, 1996.[17] The Constitutional Assembly adopted the Final Constitution as Act 108 of 1996. President Mandela signed the act on December 10, 1996, and the Final Constitution went into force February 4, 1997 (Berger, 2008, p. 42; Dugard, 2011, p. 50).

This reformed judiciary has tended over time toward an even more concentrated form of review, despite originally manifesting elements of both centralized and decentralized review. Under the Interim Constitution, the newly established SACC had exclusive power to review laws for constitutionality. It also lacked jurisdiction over nonconstitutional issues. Instead these nonconstitutional questions could be appealed to the Supreme Court of Appeal and no further. This had a complicating effect: any appeal from a High Court decision required bifurcation, with ordinary legal issues proceeding to the Supreme Court of Appeal and constitutional issues heading to the SACC. Any appellant was thus required to file two separate appeals in a single case. Several justifications counseled in favor of this initial setup. Perhaps most obviously, the long history of parliamentary superiority led to concerns about courts' willingness to go beyond a positivist interpretation of legislation; as a result, a new and separate court would address the Kelsenian concern (see

Chapter 2) that constitutional law be adjudicated in a forum and in a manner distinct from nonconstitutional legal issues. Beyond this theoretical concern, a separate constitutional court allowed drafters to resolve a politically nettlesome issue: how to deal with the judges appointed during the Apartheid regime. These judges were politically problematic both because of their tenure during a time of questionable judicial legitimacy and because they represented a holdover from a period of judicial deference (Berat, 2005). Creating a new institution filled with politically untainted members embodying a new culture of review seemed a suitable solution.

Despite these advantages, this division of powers between the SACC and the preexisting Supreme Court of Appeal did not outlive the Interim Constitution. Under the Final Constitution, the SACC enjoyed final—but not exclusive—constitutional review powers. Instead, all courts at the High Court level and above received concurrent jurisdiction over constitutional issues. This remedied the difficulties engendered by issue bifurcation between the SACC and the ordinary courts. In addition, allowing wider adjudication of constitutional issues promised a prospective, rather than reactive, approach to the country's legal culture. Instead of, in effect, quarantining constitutional issues from review by preexisting courts, concurrent review offered the possibility of instilling in the entire court system a deeper respect for the constitutional ramifications of nonconstitutional legal issues.

The result, ironically, has been an even greater concentration of judicial power in the SACC. Under the Final Constitution, any appeal dealing with constitutional issues can now proceed through the High Courts and to the Supreme Court of Appeal. Once the latter has pronounced judgment on all legal issues in a case, litigants have the option of appealing constitutional issues to the SACC. The determination of just what constitutes a constitutional issue, however, is determined by the SACC.[18] It has essentially ruled that *all* matters are potentially within its jurisdiction, as the common law must be adjudicated in line with constitutional requirements.[19] This has allowed the SACC to act as an apex court for the entire judicial system in an expanded realm of constitutional issues.[20] The central role of the SACC was confirmed by Parliament in 2001 when it amended the constitution to recognize the head of the court as "Chief Justice of South Africa," a title formerly held by the head of the Supreme Court of Appeal.[21]

The central role of the SACC is also underscored by the court's exclusive ability to render null and void any act of Parliament, the president, or a provincial government. Although the High Courts and the Supreme Court of

Appeal enjoy concurrent jurisdiction on constitutional issues, no finding of unconstitutionality takes force unless certified by the SACC. Indeed, court rules require that any other court's finding of constitutional invalidity be referred immediately to the SACC.[22] This is an important point of contrast with systems such as that in the United States or Colombia, where the highest court can avoid issues by failing to grant review. In contrast, the SACC is necessarily implicated in constitutional issues as a result of the immediate referral system. Similarly, the court has exclusive jurisdiction to decide on the constitutionality of amendments to the constitution.[23]

Finally, the politically central role of the SACC can be seen in the constitution's treatment of abstract review of legislation. The president—and only the president—has the right to refer pending legislation directly to the SACC for abstract review.[24] Neither members of the national legislature nor those of the provincial legislatures can avail themselves of this tool. Instead, members of the National Assembly retain the right to challenge legislation after it has passed and been signed by the president but before it has gone into effect.[25]

The inclusion of this distinction between presidential and legislative access to the SACC was informed by the politics of the transition and highlights the important role the court plays in balancing minority and majority interests. Originally, the Interim Constitution envisioned abstract review challenges by members of the National Assembly. The head of the National Assembly, the Senate, or a provincial legislature could bring a request for prior constitutional certification when requested to do so by the membership of one third of the chamber in question.[26] It became clear very early on, however, that this could become subject to abuse by minority members of the legislature. Members of the Gauteng provincial legislature[27] and the Democratic Party, the National Party, and the Inkatha Freedom Party[28] seized on this procedure as a means of stalling legislative activity in national education policy in the first years of the Interim Constitution. Their claims were ultimately rejected by the SACC, but legal maneuvering prompted the negotiating parties to restrict the use of similar tactics in the Final Constitution. Under the Final Constitution, legislators, unlike the president, can only bring claims *after* enactment.[29]

The result of this period of constitutional development and reform is a constitutional court at the center of political attention. The SACC has the exclusive ability to render acts null and void. It has also gained the ability to oversee all other courts in the judicial system. Its important political role is also made clear by the debates over legislative and National Assembly access to the SACC. This concentration of review power also places the court in a potentially tenuous position, as political actors can easily monitor the court's output. Surprisingly, this elite support orientation has not prevented the SACC from developing a reputation as an institution that delivers legally legitimate rulings. It regularly renders decisions against the government in numerous issue areas. Its ability to do this successfully can be attributed to its flexible institutional environment.

A Flexible Procedural Environment

As a result of the constitutional transformation, the SACC enjoys a high degree of procedural flexibility when accepting cases and rendering decisions. Under the Final Constitution, the court determines what is considered a constitutional matter, in effect determining the contours of its jurisdiction.[30] The constitution also includes a broad grant of direct litigant access to the SACC, allowing the court to sit either as a court of first instance or as on appellate court. In either situation, access is granted "when it is in the interests of justice and *with leave of the Constitutional Court*."[31] This means that, theoretically, the SACC could hear cases from litigants across the country without waiting for cases to filter through the appeals process. The requirement that cases come "with leave of the Constitutional Court" also allows the court to avoid granting access to its docket.

In addition, the SACC has been able to develop its internal court procedures free from political interference. It is these procedures that provide the rules for when and how litigants gain access to the court. Under a 1997 amendment to the court's bill, the president of the SACC is empowered to "in consultation with the Chief Justice, by notice in the *Gazette* make rules relating to the manner in which the Court may be engaged in any matter in respect of which it has jurisdiction."[32] This extremely broad grant of authority goes beyond even that enjoyed by the U.S. Supreme Court.[33] This flexibility has been key to the SACC's ability to affirm international human rights while minimizing confrontations with the government.

Lastly, as described earlier,[34] the Final Constitution's provisions on international law provide the SACC with a high degree of interpretive flexibility. This—combined with the SACC's control over constitutional jurisdiction, access, and court procedures—provides the court with the ability to control its docket, the manner in which it interprets international law, and the forms of remedies it offers in rulings. This level of flexibility has been critical to its institutional strength in the face of the ANC's ongoing electoral dominance. To understand the importance of this flexible environment, it is essential to first examine the political situation in which the court operated during and after the national transition to democracy.

As a foundational issue, the SACC was undoubtedly established in order to protect rights and act as a check on government action. At the time of transition, not only was a new minority concerned with protecting its rights from a new majority (Hirschl, 2007), but the Interim Constitution Negotiating Council itself represented a broad array of societal actors and was thus not dominated by any one faction. Because the majority of South Africans were at the time denied suffrage rights, the Negotiating Council was not created through direct elections; instead it was composed of a broad range of competing stakeholders and political parties. In such a setting, the establishment of a constitutional court is consistent with insurance theories of judicial independence; elite actors were concerned with creating an institution insulated from direct electoral concerns that could enforce rights agreed upon at the negotiating table. What is surprising is the court's ongoing activity following the transition, when subsequent elections confirmed the ongoing popularity of the ANC. Theories of judicial independence would suggest that the ongoing electoral dominance of the ANC would limit the court's ability to perform any power-balancing function (Ramseyer, 1994; Stephenson, 2003). Table 4 reports the share of the vote received and seats in the national legislature, as well as the number of provincial legislatures held by the ANC in each of the posttransition elections.[35] Other major parties are listed for sake of comparison.

As Table 4 makes clear, the ANC's dominance has been consistent at the national level throughout the post-Apartheid era and has increased in the provincial legislatures. As a result, throughout the 1990s and 2000s, the ANC had a majority in the National Assembly that enabled it to pass legislation unilaterally. Indeed, from 2004 to 2009, the ANC maintained the minimum two-thirds majority of all seats in the National Assembly necessary to unilaterally amend most provisions in the constitution.[36] In such an atmosphere of political domination by one party, competing power centers such as the SACC are undoubtedly on questionable institutional footing.

Yet, in the face of this potentially hostile environment, the SACC has produced a long list of cases interpreting international law, enhancing its institutional prerogatives, and engaging with a broad range of policy questions. The court's willingness to rule against government interests seems clear across

Table 4. Party Strength in National Elections in South Africa

Party	*Measure of Party Strength*	*1994*	*1999*	*2004*	*2009*
African National Congress	National vote share	62.65%	66.35%	69.69%	65.90%
	National Assembly seats	252	266	279	264
	Share of seats in National Assembly	63.00%	66.50%	69.75%	66.00%
	Provincial legislatures controlled	6	7	7	8
Democratic Alliance/ Democratic Party	National vote share	1.73%	9.56%	12.37%	16.66%
	National Assembly seats	7	38	50	67
	Share of seats in National Assembly	1.75%	9.50%	12.50%	16.75%
	Provincial legislatures controlled	0	0	0	1
Inkatha Freedom Party	National vote share	10.54%	8.58%	6.97%	4.55%
	National Assembly seats	43	34	28	18
	Share of seats in National Assembly	10.75%	8.50%	7.00%	4.50%
	Provincial legislatures controlled	1	0	0	0
(New) National Party	National vote share	20.39%	6.87%	1.65%	n/a
	National Assembly seats	82	28	7	n/a
	Share of seats in National Assembly	20.50%	7.00%	1.75%	n/a
	Provincial legislatures controlled	1	0	0	n/a
Minor parties (<10% of national vote share each)	National Vote share	4.69%	8.64%	9.32%	12.89%
	National Assembly seats	16	34	36	51
	Share of seats in National Assembly	4.00%	8.50%	9.00%	12.75%
	Provincial legislatures controlled	0	0	0	0

Table includes parties that garnered at least 10% of the national vote share or held at least one provincial legislature in a national voting cycle. Nine provincial legislatures exist; numbers for each election do not sum to nine because several provincial legislatures had no single party in control.

issue areas, with cases ranging from criminal procedure protections to affirmative action to the right to housing.[37] It is at least in part because of this activity that the SACC has garnered such positive reviews by court watchers around the world.

This record masks an underlying truth, however. In terms of access, the court's flexible procedural environment has allowed it to limit the number of opportunities for direct conflict with the political branches. This reduction has taken two primary forms. First, the court has drastically limited the number of direct access cases it is willing to hear, a limitation that has been the subject of much academic consideration.[38] One study found that the SACC accepted a mere eight direct access cases in the first 4 years of its operation (Berat, 2005); another found no improvement over time, with the court accepting a mere nine direct access cases from 1995 through 2005 (Dugard, 2006). Second, the SACC has avoided political conflict by limiting the constitutional right to legal representation. Namely, the court has failed to adopt any right to representation in civil proceedings (Dugard, 2013).

The result can be seen in Figure 12, which reports the number of cases decided in each year since the SACC was created in 1993.[39] The SACC's extremely flexible institutional environment has had a clear outcome: the docket has remained remarkably small in terms of total output. On average,

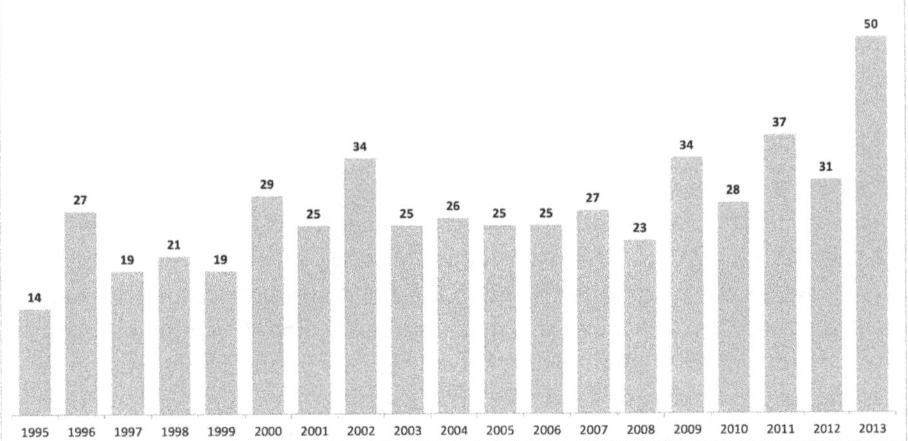

Figure 12. Annual Caseload of the South African Constitutional Court, 1995–2013.

the court rendered an opinion in only 27 cases per year in the two decades following its founding.

Limitations on direct access and lack of support for civil trials have greatly restricted the number of cases the SACC hears, shutting off the court's supply of litigation from a large segment of the population. Importantly for the theory examined here, the restrictions are in large part due to the court's own jurisprudence. After all, the constitution empowers the SACC to act as a court of first instance and to interpret constitutional rights to a fair trial in civil matters. Rather than expanding access, however, the court has limited the number of cases in which it might come into conflict with the political branches. Rather than embracing a public support orientation, the court early on adopted a stance that oriented it toward elites. Given the broad public's overwhelming support of elected officials—the ANC—adopting a public support orientation simply would not have served as a counterbalance against political elites. Instead, the SACC used its control over the levers of access to limit the likelihood that a flood of litigation would put it on a collision course with those same political elites.

Of course, its power in this area is not complete. The jurisdictional grant in the Final Constitution ensures that the SACC hears some cases it might prefer to avoid. In particular, any ruling of unconstitutionality by a High Court or the Supreme Court of Appeal must be affirmed by the SACC before the law is considered invalid.[40] In addition, the SACC does not benefit from the use of an American-style "political question" doctrine that might allow it to openly refuse to hear a case (Roux, 2003, p. 95). As a result, the SACC will undoubtedly hear cases with the potential to invite backlash. Limiting access can only proceed so far—other methods must be found.

Given this constraint, the court has managed to limit political confrontation through its procedural rules and adjudicatory standards in those cases that it does hear. Its use of adjudicatory standards has allowed it to restrict the applicability of international human rights law while affirming basic rights. In its remedial orders, the court has, at times, ruled that the government was in breach of rights while simultaneously taking into consideration government costs and refusing any ongoing structural oversight role of government policy. In short, the SACC chooses legal outcomes that affirm basic human rights and restate the court's own powers but that avoid any direct challenge to government prerogatives. Two of these situations are examined next: the rights of individuals with HIV and rights under the criminal law.

Subcase 1: Socioeconomic Rights of Individuals with HIV

My initial review of primary and secondary sources revealed that one of the most consistent sources of criticism of South Africa's implementation of international human rights law was in the area of socioeconomic rights. The particular area of concern was the right to health, with a focus on individuals living with HIV. In the 20 years of human rights reports I reviewed, this issue appeared in 11 of those 20 years.

The ongoing relevance of socioeconomic rights adjudication in the post-1993 era is perhaps not surprising, given the high level of economic inequality arising under the Apartheid regime. Under Apartheid, the commitment to a laissez-faire model of capitalism encouraged the concentration of wealth (de Wet, 1996), and the strict racial formation of the political community helped ensure a lack of ameliorating redistributive policies (Lieberman, 2001). As a result, the ability and willingness of the court to engage in enforcement of second-generation human rights has, from the court's founding, been a source of political controversy.

Concerns over the likelihood of economic redistribution under majority rule led the constitutional drafting committees to exclude many of these rights from the Interim Constitution. Their inclusion in the 1996 constitution was the result of increased leverage gained by the ANC in the intervening years. As a result, the Final Constitution differed from its predecessor in key ways. First, it included a requirement that citizens' rights were not only to be a shield against the government but that they also represented government obligations that the state had to "promote."[41] Second, the panoply of rights was accordingly expanded to include health care, food, water, and economic security.[42]

The SACC gave an early boost to socioeconomic claims by rejecting the argument that socioeconomic rights were fundamentally nonjusticiable. During the constitutional certification process, several parties had objected to the inclusion of socioeconomic rights in the Bill of Rights on the grounds that court intervention in this area would require judicial action on policy and budgetary matters and thus represent a fundamental breach of the separation of powers principle.[43] The SACC rejected this argument through comparison to judicial enforcement of first-generation rights, stating that "even when a court enforces civil and political rights . . . the order it makes will often have such implications. . . . In our view it cannot be said that by including socio-economic rights within a bill of rights, a task is conferred upon the courts so different from that ordinarily conferred upon them by a bill of rights that it results in a breach of the separation of powers."[44] As a result of this very early assertion of justiciability of second-generation rights and the development of a robust socioeconomic rights jurisprudence, the SACC has received laudatory reviews from court watchers both within South Africa and abroad.

Applicable Law

Despite this positive reputation, however, the SACC has had only a marginal impact on the real-world enforcement of socioeconomic rights and HIV treatment in particular. This is despite a wide range of legal sources on which the court could draw. The most basic source of law for socioeconomic rights claims is the Final Constitution. It reads:

> Health care, food, water and social security
> 27. (1) Everyone has the right to have access to
> a. health care services, including reproductive health care;
> b. sufficient food and water; and
> c. social security, including, if they are unable to support themselves and their dependants, appropriate social assistance.
> (2) The state must take reasonable legislative and other measures, within its available resources, to achieve the progressive realisation of each of these rights.
> (3) No one may be refused emergency medical treatment.[45]

Given the timing of South Africa's constitutional transformation, this inclusion of health rights in the constitution is not surprising; constitutionalizing the right to health is heavily influenced by the timing of constitutional change, with later adopted constitutions much more likely to include this right as international norms and treaty instruments have increasingly come to recognize a right to health (Kinney & Clark, 2004). This effect was evident in South Africa's case, where NGOs and the ANC relied heavily on the International Covenant on Economic, Social and Cultural Rights (ICESCR) and international support for the right to health during the constitutional drafting process (Heyns & Viljoen, 2002a, pp. 42–43).

The South African commitment to second-generation rights is, however, complicated by the country's dilatory treaty ratification record in this area. Of the treaties comprising the International Bill of Human Rights, South

Africa signed and ratified the ICCPR, two of its optional protocols, and the Universal Declaration of Human Rights.[46] Although South Africa signed the ICESCR, the third major instrument in the International Bill of Human Rights, it did not ratify it until 2015. As such, any treaty provisions in the ICESCR were not directly binding during the time the cases studies here were decided.[47] Instead, the otherwise nonbinding ICESCR treaty provisions and any decisions by ICESCR bodies would have been considered interpretive guides under SACC precedent.[48]

South Africa did, however, ratify the African Charter on Human and Peoples' Rights (the Banjul Charter) in July 1996, just before the Final Constitution came into force. The Banjul Charter provides that "every individual shall have the right to enjoy the best attainable state of physical and mental health" and that "States parties to the present Charter shall take the necessary measures to protect the health of their people and to ensure that they receive medical attention when they are sick."[49] The Banjul Charter, as a duly ratified treaty, acts as a binding constraint for the government under the South African Bill of Rights.

The Case

It was in this relatively hospitable legal environment that the SACC became involved in the HIV treatment issue. The primary case dealing with HIV treatment in South Africa is the landmark *Minister of Health and Others v Treatment Action Campaign and Others (No. 2)*,[50] or *TAC 2*. Although *TAC 2* dealt with a specific scenario—patients' access to antiretroviral drugs limiting the transmission of HIV from mother to child—the importance of this case in South African politics cannot be overstated. At the time of the *TAC 2* decision, approximately five million South Africans were infected with HIV, the highest number of infected individuals in any country (Fassin & Schneider, 2003). Transmission from mother to child accounted for 10% of new cases (Makgoba, 2000). The SACC itself noted in its opinion that, according to government publications, the HIV/AIDS pandemic had cost millions of South Africans their lives, threatened the economy, and produced one of the greatest challenges facing the posttransition democracy.[51]

The Treatment Action Campaign (TAC) originally brought an application against the government in the High Court in Pretoria.[52] TAC is an advocacy group focused on expanding access to safe and effective treatment for individuals diagnosed with HIV. The organization brought the case in order to challenge the government's policy limiting access to nevirapine, a drug that had been tested as effective at reducing the incidence of mother-to-child transmission of HIV during birth, and which had been approved for use in South Africa since 1998.[53] Under the government's program, nevirapine was only made available in public health facilities at two pilot sites (one rural, one urban) in each of the country's nine provinces (Richardson, 2007).

In December 2001, the High Court found in favor of the applicants, specifically ruling that the government had acted unreasonably by (1) failing to make nevirapine available in the public sector when a medical doctor deemed it necessary and (2) failing to set a time frame for implementation of a national program to prevent mother-to-child transmission of HIV.[54] The court found that the constitution and case law required the government to move toward progressive realization of the right to health, something that government policy did not achieve. The court, therefore, ordered the government to make nevirapine available at all public health facilities to women, when medically indicated, and to create "an effective national programme to prevent or reduce the mother-to-child transmission of HIV."[55] Importantly, the High Court maintained jurisdiction over the case, requiring follow-up reports from the government at specified dates.[56]

The government appealed the case, and the SACC granted expedited review. In a unanimous ruling, the SACC agreed with the Pretoria High Court that the government's restriction of nevirapine to 18 test sites was not in compliance with constitutional mandates. The SACC also agreed that the constitution required the development and implementation of a national program providing access to treatment preventing mother-to-child transmission of HIV.[57] Despite this, the SACC vacated the Pretoria High Court's orders requiring development of a program within a specified time frame and allowing for continued court oversight. In their place, the SACC ordered the government to make nevirapine accessible throughout the public health system and to develop a national program, but without any timeline and without maintaining the SACC's jurisdiction.[58] Instead, the SACC indicated that it could rely on the good faith of the government to comply with the ruling.[59]

Court Restrictions

The SACC's ruling received a positive reception both in South Africa and abroad. Despite this positive reception, the SACC's decision in *TAC 2* was in many ways self-limiting. The court built on a jurisprudential foundation that allowed it to use procedural and interpretive tools to affirm basic rights without antagonizing reluctant government actors. Specifically, the court adopted adjudicatory standards that limited the reach of international human rights law and applied remedial orders that avoided any direct oversight role for the court. In this way, the SACC avoided confrontation with the government, maintained and even strengthened the legal legitimacy of its rulings, and avoided any threats to its institutional prerogatives.

ADJUDICATION AND STANDARDS

Perhaps most importantly, the SACC was able to limit the extent to which it would rely on standards of international law when interpreting socioeconomic rights. It did so by adopting a less rigorous standard of review for the rights in question than it might have chosen. Whereas international law has developed a "minimum core" standard for adjudicating whether or not a right has been fulfilled, the SACC chose instead to rely on a "reasonableness" standard that guaranteed the maximum flexibility for government actors and the court itself.

This standard was first adopted by the court in the earlier landmark case of *Government of the Republic of South Africa and Others v Grootboom*,[60] which dealt with the right to housing under the Final Constitution, §26. In *Grootboom*, the appellants had asked the SACC to adopt the minimum core standards used by the UN Committee on Economic, Social and Cultural Rights (CESCR), which monitors implementation of the aforementioned ICESCR. This would have set "minimum essential levels" for the right that the state would be obligated to provide using "all the resources at its disposal."[61] The SACC noted that some of the language of §26 of the Final Constitution was itself "taken from international law and Article 2.1 of the Covenant [ICESCR] in particular,"[62] and that the court was obliged to consider international law and interpretations by relevant international tribunals.[63] Despite this, the court justices unanimously decided to disregard the CESCR's interpretive guide to the language. In this, it deviated from the actions of other South African institutions, most notably the Human Rights Commission,[64] which employs the CESCR's minimum core standards when evaluating government compliance with guarantees of socioeconomic rights (Heyns & Viljoen, 2002a, p. 52, fn. 126).

The SACC instead adopted a "reasonableness" standard to evaluate the government's policy. One key problem with this approach is that it fails to provide any content to the rights in question (Bilchitz, 2003). Whereas a minimum core approach requires provision of basic essential services, the SACC's reasonableness standard is entirely context-specific: "The state's obligation to provide access to adequate housing depends on context, and may differ from province to province, from city to city, from rural to urban areas and from person to person."[65] Because it is context-specific, it also limits the court's capacity to determine the extent of the right:[66] "Even if it were appropriate to do so, it could not be done unless sufficient information is placed before a court to enable it to determine the minimum core in any given context. In this case, we do not have sufficient information to determine what would comprise the minimum core obligation in the context of our Constitution."[67] Instead of seeking more information, the SACC issued a declaratory order requiring the government to establish a program that would progressively meet the right of access to adequate housing.[68]

The SACC built on this analysis in *TAC 2*. In doing so, it effectively reaffirmed the idea that a "minimum core" was not so much a basic rights guarantee as it was an adjudicatory standard: "It is impossible to give everyone access even to a 'core' service immediately. All that is possible, and all that can be expected of the state, is that it act reasonably."[69] The court reiterated that §27 of the Final Constitution did not require satisfaction of a particular right's minimum core: "The socio-economic rights of the Constitution should not be construed as entitling everyone to demand that the minimum core be provided to them." Rather, the concept of a minimum core would be "possibly relevant" to determining whether the government program was reasonable.[70]

The SACC used adjudicatory standards to accomplish two goals. First, it reiterated the importance of international law in interpreting the South African Bill of Rights. As such it ensured the ongoing availability of this tool and maintained the legal legitimacy of the court's rulings in the eyes of court watchers. Second, the SACC eschewed any direct usage of the minimum core standards found in international law, instead recharacterizing them as interpretive aids—but aids in interpreting standards, not rights. This enabled it to affirm a basic human right while simultaneously removing itself from direct conflict with the government over determination of that right's content and implementation.

REMEDIES

The SACC followed a similar pattern when choosing which remedies to apply in *TAC 2*. While agreeing with many of the substantive findings of the High Court, the SACC replaced that lower court's structural interdict with a declaratory order. In effect, the SACC simultaneously affirmed the appellant's claim of right and removed the possibility of the type of court oversight that might maintain pressure on the government to ensure fulfillment of that right.

The Final Constitution provides the SACC with substantial leeway in its determination and application of appropriate remedies. Specifically, §38 allows the court to provide "appropriate relief"; and §172(1)(b), dealing with the Bill of Rights, empowers courts to "make an order that is just and equitable." Theoretically, this provides the SACC with the ability to award money damages, declare laws invalid, provide declaratory relief, or issue structural interdicts granting the court supervisory powers, to name only a few remedies.

It is likely that a structural interdict was appropriate in this case, given the prevailing legal standards for such orders. A structural interdict would have allowed the court to maintain jurisdiction, require follow-up reporting by the government, and provide easy access to the court for the applicants in case of government noncompliance. The SACC instead chose to rely on the government's good-faith efforts to comply. Under the court's own precedent, structural interdicts are considered appropriate when a failure to comply—even given good-faith efforts—is likely to have a dramatic negative impact (Roach & Budlender, 2005, p. 333). It seems clear that the facts in *TAC 2* met this standard, given estimates that a universal nevirapine program could prevent as many as 35,000 HIV transmissions annually (J. M. Berger & Kapczynski, 2009, p. 7) and that every day the program implementation was delayed could result in as many as 10 additional HIV infections.[71]

Despite this, in *TAC 2* the SACC overturned the High Court's use of a structural interdict to oversee government compliance and instead articulated a more restrictive standard under which oversight would only be appropriate where "necessary." As one commentator has noted, it is difficult to imagine a case in which the SACC would, in advance, know that such oversight was necessary absent clear evidence that a government actor was incompetent or acting in bad faith (Bishop, 2008, p. 9.2[c][ii][aa]). Even so, the facts in *TAC 2* arguably met even this heightened standard. The SACC itself noted that its inquiries to parties throughout the case's litigation had elicited "contention" instead of "enlightenment,"[72] and that parties' interactions entailed "a regrettable degree of animosity and disparagement."[73] The court deemed the government's lack of transparency "regrettable."[74] In sum, the court found that the "unusual degree of political, ideological and emotional contention" surrounding the issue of HIV in South Africa not only "bedevil[s] future relations between government and non-governmental agencies that will perforce have to join in combating the common enemy, but it could also have rendered the resolution of this case more difficult."[75] If ever SACC oversight were necessary, this seemed to be the case.

The SACC nevertheless undertook this tactical retreat, all the while maintaining its prerogatives in future cases. The government's position had been that when a court finds government policy lacking under the constitution, "the only competent order that a court can make is to issue a declaration of rights to that effect." In short, the government argued that separation-of-powers concerns should prevent courts from issuing mandatory orders or maintaining a supervisory role over implementation of court orders. The SACC rejected this argument, citing both case law and the constitutional imperative that the court grant "appropriate relief" and "make any order that is just and equitable,"[76] and stating that the court was empowered to "exercise some form of supervisory jurisdiction to ensure that the order is implemented."[77] These strong institutional claims were, however, not joined with action. Rather than maintaining jurisdiction, the SACC chose to rely on the government's good faith, concluding that "[t]he government has always respected and executed orders of this Court. There is no reason to believe that it will not do so in the present case."[78] In place of the structural interdict, the SACC provided declaratory relief that found the government policy inconsistent with the Final Constitution and ordered the government to make nevirapine available at public health facilities other than the testing sites.

On balance, the SACC retreated from the oversight contemplated by the High Court, avoiding direct confrontation with the government. In doing so it also provided greater flexibility for the government. The High Court's order had required development of a national program and submission of a progress report to the court within three and a half months; the SACC, in contrast, did not impose any timeline for the development of a national program. The SACC ruling also specifically allowed the government to deviate from the nevirapine order if other, "equally appropriate," methods became available.[79] The court affirmed human rights and its own powers under the constitution, all the while crafting a remedy that allowed the government significant room to effectuate its policy free of ongoing court interference.

Outcome

Can SACC intervention in this policy area be considered effective? It seems clear that the failure of the SACC to clearly define the content of the right in

Table 5. Expansion of HIV Treatment Coverage in South Africa

Year	*Treatment Coverage*
2000	<3%
2001	<3%
2002	<3%
2003	5%
2004	10%
2005	<30%

question and to engage the government through a structural interdict limited the ruling's effect on nonlitigants and on the policy area more generally. Table 5 reports the general increase in the use of antiretroviral drugs to prevent mother-to-child transmission before and after the SACC's ruling (Chigwedere et al., 2008). The progress is less than impressive, given the court's order to make nevirapine available in all public health facilities and given the fact that the government faced little financial cost. (In the summer of 2000, nevirapine's manufacturer had offered to supply the drug free of charge for 5 years.[80]) By 2005, 3 years after the ruling, treatment coverage had still not passed the 30% mark.

This compares poorly to policy outcomes in Botswana and Namibia, countries of similar economic means[81] and with similar exposure to the HIV/AIDS pandemic. Botswana had reached 85% treatment coverage by 2005; Namibia had reached 71% coverage in that same year, more than double the proportion achieved by South Africa (Chigwedere et al., 2008). Instead, the anticipated "good faith" efforts by the government were slow in coming. Though the declaratory order in *TAC 2* required immediate development and implementation of a national program, the government did not implement a national treatment plan until 2004. By 2005, as many as half of all pregnant women had not even been tested for HIV. It was not until 2007 that the government adopted the more ambitious national strategic plan; despite this, as recently as 2012, 15% of public health facilities were still not equipped to initiate antiretroviral treatments (Barron et al., 2013).

Use of indicators and data are critical to increasing coverage, but the lack of a structural interdict meant the court was not involved in this monitoring process. This instead meant that activists and litigants were tasked with ensuring enforcement. Follow-up litigation is a common means of ensuring government compliance, but this presents particular difficulties in a country such as post-Apartheid South Africa with its lopsided allocation of legal resources.[82] Luckily, in *TAC 2*, follow-up litigation was possible because of the participation of a large, institutionalized actor. TAC filed (or threatened to file) contempt-of-court proceedings to force recalcitrant provinces to comply with the SACC's order (Heywood, 2003, p. 314; Heywood & Hassim, 2008, p. 265). Even given the participation of this repeat player, however, follow-up litigation was often impeded by the unwillingness of government bureaucrats to act as whistleblowers (J. Berger, 2008, p. 73). As a result, TAC reverted to direct action techniques. These included a march to Parliament of 20,000 people in February 2003 and a recurring civil disobedience campaign against the government in 2003 to force compliance with the 2002 ruling (Heywood, 2009).

The biggest change may have been in the tone of government rhetoric, but even here the SACC's ruling was only one of many influences. In April 2002 (just 2 months before the ruling in *TAC 2*), President Thabo Mbeki finally distanced himself from those groups arguing against a causal link between HIV and AIDS; this was followed by a cabinet statement in October 2002 supporting wider access to antiretrovirals (Fassin & Schneider, 2003). At the same time, it seems clear that pressure was already mounting on the government, both from within and without. At the time of *TAC 2*, a split had already developed among the provinces over how fast to proceed with the nevirapine program rollout, and consensus had broken down within the ANC. For example, in early 2002 before the decision in *TAC 2*, the ANC premier, Mbhazime Shilowa of the province of Gauteng, continued with an expansion of that province's nevirapine delivery program in defiance of the ANC's national minister of health (Heywood, 2003). As litigation proceeded, additional provinces likewise announced their intention to expand their nevirapine programs (Roux, 2013, p. 295).

Despite a shift from outright government denialism of a causal link between HIV and AIDS,[83] it seems clear that, unlike in the provincial governments, no radical policy changes were implemented or even advocated for by the national government in the immediate aftermath of *TAC 2*. On the contrary, a review of cabinet meeting statements from December 2000 through the end of 2002 reveals that there was little shift in policy emphasis as a result of the court's ruling. Both in 2001 and 2002, approximately one third of cabinet statements addressed the HIV/AIDS crisis in some way: 36% in 2001, and 39% in 2002. The percentage of statements addressing the crisis actually fell after the ruling, from 50% of the 10 statements issued immediately before the ruling to 40% of the 10 statements issued immediately after the ruling.

Indeed, the greatest period of emphasis on HIV policy in general, and mother-to-child transmission in particular, came during the period after the High Court issued its ruling but before the SACC heard oral arguments on appeal. During this 5-month window, four of seven cabinet statements dealt with the HIV crisis in South Africa. All of these offer a defense of the government's existing program rollout or otherwise indicate that the then-current program would continue.

In addition, two statements attempt to reframe the court battle as one not of policy but of the proper role of the judiciary in the democratic framework. For example, the February 21, 2002, cabinet statement asserts, "Government is appealing against this judgment. This is not because we are against expanding the mother-to-child programme—that process continues. It is because we need to gain clarity on whether the courts or the elected government decides on the detail of providing health services: This is a critical question about the division of powers in our democracy."[84] Similarly, the April 30, 2002, cabinet statement reiterated this framing of the issue, stating that the SACC case "will be treated in its proper context as seeking clarification on the issue of division of powers rather than a debate on access to nevirapine."[85] It should be noted that all of these statements came during the period of time when the government was under the threat of the High Court's structural interdict.

Lastly, there is also little evidence of any lasting policy shift among the ANC leadership more generally. A review of the ANC's important annual policy position statements—the "January 8th statements"—failed to reveal any major changes in the governing party's approach to HIV treatment following the SACC ruling. The January 8th statements for 2003 and 2006 only mentioned a general need to increase teaching and awareness;[86] those for 2004 and 2005 did not contain any reference to AIDS or HIV at all. The first mention of any policy change occurred in 2007, and even then the statement thanked the Ministry of Health for its work and called only for a finalization of the government's national strategic plan.[87]

Overall, the court's decision to adopt a reasonableness standard and to rely on declaratory remedies limited the ruling's policy impact. This treatment has been consistent across areas of socioeconomic law, including those outside the right to health. The SACC's rejection of a minimum core standard was first applied to the right to housing in *Grootboom* and later to the right to adequate water.[88] The SACC's ruling in *TAC 2* is thus indicative of an ongoing pattern, whereby the court has been willing to affirm rights while reducing the applicability of international law and deferring to government judgments about what is reasonable given available resources. At the same time, the progressive nature of socioeconomic rights might suggest that they are ideal cases for standing orders. Unfortunately, this has not been the case. Instead, the SACC has preferred declaratory orders that require no follow-up, provide no concrete relief to rights advocates, and avoid involving the court in any ongoing policy dispute with the government.

Subcase 2: Rights and Protections Under the Criminal Law

This pattern of restricting the substantive impact of international human rights law while limiting the effect of rulings appears in the second area of law explored in this study, that of citizens' rights under the criminal law. These rights represent an additional policy area of international human rights law in which South Africa has received consistent criticism in the post-Apartheid era. In the 20 years of human rights reports reviewed, this issue appeared in all years. However, unlike the health considerations under the HIV case, rights under the criminal law appeared across a wide range of topics, from individual claims of police malfeasance to challenges against the amnesty that arguably formed the basis of the transition from Apartheid. Taken together, these claims reveal a constitutional court that has had difficulty matching the strong human rights language of the new constitutional settlement to the facts on the ground.

Applicable Law

The rights of individuals in criminal proceedings represent one of the longest standing, and thus most heavily legalized, areas of international human rights law. They range from those defending the individual against overbearing state power in criminal matters—protections against inhuman or degrading treatment,[89] the right to a fair trial,[90] and prohibitions on arbitrary detention[91]—to affirmative rights that impose burdens on the state, such as the right to an effective remedy against state violations.[92] In sum, they constitute rights to engage the state's criminal law apparatus in a fair and humane manner. In addition, the vast majority of these protections have analogues in South

African constitutional and statutory law (Killander, 2010, p. 386). In particular, the rights were entrenched in the fundamental rights sections of the Interim Constitution[93] and again in the Final Constitution's Bill of Rights.[94]

Despite this heavy legalization at both the international and domestic level, the SACC adopted a restrained approach to rights enforcement similar to what it followed in the area of socioeconomic rights. First, the SACC interpreted the constitution in ways that limited the reach of international law's direct applicability in the domestic court system. Moreover, it adopted remedial approaches that affirmed rights without imposing extensive material costs on the government. At the same time, it has found ways of incorporating even nonratified treaty law into the domestic system through its role as final interpreter of the constitution. The result, as in the socioeconomic arena, is a preservation of the SACC's institutional prerogatives and a general affirmation of basic human rights without undue interference with government policy.

Court Restrictions

ADJUDICATION STANDARDS: LIMITING THE APPLICABILITY OF INTERNATIONAL LAW

The SACC has avoided conflict with the political branches primarily by narrowing the applicability of international law. In the well-known case *Azanian Peoples Organization (AZAPO) and Others v President of the Republic of South Africa and Others*,[95] the SACC limited international law's domestic applicability in order to enable the Truth and Reconciliation Commission to act. Applicants argued that the act creating the commission[96] contravened both international law and South African constitutional law by granting amnesty to perpetrators of gross human rights violations during the Apartheid era.[97] The applicants argued that the establishment of the commission violated §22 of the Interim Constitution, which provided that a court or other forum settle justiciable disputes,[98] as well as international law protections under the Geneva conventions.[99]

The SACC allowed the enabling act to stand by making reference to the Interim Constitution's rights limitation clause, as well as to general principles of national unity and reconciliation found in the epilogue to the Interim Constitution. While acknowledging that amnesty breached claimants' right of access to the courts, the need for national unity rendered this limitation permissible. Perhaps most tellingly, the court also recognized that without the amnesty provisions the new constitution would most likely never have come into being.[100]

The court also hedged on the question of legality under international law, first by finding that international law was not binding in this case, and second by asserting that "there is no single or uniform international practice in relation to amnesty."[101] The SACC found that human rights protections such as those of the Geneva conventions could not apply directly, because they had not been transformed by parliamentary act into domestic legislation.[102] Moreover the court skirted the issue of whether these would be violations under customary law (and thus not require transformation) by concluding that the Interim Constitution did not require adoption, but rather mere consideration, of international law when dealing with questions of fundamental rights.[103] As a result, the SACC took note of international practice and drew a distinction between unrepentant regimes—which the court reasoned could not legitimately grant themselves impunity—and transitional regimes, such as South Africa's, which could accept conditional amnesty as part of a constitutional pact entered into by all segments of society.[104]

This pattern of limiting international law's reach is reflected in subsequent cases dealing with rights under the criminal law. In *S v Williams and Others*,[105] the SACC was presented with the question of whether South Africa's subjection of juveniles to corporal punishment could be sanctioned under the constitution and international law. Six juveniles in five different cases were sentenced to whipping using a light cane under the Criminal Procedure Act.[106] The court began by noting that the protections in the constitution against torture and cruel treatment conformed "to a large extent with most international human rights instruments."[107] Despite this, the SACC was clear in treating international law as nonbinding. This was entirely justifiable, given that, at the time of the case, South Africa had signed but not yet ratified the ICCPR.[108] Yet the SACC did not take this obvious path. Instead, by failing to distinguish nonratified from ratified treaties, the court adopted an approach that allowed it to focus on domestic concerns while deemphasizing international law full stop. Namely, it noted that while "valuable insights" might be found in international law and the judgments of foreign courts, any judgment had to comport with "contemporary circumstances" in South Africa.[109] (The court avoided discussing similarly signed-but-unratified treaties, such as the Convention Against Torture[110] and the Convention on the Rights of the Child,[111] despite a lengthy discussion of torture and child rights by foreign jurisdictions.) Despite this downgrading of international law's importance, the SACC ultimately found that the use of corporal punishment on children violated constitutional protections and was inconsistent with the purpose of the rights enshrined in the Interim Constitution and which were informed by international standards.[112] As such, the offending section of the statute was to be treated as having no force or effect.[113] The government subsequently repealed section 294 of the Criminal Procedure Act, along with all other laws allowing for corporal punishment.[114] This result allowed the court to split the difference: it could claim fealty to the normative demands of international law while focusing squarely on domestic concerns.

Even in cases where South Africa has already signed and ratified a treaty, moreover, the SACC has taken a conservative approach to direct domestic applicability of treaty provisions. As previously noted,[115] the Final Constitution generally requires enabling legislation for ratified treaties except for self-executing treaty provisions. What constitutes a self-executing treaty provision is up for debate, but an early definition treats as self-executing any treaty "which of its own force furnishes a rule of municipal law for the guidance of municipal courts in deciding cases involving the rights of individuals" (Henry, 1929, p. 776).[116] Beyond this basic definition, little is agreed, most importantly which treaties or provisions qualify. In the cases of *Goodwin v Director-General, Department of Justice and Constitutional Development and Others* and *President of the Republic of South Africa and Others v Quagliani*,[117] both of which dealt with an extradition treaty with the United States, the SACC had the opportunity to clarify which treaty provisions were to be treated as self-executing. The cases arose following competing rulings on the issue in the High Courts.[118] The SACC chose to sidestep the issue altogether, finding extradition permissible based on prior South African law while avoiding any decision on self-execution.[119]

The failure to clarify which treaties are self-executing has led to limited treaty enforcement in later cases, most famously for the appellant in *Claassen v Minister of Justice and Constitutional Development*.[120] In that case, the appellant was seeking to overturn the dismissal of his claim for damages for unlawful detention. The High Court recognized that South Africa had a duty not to unlawfully detain its citizens under §12 of the Bill of Rights; the High Court likewise acknowledged the right to a private law remedy in damages for unlawful detainment in Article 9(5) of the ICCPR,[121] which at the time of ruling had been duly ratified by South Africa.[122] The High Court ultimately held, however, that because the ICCPR was not self-executing, the relevant article was not binding on the court. This was a critical distinction, for although the language of the Bill of Rights closely tracked the ICCPR, the Bill of Rights failed to include any clear right to compensation for a rights violation (Killander, 2010, p. 387). Hence, the court was not required to provide a private right of action, and the appeal was dismissed.[123]

DEVELOPMENT OF THE COMMON LAW

The SACC's reluctance to treat international law as domestically binding has not been consistent. On the contrary, the court has maintained its flexibility to determine the applicability of international law even when no ratified treaty law is available. The SACC has accomplished this by what it terms "developing the common law." It is not surprising, given South Africa's constitutional transformation, that much of the pre-1993 common law either contains legal lacunae or is in direct opposition to jurisprudential considerations inherent in the new constitutional settlement. As a result, the development of the common law is an active area of jurisprudence for the SACC as it endeavors to bring decades of case law into accordance with new human rights protections. Indeed, this is a constitutional imperative: when applying a provision of the Bill of Rights, any court in South Africa "must apply, or if necessary develop, the common law to the extent that legislation does not give effect to that right."[124] The result has been a legal environment in which the SACC affords itself maximum latitude, at times cabining international treaty or customary law while at other times relying on international law, even nonratified treaties, to develop the common law.

In *Carmichele v Minister of Safety and Security*,[125] the SACC relied both on the constitution and international human rights law to develop the common law in such a way as to increase the liability of police and prosecutors. In that case, the appellant, Carmichele, argued that the police service and public prosecutors had negligently failed to protect her from attack by a known sex offender who had been released from custody pending trial. The court acknowledged that the legislature had the primary role of reforming the country's laws.[126] At the same time, the SACC stated that the courts themselves could not eschew their obligations to ensure the common law comported with international standards. It specifically cited statutory guidelines requiring the national director of public prosecutions to encourage prosecutors' compliance with the principles found in the UN Guidelines on the Role of Prosecutors.[127] It noted that South Africa had signed and ratified CEDAW, and that CEDAW required the state to take "reasonable and appropriate measures" to protect women's rights.[128]

Importantly, the SACC did not cite any binding law, either domestic statute or international treaty, for the issue at hand: whether police and prosecutors could be subject to liability for a failure to prevent a rights violation. Instead, the SACC made reference to UN committee recommendations that states may be liable for compensating victims.[129] The court found the appellants could be held liable and remanded the case to the High Court for further proceedings and to assess damages.[130]

Developing the common law has also allowed the SACC to ignore the constraints it seemed to apply in recognizing nonratified or nonincorporated treaty law. In *Government of the Republic of Zimbabwe v Fick and Others*,[131] the SACC instead chose to develop the common law in such a way as to allow domestic South African enforcement of an international tribunal's costs order. In that case, the Zimbabwean government had argued that the tribunal's order was not enforceable in South Africa because the latter had ratified but not legally domesticated the treaty establishing the Southern African Development Community (SADC) Tribunal. The SACC held, however, that the constitution required the courts to develop the common law in line with international law, and as such ratification rendered the treaty "binding on South Africa, at least on the international plane."[132] The court ignored any number of issues that could have provided grounds for questioning the binding nature of the SADC Tribunal's order: no South African enabling legislation directly incorporated the treaty; the order to be enforced was a tribunal's finding and not part of the original treaty; and the requirements for consideration of international law are less stringent when the SACC is not interpreting the Bill of Rights. It instead used the opportunity to develop a new common law rule treating international tribunals analogously to foreign domestic courts in terms of judgment recognition.[133]

DAMAGES

By refusing to be pinned down on the issue of when international law is actually binding, the SACC has ensured its ability to avoid direct confrontations with the government. At the same time, even when the court has found against the government, it has done so in ways that have limited the material impact of its rulings to the immediate case and prevented more widespread systemic effects. This can be seen in the SACC's rulings that have awarded damages. In *Carmichele*, the court recognized that the state's negligence allowed the victim to sue for damages. The court reached a similar outcome in *Zealand v Minister for Justice and Constitutional Development and Another*,[134] a case dealing with a claim of wrongful imprisonment. In *Zealand*, the SACC found that the constitution's protection against unlawful detention[135] enabled the applicant to sustain a claim of damages against the government.[136] Although the court, as in *Carmichele*, referred to the ICCPR, it instead relied on the constitution as "sufficient" grounds for its ruling.[137] Together, these cases would seem to bode well for victims of government abuse or neglect.

Unfortunately, the SACC has been unwilling to create a greater incentive structure for government compliance with rights protections. It has done so by limiting damages to those compensatory rights available in delict while avoiding punitive damages. In *Fose v Minister of Safety and Security*,[138] the appellant had claimed a right to damages under the constitution for police abuse. Although the court agreed that he was entitled to damages for the violation of an entrenched right, it refused to award any *punitive* constitutional damages as a means of deterring future governmental violations. Doing so, the SACC decided, would place a great demand on public coffers already overburdened by a multiplicity of policy demands; moreover, the court reasoned that there would be no guarantee of punitive damages' effectiveness.[139] (Of course, the demand on public coffers would be the exact reason punitive damages might indeed be effective.) In short, although the appellant was entitled to damages for violation of a constitutional right, real-world considerations counseled against a reward that would significantly impinge on government policy prerogatives. Lack of punitive damages ultimately meant that there was reduced incentive for government actors to comply with precedent. Indeed, the issue of punitive damages was not even addressed in subsequent cases, such as *Carmichele* or *Zealand*.

Outcome

The SACC in its early years appeared to be focused primarily on its role as an enabler of the post-Apartheid transition, as evidenced by the court's willingness to distinguish amnesty in South Africa from crimes covered in international treaties. This early focus on the South African experience carried through later cases, when the SACC continued to limit the applicability of international law in favor of a concern for the special circumstances of South African sociopolitical considerations. The result was a court that limited its rulings in ways that prevented any serious conflict with political actors and recognized the broad powers of the government to set policy.

One explanation for the SACC's behavior is that it became less assertive over time due to its altered political footing as the ANC gained power (Roux, 2013, pp. 176–177). According to this argument, the court in its early years was willing to act as a check on government because the ANC was not yet a dominant actor politically during the immediate posttransition era. As a result, any decisions against the government in early cases served to strengthen the institutional footing of the young court by asserting its role as a trustworthy guardian against overzealous majoritarianism.[140] In contrast, the court in later cases operated in a more precarious institutional setting, one where the ANC's dominance and deepening control over state levers of power cast doubt on the SACC's ability to act in overt opposition to government policy.

The cases reviewed here suggest an alternative phenomenon. Instead of changing its tactics across time, the SACC has consistently sought to hand down legally legitimate rulings that accrete into broader institutional legitimacy while limiting the immediate threat to political actors. *AZAPO* occurred against the backdrop of negotiations with a not yet vanquished National Party, and the court recognized this by crafting a legally legitimate decision that distinguished the South African scenario under international law and allowed the peace process to continue. In *Williams*, *Carmichele*, *Zealand*, and *Goodwin/Quagliani*—cases spanning a 14-year period—the SACC consistently recognized the role of international law in its criminal law jurisprudence but ultimately limited its direct applicability in favor of domestic considerations. It also limited the costs of those rulings for the government, even when increasing government costs was the only way to achieve the desired systemic effects of the SACC's ruling.

By doing so, the court, as predicted by theory, has maneuvered within a flexible institutional environment to maintain its legitimacy without inviting political attack. It has done this not by capitulating on rights, but by crafting decisions that are palatable to government actors. By using international law as an interpretive aid but not as directly binding, the SACC has been able to frame its jurisprudence in ways that legitimate broad human-rights–informed policy goals while referencing the ongoing special circumstances of South Africa. Its rulings have also afforded the court a high degree of maneuverability in future rulings by hedging on the binding nature of international human rights law. In some rulings, the SACC has limited the direct applicability of international law that has not been ratified. In separate rulings, duly ratified treaties were not applied because the SACC had not determined which treaties were self-executing. In yet other rulings, the court treated nonratified treaties as key to developing the common law in the new constitutional settlement. The unifying theme in these cases has been flexibility—the SACC can apply international human rights law according to its needs in individual cases. As a result, the court's use of international law to lock in democratic change has been subtle and marginal, and the SACC itself is under little threat of political retaliation for adverse rulings.

Linking Theory to the Subcases

My theory postulates that courts act according to competing drives as a result of their combined legal and political nature. In order to maintain legal legitimacy, they must, whenever possible, render legally plausible rulings. To maintain a meaningful role as policy spaces in the domestic environment, they must avoid inviting backlash from the government. These roles are often in tension, and this tension is at the heart of the first dimension that courts must consider: their relationship with political branches. How successful courts are in achieving their legitimacy-seeking goals also depends on whether they are able to engage the public and do so within the limits imposed by international law. How a court deals with these two additional dimensions of concern depends in large part on how flexible its procedural environment is. For the SACC, the court has used its flexibility to diminish the potential constraining effects of the second dimension (embedded internationalism) and effectively cut off the third dimension (public concern). This has allowed it to focus its attention on the first dimension (political actors) without sacrificing its legitimacy.

Where a court is able to engage the public, one option is to balance public opinion against the threat of political backlash. In a system such as South Africa's, however, such a balancing act is not feasible due to the extreme electoral dominance of the ANC and the large portion of the population that identifies with the party. The constitutional settlement did, however, endow the SACC with high levels of flexibility over its own docket and the terms on which it hears cases. The SACC has used this flexibility to maintain an extremely low number of cases and to avoid diverting public policy questions into the courts.

By limiting access in this way, the SACC has avoided confrontation with the government, but the cost of this strategy has been the inability to build a public support orientation. A 1997 survey of public opinion could be summed up as finding that the SACC was itself on probation. All South African ethnic groups registered higher levels of support than opposition for the court, but all groups also demonstrated an overall willingness to abolish the court if it regularly ruled against respondents' preferred policy outcomes. Overall, 55.4% of the population said that the court could be trusted (Gibson & Caldeira, 2003, pp. 9–11). A 2004 follow-up survey found that this number had barely moved, with 57.6% of the population trusting the court. The court's overall lack of relevance to the population can be seen in the fact that the same survey found that a full 20% of South Africans had not even heard of the SACC (Gibson, 2008, p. 243). This lack of public confidence or even awareness has led commentators to view the SACC as an "institution of elite politics."[141]

Given the relative poverty of the South African population, the levels of social need, the limited resources of the government, and the simple fact that, until recently, supermajorities of the population supported the ANC during elections, the court perhaps wisely chose to avoid becoming the locus of broad policy disputes with the government. It could not limit access in all cases, however, and again the systemic variables explored in this chapter explain the SACC's behavior. The court's failure to engage the public meant that it ceased to participate in a triangular game with the public and political branches; instead, it found itself in an institutional environment characterized most readily by the relationship between an apex court and the government. Absent moderating factors, this might have created a situation in which the SACC would be forced to choose between its legal legitimacy and the probability of inviting backlash. Moderating factors did exist, however, in the form of procedural flexibility. This allowed the SACC to limit the direct impact of international law and avoid conflict with the government through relaxed adjudication standards and limited remedies. In line with the SACC's moderate predisposition toward enforcing international law, the court rendered verdicts that moved the nation's legal environment toward greater conformity with international law standards, but subtly and marginally, and often without immediate effect that would provoke backlash.

This can be seen in both subcases. In the realm of socioeconomic rights, the SACC rendered a verdict that went against the government but did so in a way that did not require immediate implementation. Nor did the ruling directly rely on developing international law standards such as the minimum core, instead focusing on the reasonableness of the government's approach and allowing political actors to determine the precise course of action. Nevertheless, the ruling did validate an alternative approach to that which the government had been pursuing and reaffirmed the right to health in the HIV realm, despite its lack of immediate effects on the government.

In the criminal law cases, a similar pattern emerged. The SACC avoided the direct applicability of international human rights standards in favor of recognizing South Africa's special circumstances. The SACC also did not impose costly remedies, instead requiring protection of rights but avoiding pronouncements on the appropriate allocation of the government fisc. At the same time, international law standards were embedded more deeply into the nation's legal system through development of the common law and the acknowledgment of generally recognized human rights. In both first-generation and second-generation rights, the SACC has acted according to theoretical expectations, crafting legally legitimate rulings that recognize international law but limit the immediate effects to those that are palatable to the government.

Conclusion

The South African Constitutional Court has garnered attention from observers of international law and comparative court watchers because of its many rights-affirming rulings. In a deeply divided state recovering from decades of institutionalized racism, it is easy to understand why so many would be keen to affirm the new court's role. Interestingly, the SACC's laudable rulings have often used rights rhetoric and strengthened the SACC's reputation without providing any meaningful, immediate relief to those claiming the protection of international human rights law. Instead, the court has taken a gradualist approach, affirming international human rights but focusing on domestic sources of law and marginal enforcement.

This outcome can be explained by the variables examined in this project. First, like independent courts in other democracies, the SACC can rely on the rhetoric of international human rights law that is ensconced in treaties and in the domestic legal structure. South Africa's transformation from the Apartheid regime was itself at least partially grounded in the interaction between domestic resistance and international rhetoric, an interplay that flowed outward from South African activists seeking to undermine the legitimacy of the Apartheid regime but also flowed back into the domestic system by reliance on this same international human rights rhetoric and emergent international law principles. In addition, the beneficiaries of the previous ruling regime themselves had an incentive to rely on and accept incorporation of international human rights law as part of the transition. Whereas the elite in the

Apartheid era eschewed any calls for compliance with international human rights law, under the new regime these same laws and rights became a shield against domination by a newly empowered democratic majority. As a result, the role of international human rights law was accepted, institutionalized, and internalized by the constitution, the political elite, and the newly appointed justices of the SACC. This internalization was moderated, however, by the special needs of a South African society in transition.

The outcome also turns on the second variable under consideration: the relative lack of a public orientation for the court system. The concentration of economic and legal power during the Apartheid era was one argument seized upon by advocates of a new constitutional court. The previous judicial system's complicity—or at the very least acquiescence—with Apartheid-era government abuses meant that many in the ANC and other resistance groups were unwilling to accept a strong, independent judiciary staffed by pretransition judges. A new constitutional court addressed this concern, but it could not overcome the racial imbalance in the overall judiciary or the legal community more generally. As a result, while steady progress has been made toward an increasingly diverse court system nationwide, the SACC has remained the focus of political attention and has even seen its role as apex court strengthened over time. The result has been the lack of a public support orientation that would allow the SACC to serve as a link between the people and the international human rights ensconced in the constitution. This has also meant that the SACC is aware of the political importance attached to its rulings and has further limited its docket and the reach of its rulings in ways that avoid overt backlash.

Lastly, this desire to incorporate substantive rights buttressed by a new and independent constitutional court was accompanied by a procedural environment that granted a high degree of flexibility to the SACC. Although the substance of rights was debated during the constitutional drafting process, legal procedures were left to the court—in the name of judicial independence but also as a holdover of the broader common law traditions of the judiciary. As a result, the SACC has been able to constrict access over time, ensuring that it remains a relatively elite institution, insulated from the legal demands of a diverse but poor population. Constrained access is matched by minimally restrictive policy outputs that proclaim broad principles but do so without creating follow-up monitoring mechanisms, requiring significant outlays of money, or establishing standards that go beyond reasonableness or context-sensitive considerations.

The result has been a court that has affirmed the role of international human rights without taking it upon itself to effectuate those rights directly. The SACC has gained a strong reputation for legal legitimacy by embracing the international human rights articulated in treaties and in the Final Constitution; it has also laid the seeds for an expansion of these rights by declaring that the common law must be developed in line with international law. At the same time, it has guarded its institutional legitimacy by establishing precedent that respects the separation of powers—avoiding rulings that would create an ongoing antagonistic relationship with the government. It has used its control over procedures to ensure a limited level of access to the court alongside marginal demands for governmental implementation of those few rulings it does offer.

CHAPTER 5

Mexico: Rigid Reform

> When dealing with amparo suits, actions of unconstitutionality, constitutional controversies and ordinary federal suits, among others, the Supreme Court is an expeditious court for imparting justice, as indicated in the Constitution, but when dealing with the investigatory function envisioned in the second paragraph of Article 97, it is not. It cannot impart justice, even if it wishes.
>
> —*Ruling on the request to exercise special investigatory powers* (minority opinion), 2009

Introduction

Constitutional transformation and human rights incorporation have been hallmarks of democratic change over the past 30 years, as evidenced by the Colombian and South African experiences. This pattern has been replicated throughout much of Latin America: Bolivia (2009), Brazil (1988), Colombia (1991), Costa Rica (1989), Ecuador (1998 and 2008), Paraguay (1992), Peru (1993), and Venezuela (1999) all adopted new constitutions during this period.[1] Mexico, however, followed a different path. Rather than adopt a new constitution, Mexican politicians subjected the century-old Carta Magna[2] to a series of reforms beginning in 1994.[3] The reasons for the 1994 reforms are up for debate. They have been interpreted as a means of cracking down on corruption, representing merely another attempt to strengthen the oversight capacity of a waning authoritarian state (Domingo, 2000, p. 78). Alternatively, they may have been motivated by President Ernesto Zedillo's desire to recover lost legitimacy on the part of the governing party and the Supreme Court following earlier controversies (Oseguera, 2009). The most well received theory, however, is that proposed by Finkel (2003). She argues persuasively that the reforms were a form of political insurance on the part of the then-dominant political party, the Partido Revolucionario Institucional (PRI). As the party's electoral dominance declined in the late 1980s and early 1990s, the institution of an independent judiciary would ensure that the PRI had ongoing political access in the event the party lost its congressional majority or the presidency (Finkel, 2003).[4]

To ensure this access, the reforms focused on a purportedly nonpolitical institution: the Supreme Court of Justice of the Nation (SCJN). The reforms strengthened the SCJN across several dimensions. They expanded the court's jurisdiction over constitutional issues, allowing minority legislative parties to challenge the constitutionality of laws before they went into effect. The reforms also expanded the stakeholders in the appointment process of SCJN justices, providing for presidential selection of a three-person pool from which the Senate would choose each new justice. The 25 sitting justices of the SCJN were dismissed and replaced with a total of 11 new justices who were to hold their positions for a single, nonrenewable term of 15 years.[5] Although this represented a reduction from the previous life appointment of justices, 15 years was considered long enough for justices to operate without undue presidential influence while at the same time not remaining in office so long that they suffered significant drift from popular sentiment (Domingo, 2000, p. 713).

The PRI dominated the reform process. Zedillo introduced the reforms to the Mexican Congress within days of taking office, and the changes were passed by both houses of Congress within 10 days and by the requisite number of state legislatures within a week. The constitutional amendments became binding law within 1 month of their introduction (Vargas, 1995, pp. 506–507).[6] Throughout this process, opposition parties argued that the reform bill should be the subject of a special session of Congress, but the PRI rebuffed such requests. Members of the legal community, academics, and the public likewise had little input in the reform process (Fix-Fierro, 2003).

As a result, access to the judiciary by political actors remained the hallmark of the reforms. No effort was made at this point to expand standing to nonpolitical actors. Nevertheless, the newly strengthened judiciary has emerged as politically independent with the ability to exercise constitutional review powers; this has offered the possibility of rights enforcement based on human rights laws and treaties to which Mexico is a party. Indeed, the United Nations in 2013 awarded the SCJN its Human Rights Prize for the court's "important progress in the promotion of human rights through its implementation and application of the Mexican Constitution and its obligations under International Human Rights."[7]

This transformation, however, took nearly two decades and further rounds of reforms by political actors. The evolution from a newly strengthened SCJN with a focus on political disputes to a coequal branch able to enforce human rights has been slow in coming. It is my argument that procedural constraints on the SCJN limited its ability to enforce human rights in any meaningful way for most of the years of this study. The court exhibited a relatively superficial level of embedded internationalism, limiting the likelihood that justices would look to treaty law when considering human rights disputes. In addition, the reforms that strengthened the SCJN left the court with a limited public support orientation that left the judiciary subject to relatively efficient monitoring by political actors. Lastly, a lack of procedural flexibility has rendered the SCJN unable to avoid politically problematic cases or, alternatively, to balance public opinion and empower rights entrepreneurs against potentially hostile political actors. As a result, the post-reform SCJN failed to provide a hospitable venue for rights enforcement, and the court's role would expand primarily at the initiative of political actors outside the judiciary.

The Mexican case allows a deeper understanding of the impact of these variables because of the changing role of the SCJN over the past two decades. This institutional evolution has not been accompanied by a larger constitutional revolution of the type seen in Colombia and South Africa, where entirely new institutions assumed the role of constitutional arbiter. Instead, the reform of Mexico's judicial system occurred within an otherwise static constitutional framework. In addition, the Mexican judiciary has slowly evolved from a negative case, with very little judicial enforcement of rights, to a case where the highest court is beginning to test the waters of rights enforcement. This internal variation allows for a deeper understanding of the country-specific variables that have influenced judicial institutional outputs and societal leveraging of court enforcement mechanisms over time. The period of study begins with the 1994 judicial reforms and continues through 2013, covering the complete ninth and early tenth "epochs" of SCJN activity.[8]

The Mexican Institutional Setting

To begin, I position the Mexican case study in the larger theory outlined in Chapter 2. The theory emphasizes three variables that explain a court's ability to maintain or expand over time its enforcement of international human rights law obligations: the level of embedded internationalism, the support orientation of the court system, and the procedural flexibility of the court. I explore these variables in this section with regard to the SCJN. In the subsequent subcases, I examine how these institutional characteristics determine the SCJN's interactions with the political branches and litigants. In summary, the SCJN during the period of study is best categorized as presiding over a system with an initially superficial level of international embeddedness that, over time, slowly shifts to a moderate level; a limited public support orientation; and procedural rigidity. As a result, the SCJN has played a relatively minor role in the domestic enforcement of international law until recently. The low to moderate degree of international embeddedness has led the SCJN to deemphasize international human rights in its legal rulings and thus not treat international law as a core element of its legitimacy calculus. The court's output has been further constrained by the remaining two factors. The limited public support orientation of the system has allowed for relatively easy monitoring of the court's behavior over time. The lack of procedural flexibility has limited the SCJN's ability to selectively engage in rights enforcement. The result has been a court that has been unable to either avoid contentious rulings or selectively enforce rights in particular areas of the law. To the extent that the SCJN has expanded its role over time, this has been at the behest of political leaders, not as a result of the court's own initiative.

Superficial Internationalism

The status of international law in the Mexican constitutional framework was historically ambiguous, and the courts played only a tentative role in the domestic enforcement of international law. Only in the past two decades has the legislature clarified that international treaty law may have direct effect. For most of modern Mexico's history, the relationship between domestic and international law was governed by the constitution's Article 133 supremacy clause, which provides that both federal laws and duly ratified treaties shall be recognized as the supreme law of the union.[9] This article also binds the judges of the nation to enforce the federal constitution, laws, and treaties when in conflict with state laws. It is clear from the text of Article 133 and from later interpretations by the SCJN that the article is primarily concerned with federal supremacy over states, not with creating a hierarchy of laws that could place federal statute above or below ratified treaties. The constitution was also completely silent with regard to other forms of international law, such as custom or the pronouncements of international judicial bodies.

As such, the relation between federal statute and international law has been left to judicial interpretation. While the judiciary has addressed the question of whether international law can serve as a source of law to override domestic statutes, it has failed to provide a consistent answer. In several cases, the SCJN has found that federal law cannot be constrained by international treaties. In 1981, the court clarified that Article 133 is primarily concerned with the hierarchy of federal and state laws, not the relationship between laws and treaties: "It is, therefore, a rule of conflict to which Mexican authorities must subject themselves, but at the same time it cannot establish that treaties are of a greater obligation than laws of Congress."[10] In another ruling that year, the SCJN stated that "Article 133 does not establish any preference" between congressional statutes and duly ratified treaties.[11] The court reiterated this stance in 1991, finding that an "international treaty cannot be the criteria by which to determine the constitutionality of a law, nor vice versa."[12]

Despite this, the SCJN has in more recent jurisprudence suggested an elevating of treaty law's role in the domestic hierarchy. In a 1998 case dealing with labor rights, the court concluded that "this Supreme Court of Justice considers that international treaties find themselves on a second plane immediately below the Fundamental Law and above federal and local law."[13] Indeed, in articulating the ruling, the SCJN directly cited its earlier 1991 ruling and stated that it was "appropriate to abandon" the earlier interpretation, and that the court would view treaties as occupying a higher level in the legal hierarchy "even against federal law."[14] In such a framework, international treaty law could be used by the courts to strike down federal statutes.

It is difficult to imagine a clearer repudiation of its earlier stance, and yet the SCJN subsequently hedged. Without declaring yet another interpretation of Article 133, the court has indicated that the elevation of international treaty law above federal statute is not a general rule. In a subsequent speech, Justice Sánchez Cordero explained that because the SCJN in its 1998 ruling was addressing an issue of union organization rights, the treaty right paralleled a fundamental right in the Mexican constitution. As such, the elevation of treaty law in the national hierarchy was primarily an elevation in terms of its interpretive value as a means of supporting the reasoning of the court in its finding of unconstitutionality. This should not be taken, she stated, as indicating that treaties were situated unequivocally higher than statute.[15] Although this interpretation was provided by a single justice, the SCJN subsequently published online an edited version of the comments that included this reasoning, under the title "The Constitution and International Treaties," suggesting that the view is at the very least not contrary to the understanding of a majority of justices.[16]

The greatest changes in treatment of international law have come not at the hands of the SCJN but through the political process. In June 2011, President Felipe Calderón signed into law a package of constitutional changes that elevated human rights protections to constitutional status.[17] These changes were part of a larger set of reforms over the previous 3 years that included changes to the criminal justice laws, electoral processes, and expansion of protective claims against the government (Colli Ek, 2012, p. 7). The changes to Article 1 of the constitution were of particular importance, incorporating for the first time the direct protection of human rights. Whereas previous iterations of Article 1 indicated that all Mexicans enjoyed the rights *granted by* the constitution, the 2011 reforms expanded those protections to encompass all human rights *recognized by* the constitution or international treaties to which Mexico is a party. This not only expanded the range of rights protected to include those in international treaties, but the reform also made clear that the Mexican constitution was no longer to be considered the source of those rights. Instead, these rights were to be protected in the manner that would provide the broadest possible protection. Accordingly, the title of the chapter was changed from "individual rights" to "human rights," indicating the more expansive nature of the protections (Colli Ek, 2012, p. 9).[18]

This combined textual and rhetorical transformation has enhanced international law's status throughout the constitution. Of particular importance are the parallel changes found in the provisions regulating the amparo proceeding.[19] The amparo is a protective suit against the government for the failure to respect or enforce rights, particularly those rights ensconced in the first 29 articles of the constitution.[20] Prior to the 2011 reforms, any use of this suit was restricted to individuals claiming a "legal interest" in the proceedings. This strict language was expanded in 2011 to allow suit by any individual or group with a "legitimate interest"—a much less textually stringent standard that matches the new human rights rhetoric.[21] The reforms also increased the powers of the National Human Rights Commission. Whereas the commission could previously bring claims in the SCJN for violations of constitutional rights, the revisions allowed the commission to bring claims arising from rights under treaty law.[22] In practice, these combined changes offered the possibility of a greater range of cases reaching the SCJN, as well as a more deeply embedded internationalism.

Despite this late constitutionalization of international law, Mexican ratification of treaty law was relatively robust even before the democratic transition and constitutional reforms of the 1990s. During the period of inquiry, Mexico was a party to the two major human rights instruments, the ICCPR (acceded, March 23, 1981) and the ICESCR (acceded, March 23, 1981), as well as to the numerous issue-specific human rights treaties governing torture, women's rights, children's rights, and the rights of migrant workers. The country was also party to numerous International Labour Organization (ILO) treaties, as well as to those regional mechanisms comprising the inter-American human rights system. A complete list of Mexico's ratifications of and accessions to major international human rights treaties is included in Appendix 2.

The high number of treaty ratifications indicates that Mexican courts should have ample legal basis for rulings that safeguard human rights. At the same time, the constitution's textual ambivalence toward international law's role provides little guidance as to how, whether, and when courts must apply these protections. The resultant institutional ambiguity suggests that the attitudes of Mexico's justices have played an outsized role in determining the extent to which international law serves as a source of binding constraint. This has varied greatly over Mexico's recent history, ranging from an early period of extreme antipathy toward international law to a more recent tentative embrace of human rights norms.

Any discussion of judicial attitudes toward international law must make note of the extreme legal nationalism that historically characterized the Mexican judiciary. In addition to the constitution's textual downgrading of international treaty law highlighted earlier, the Mexican legal system until the 1980s was extremely reluctant to enforce legal principles of any non-Mexican provenance, be they public or private principles of law. Scholars have suggested that the origins of this antipathy can be found in the foreign dominance of industry and natural resource exploitation in the years leading up to the Mexican Revolution. The resultant social inequities provided populist fervor that shaped the social provisions of the 1917 constitution and the later nationalization of foreign oil investments. This extended to the legal regime, which recognized this nationalism through the adoption of "absolute territorialism"—an aversion to recognizing foreign and international legal principles when deciding disputes. It was not until the late 1980s that the country's economic opening helped break down this resistance to foreign legal influences, resulting in the first attempts to codify conflict-of-laws principles and ratify and incorporate treaties domestically (Vargas, 2009, pp. 56–66).

This opening to international and foreign law has only slowly become a regular feature of the Mexican judicial system. Treaty compliance continues to be hindered by lack of knowledge among judges and lawyers. International human rights issues have recently become a standard part of legal curricula in Mexico, but as of 2002 only 15 schools required such training as part of the undergraduate law degree (Heyns & Viljoen, 2002b, p. 423). A more recent study indicates that human rights law continues to be but a small part of an extremely varied educational system; courses focused on human rights tend to be just one elective course among the 40 to 70 courses students complete (Pérez Hurtado, 2010, pp. 582–583). Interest in human rights may be growing, but slowly, with only 17.5% of Mexican law students indicating a concern for social justice of any kind as the reason they pursued a legal education (Pérez-Hurtado, 2009, pp. 93–94).

To determine the extent to which the justices of the SCJN are exceptions to this general lack of attention to international law, I examined the educational and professional backgrounds of all justices since the 1994 reforms. To determine whether individual justices' ideal points are reflective and supportive of international human rights law, I reviewed each justice's personal biography as included on the judiciary's website to determine whether the justice was educated in a foreign institution, worked in a foreign country, or regularly traveled abroad for conferences and presentations.[23] While not determinative of an individual justice's attitude toward international law, overseas training and work do indicate exposure to legal traditions beyond the domestic system and a willingness to engage with foreign or international legal concepts. This exposure would provide at least the possibility of embedded internationalism at a personal and professional level, if not at the level of constitutional text. The results of this review are included in Figure 13. An asterisk (*) indicates a justice whose experience includes this international exposure.

Overall, only a minority of justices have experience that provides them with any heightened sensitivity to international law concerns. Of the 20

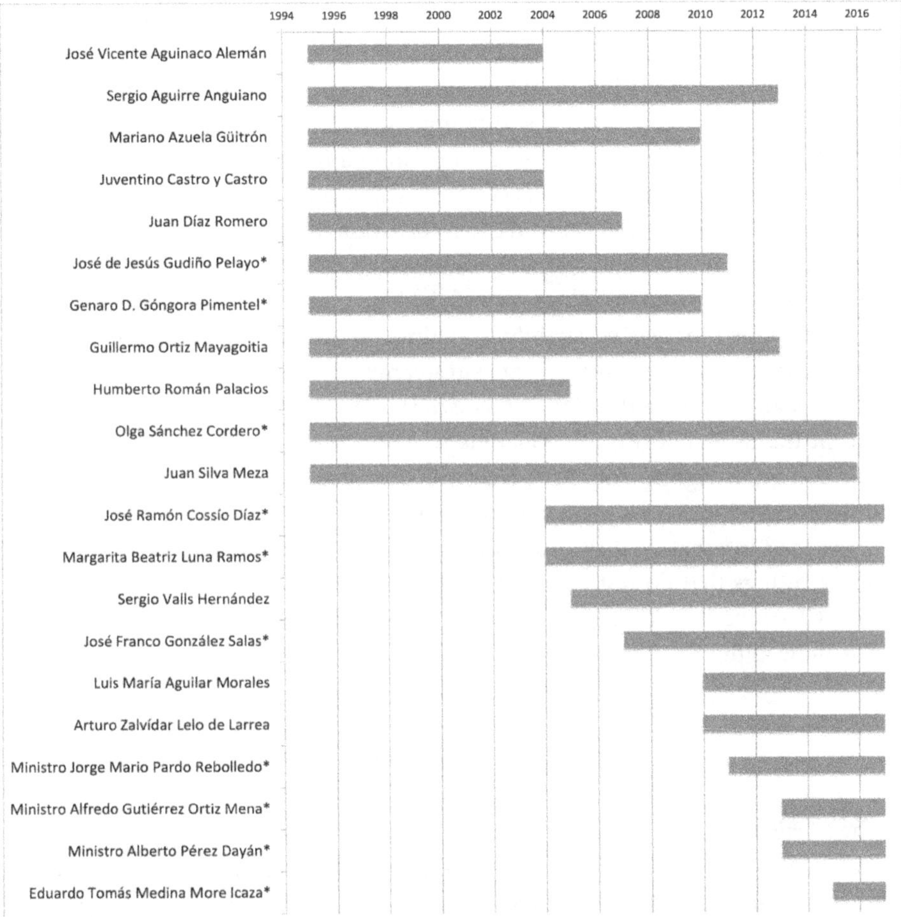

Figure 13. Justices of the Mexican Supreme Court of Justice of the Nation.

justices who served on the SCJN in the years following the 1994 reforms, only 9 had biographies listing significant educational or work experience abroad. At the collective institutional level as well, these justices rarely represented a majority. Only in the years 2007–2010 and again after 2013 did these more internationally oriented justices constitute a majority of the 11 justices.

In general, both at the institutional level and at the level of individual justices, the SCJN has exhibited only a slight orientation toward international law during the period of study, with no clear imperative to either adopt or reject international law. The textual ambiguity of the constitution has, until recently, provided little impetus for the court to consider international treaty law or broader international human rights norms. The legal training and experience of the justices have failed to overcome this institutional shortcoming. The text of the constitution and a wide range of treaty ratifications suggest the possibility for the court to enforce international human rights, but the lack of any clear textual imperative is coupled with a high court whose members have limited professional exposure to international law. As a result, the Mexican judiciary is most appropriately classified as operating in an institutional context characterized by at best superficial internationalism, with the level of embeddedness increasing slightly over time. This has created problems not just for international human rights enforcement but also for the court itself. In the years following the 1994 reforms, a lack of embedded internationalism meant the SCJN's legitimacy calculus was not deeply informed by international human rights. The 2011 reforms, however, embedded international human rights more deeply in the constitutional framework. A more deeply embedded internationalism now threatens to heighten the legitimacy gap of SCJN rulings that do not comport with international human rights law, yet the SCJN's weak links to the public and rigid procedural environment have not allowed the court to keep pace.

A Limited Public Support Orientation

The Mexican judicial system during the period of study is best categorized as having only a limited public support orientation. This results from the judicial system's admixture of diffuse and concentrated constitutional review powers. The degree of diffusion has fluctuated over time as political actors have focused attention on the SCJN and the SCJN has reacted through its rulings. Historically, the system has often adhered more closely to the diffuse model, but periodic political interventions have highlighted the politically dominant role of the SCJN in the court system. The 1994 reforms continued this process by increasing the court's ability to review laws at both the state and federal levels, but within limits set by political actors. This has allowed politicians relatively efficient monitoring of the judicial branch and prevented the SCJN from effectively utilizing the public as a meaningful alternative constituency.

Historically, the Mexican system could be categorized as diffuse in terms of its allocation of review powers because of the existence of the amparo suit. The amparo is a special judicial suit designed to protect individual rights. It was first established in 1847 and spread outward from Mexico to other parts of Latin America and the Spanish-speaking world, extending as far as Spain and the Philippines. It constitutes a multiplicity of actions, from a judicial request to overturn a lower court's ruling to the equivalent of a habeas corpus writ. The common element is the protection of a private individual's right under the constitution to be protected from government abuse by any public actor in any branch of government. Amparo suits are brought in the federal court system[24] and serve as the primary judicial means of enforcing human rights in the courts. From the time of the amparo's initial formulation, it has been designed for broad access that would allow individuals to bring claims in courts throughout Mexico (Brewer-Carías, 2008, pp. 120–129). In its basic contours, it resembles the Colombian tutela discussed in Chapter 3.

The potential power of the amparo was balanced, however, by strict limitations on the applicability of individual court rulings—any ruling in an amparo suit applied solely to the individuals in the case. This inter partes application even extended to challenges against legislative acts, meaning that although a citizen could challenge the constitutionality of legislation, any court ruling in favor of the challenger only applied to the individual; the law itself remained on the books and authorities could continue to apply it against other members of society.[25] This is consistent with the Mexican judiciary's historical basis in civil law principles, wherein the concept of binding precedent has found little purchase. The concept of binding precedent is not, however, completely absent from the Mexican judicial system. Instead, it is calibrated in such a manner as to concentrate important precedential rulings at specific points in the judicial system, allowing for easier monitoring of judicial activity by political actors. In Mexico, certain courts are empowered to establish precedent through the articulation of *jurisprudencia*.[26] This allows these legally designated courts to create binding normative rules through one of two processes.

The first is the process of "repetition," wherein the court rules on a point of law in the same way five times without contradicting itself. This obviously limits the power of the judicial branch—while even courts in the United States are considered passive because of their inability to seek out cases actively, in Mexico the repetition requirement means a passive judiciary must wait for five separate cases to make their way to the court. It also allows for more active political monitoring in two ways. First, the repetition requirement ensures that no individual court can overturn a government policy without the government having ample time to intercede, either by tweaking the policy or by appointing new judges as terms expire.[27] Second, because the primary means of enforcement of individual rights is through the amparo, and the amparo is a federal court hearing, this process of repetition ensures that the SCJN is likely to be the most effective interpreter of even state laws (Zamora, 2004, p. 85).[28] This allows the federal court system to operate as a policing mechanism over subnational government units.

The second means by which a court can create *jurisprudencia* is through "contradiction." Under this method when a high court overrules a lower court's contrary ruling on a particular legal point, a new point of law is created and becomes binding on all lower courts. Here, the political concentration of power in specific courts is much more explicit: this method of creating *jurisprudencia* is available only to the apex court in each jurisdiction, such as a state high court, the federal electoral tribunal in electoral matters, and most importantly the SCJN. The SCJN plenary chamber is also able to create *jurisprudencia* in this way when it overrules a point of conflict between its individual chambers. This means that the vast majority of courts, such as the federal district courts, are simply not empowered to create binding precedent (Zamora, 2004, pp. 83–88).

The 1994 reforms built on this history through the adoption of two new forms of judicial review: the constitutional controversy and the action of unconstitutionality. This further concentrated adjudicatory power in the SCJN, as it is the only court in the nation empowered to hear these two types of claims. Constitutional controversies comprise those suits that arise between different branches of government or between governmental units at the various levels of the federal hierarchy.[29] This marks an important departure from the use of the amparo as the only judicial means of ensuring state compliance with federal laws; whereas the amparo depends on suits brought by citizens, the new constitutional controversy can be brought by members of any level of government. This implicates the SCJN directly in political disputes between governmental actors.

Next, unconstitutionality review represents Mexico's first venture into abstract constitutional controls. The reforms enable minority party members of the legislative branch to bring claims of unconstitutionality against new legislation before it has gone into effect. This power extends to legislative minorities at the federal and the state level, as well as to the attorney general. Jurisdiction extends to state, federal, and federal district laws, allowing the SCJN to serve as a venue for political disputes throughout the nation.[30] In both constitutional controversies and actions of unconstitutionality, the SCJN also received the power for the first time in its history to hand down rulings with general (erga omnes) effect.[31]

The increased judicial powers were systematically concentrated in the SCJN, continuing a pattern that already existed with regard to amparo suits. An earlier round of reforms in 1988 removed lower court jurisdiction over constitutional issues in amparo proceedings (Zamora, 2004, p. 263). In 1994, lower-level courts received few if any additional powers; to the extent that district courts were empowered to hear cases involving the federal government, those cases were given only inter partes effect. The SCJN also retained the power of "attraction," which allowed it to immediately assert jurisdiction over any suit of overriding significance.[32] In addition, the federal government retained the explicit right to appeal amparo cases to the SCJN—a right not extended to other parties.[33] A further set of reforms in 1996 enabled the court to hear claims over the constitutionality of electoral laws.[34]

It should be noted that the enhanced role of the SCJN was focused entirely on political actors. The general populace did not gain any new access mechanisms, nor did they gain either a priori or ex post standing to bring constitutional challenges with erga omnes effect. As a result, the SCJN has remained an elite institution in terms of constitutional issues; the amparo action, meanwhile, has continued to serve as the sole method by which citizens may challenge government actions even after the judicial reforms of 1994. This has limited the court's ability to draw on the public as an alternative source of institutional support. Unlike the Colombian Constitutional Court, Mexico's SCJN cannot engage in a balancing act that plays public concerns against political actors.

Further judicial reforms in 2011 continued the trend, simultaneously enhancing the protection of human rights under the constitution and increasing the concentration of adjudicatory power in the SCJN. Any suspension of human rights during states of emergency must now be reviewed by the SCJN, automatically and immediately.[35] Political monitoring of the judiciary is, meanwhile, even more seamless: the SCJN is now required to notify the responsible government branch when any federal judicial body finds any legal provision unconstitutional for a second time.[36] Once a government actor is presented with a finding of unconstitutionality, the responsible authority has 90 days to correct the breach; only if no correction is made can the SCJN rule that the legal norm is no longer applicable, and then only with a supermajority of 8 out of 11 votes.[37] In effect, the system builds "mootness" into the review process.

On its face, these increased judicial oversight powers would suggest a court well positioned to enforce the numerous treaty-law and constitutional provisions that now protect international human rights in Mexico. The increasing concentration of these adjudicatory powers in a single court, however, has highlighted that institution's political nature and rendered it vulnerable to efficient monitoring by the political powers it might otherwise check. This does not mean the SCJN is not aware of the problem. Indeed, it has expended some degree of effort in publicizing its decisions in an attempt to make them intelligible to the broader public (Staton, 2010). Despite these efforts, the orientation of the SCJN remains focused on political actors, not the broader public. As will be explored next, this is because of the extremely rigid procedural environment in which the court operates. Whereas the Colombian Constitutional Court has been able to increase public engagement over time to balance against political actors, and the South African Constitutional Court has reduced exposure to conflict by limiting access, the SCJN has not been able to modulate its public engagement in similar ways. The result has often been a court locked in the traditional one-dimensional standoff with political actors, with deleterious effects for human rights entrenchment and the court's own institutional legitimacy.

Procedural Rigidity

The existence of the amparo suit might suggest a court well positioned to enforce human rights, similar to how the Colombian Constitutional Court transformed the tutela into a source of public support. This has not occurred. Instead, the strict political regulation of the amparo's use and the extremely rigid nature of the Mexican legal system have acted as impediments. Historically, this lack of flexibility could be attributed to two factors: the extreme dominance of the political system by the PRI and the legal system's civil law origins. Although both have become less determinative factors over time, the newly independent judiciary has inherited an inflexible procedural environment that continues to be dominated by legislatively determined court rules.

The SCJN's current lack of institutional flexibility has roots in the president's post-1917 dominance of the entire political structure. As the head both of the executive branch and the overwhelmingly dominant PRI, the president served as the fulcrum of power for Mexico's political system, an informal method of power consolidation referred to by scholars as *presidencialismo*

(Weldon, 1997). The president enjoyed ex officio constitutional power to select members of the judiciary, but under the constitution these selections were subject to Senate approval. This approval however was entirely pro forma. The president's leadership role in the PRI provided him with what have been termed "meta-constitutional" powers—namely, the selection of heads of both chambers of Congress.[38] These formal and informal powers guaranteed a seamless judicial appointment process (Ugalde, 2001). It also allowed the president to use SCJN appointments as a reward to loyal politicians, resulting in a body of justices who were party loyalists rather than accomplished jurists (Magaloni, 2003).

This arrangement had obvious negative effects on the development of an independent judiciary. Although structural safeguards existed in the constitution, the party-based system ensured an alignment of interests and the lack of any effective veto point in the judiciary. Instead, the courts followed a policy of deference to political actors. This would be an obvious outcome in any system marked by *presidencialismo*. In the Mexican judiciary, this was enhanced by the transformative nature of the 1917 constitution and the revolutionary credo of Mexico's dominant party. Any judicial attempts to counterbalance political initiatives would be seen as particularly problematic. Instead, members of the judiciary and society at large expected policy would be determined by overtly political—but purportedly representative—bodies such as the Senate (Schor, 2009).

Despite this expectation, during the period of PRI dominance the courts did act as a check on government power—after a fashion. Instead of checking Congress or the president, the federal courts acted as a rein on state and municipal power. Once laws were passed at the federal level, the federal courts monitored state and municipal application of those laws through citizen amparo suits. This allowed the party to use the courts to police the various branches and levels of government throughout the Mexican federal system. When a local official failed to apply the law correctly, the application could be challenged in federal court. The federal court system in effect became another governing mechanism for the dominant PRI (Magaloni, 2003, pp. 291–294).

The judiciary's role as enforcer of PRI policy prerogatives had an important secondary effect: the SCJN historically has not been empowered to develop its own procedures. Given the importance of the amparo in the system of vertical checks and balances, the political branches have been attuned to the potential substantive importance of seemingly procedural questions. As a result, the legislature has been historically very active in articulating the jurisdiction and procedures governing the federal courts' use of the amparo. The legislature designed the amparo to be limited in applicability. Litigants can only use the procedure to challenge official acts, and a ruling in an amparo proceeding applies only to that case—no general effects arise from the decision (Brewer-Carías, 2008, p. 82). In short, were an adventurous court to overrule one of the PRI's preferred policies, it would still only apply to the case at hand.

Lastly, the SCJN's tight alignment with party mechanisms has limited the court's efforts at institutional innovation. Unlike in the United States, binding precedent and the ability to override laws are not judicially created legal concepts. On the contrary, the ability of the Mexican courts to serve as a check on the legislature has been a political project self-consciously undertaken by the legislature. It was the federal Congress that introduced the idea of binding precedent with the 1882 amparo law; in 1950, the potential for binding through repetition became part of the constitution as Article 107.[39]

For its part, the SCJN has historically avoided attempts to expand its powers. Partially, this was a result of the president's unilateral control over judicial appointments and the tight alignment of judicial attitudes with party doctrine. Deference was further buttressed by the fact that the judiciary did not represent a long-term career path for the majority of the SCJN's justices. Although the constitution protected life tenure, presidents throughout the period of PRI dominance appointed, on average, more than 50% of the bench as sitting justices cycled off the court. As Magaloni (2003, p. 290) demonstrates, political posts represented the single largest identifiable career path for justices leaving the judiciary during the era of PRI dominance. As such, there was little incentive for justices to concentrate on institutional strengthening of the courts. It was only at the behest of Congress that the court's institutional role grew over time.

This dominant legislative role was likewise supported by the country's civil law tradition.[40] As mentioned previously, the amparo suit is a Mexican innovation. As such, its origins cannot be traced to the Spanish legal system or European systems generally (Brewer-Carías, 2008, p. 81). Nevertheless, the implementation of the amparo suit has followed the civil law tradition of reliance on extensively codified legal doctrines to create a fully conceptualized understanding of the law prior to its implementation in the courts. In particular, the Mexican legal system has, since its founding, relied on numerous regulatory statutes (*leyes reglamentarias*) that provide the content for constitutional doctrines and also outline the procedures through which courts

Table 6. Party Strength in Congress in Mexico's Post-Reform Era

Party	*Congressional Body*	*1997*	*2000*	*2003*	*2006*	*2009*	*2012*
PRI	Senate (Seats)	n/a	60	n/a	33	n/a	54
	Senate (Percent)	n/a	47%	n/a	26%	n/a	42%
	Deputies (Seats)	239	211	225	104	237	213
	Deputies (Percent)	48%	42%	45%	21%	47%	43%
PAN	Senate (Seats)	n/a	46	n/a	52	n/a	38
	Senate (Percent)	n/a	36%	n/a	41%	n/a	30%
	Deputies (Seats)	120	206	152	206	143	114
	Deputies (Percent)	24%	41%	30%	41%	29%	23%
PRD	Senate (Seats)	n/a	16	n/a	29	n/a	22
	Senate (Percent)	n/a	13%	n/a	23%	n/a	17%
	Deputies (Seats)	126	50	96	126	71	103
	Deputies (Percent)	25%	10%	19%	25%	14%	21%
Minor parties	Senate (Seats)	n/a	6	n/a	14	n/a	14
	Senate (Percent)	n/a	5%	n/a	12%	n/a	11%
	Deputies (Seats)	15	33	27	64	49	70
	Deputies (Percent)	3%	7%	5%	13%	10%	14%

Minor parties are those that garnered less than 10% of the seats in either house of Congress. Elections to the Chamber of Deputies are held every 3 years; Senate elections are held once every 6 years. The total number of seats in the Chamber of Deputies is 500; the total in the Senate is 128. Percentages do not sum to 100% due to rounding. PAN = Partido Acción Nacional; PRD = Partido de la Revolución Democrática; PRI = Partido Revolucionario Institucional.

may implement these doctrines. Because codes are intended to be complete and self-explanatory, judicial interpretation (as opposed to application) is considered to be unnecessary (Zamora, 2004, p. 81). As one commentator has put it, the law "was identified with legislation, and the judiciary was its servant" (Concha Cantú, 2006, p. 364).

The 1994 reforms signaled a conscious attempt to break with this past, but despite institutional strengthening and increased judicial independence, much of the rigid procedural framework has persisted. After President Zedillo and the PRI enacted court reforms in 1994, the party slowly lost its electoral dominance, giving credence to Finkel's insurance theory mentioned at the beginning of the chapter (Finkel, 2003). Table 6 provides an overview of political party power in each of the two houses of the Mexican Congress in the post-reform era.[41] The lack of a dominant party indicates the declining utility of meta-constitutional control structures. Indeed, under 1996 electoral reforms, it is now structurally impossible for any party operating alone to amend the constitution: while constitutional amendments require a two-thirds vote of the legislature, the constitution limits any one party to a maximum of three fifths of the seats.[42] Zedillo's successors, Vicente Fox (2000–2006) and Felipe Calderón (2006–2012) of the Partido Acción Nacional put forth modest legislative reforms, but during this time no party maintained a majority in either house of Congress.

Given this lack of a dominant party in the political branches, theories of divided government would suggest this period would be ideal for the SCJN to assert its institutional role in the political structure (Epstein, Knight & Martin, 2001; Ferejohn, 2002; Ríos-Figueroa, 2007). This has not been the case. The reason can be found in the rigid procedural environment in which the SCJN continued to operate following the 1994 reforms. The declining electoral fortunes of the PRI mask this phenomenon. As in past periods, the focus of procedural innovation in 1994 and subsequently has been the president acting through the legislature, and reforms have been accompanied by the articulation of rigid jurisdictional delineations and procedural mechanisms that provide little leeway for court-generated innovation.

As described earlier, the 1994 reforms that strengthened the judiciary were exclusively the work of political actors; members of the court system had little role in designing them.[43] The reforms extended access to the SCJN but did so in an extremely focused manner, emphasizing the ability of legislative minorities to bring abstract constitutional review challenges. The reforms also extended the SCJN's constitutional review powers, but again outlined the types of cases to which these powers would apply—primarily intergovernmental disputes. The reforms also provided specific jurisdictional carve-outs, including electoral cases. In short, the reforms strengthened the institutional bases of judicial independence and ensured that the SCJN was free to decide issues on their merits; but it also did little to enhance the court's ability to embark on procedurally innovative methods of engaging litigants.

The ongoing rigidity of the procedural environment can be seen both at the level of the constitution and in the regulatory laws. The constitution continues to set out an extensive framework for when and how courts can hear amparo suits, comprising more than 50 paragraphs and 2,800 words. The sections lay out in extreme detail the types of cases that litigants may bring; the conditions under which courts may accept cases, render rulings, and allow appeals of decisions; and the extent to which a suit is binding on nonparties to the dispute.[44]

The control of procedural instruments extends beyond the constitution, with statutes providing further regulation. The constitution contemplates further statutory regulation for the courts in the timing of declarations of unconstitutionality of general legal provisions;[45] the conditions under which a court may suspend an official act pursuant to an amparo hearing;[46] and certain venue decisions.[47] The amparo law[48] has long provided detailed regulations for that instrument's use—details that are so intricate that by 1992 as many as four out of five amparo suits were dismissed because of lack of conformity with procedural technicalities (Rubio et al., 2000, p. 64). The creation of new constitutional controversies in 1994, however, was accompanied by a further expansion of statutory directions to the court. An entirely new federal code of civil procedure was passed in 1995 to define in extreme detail the contours of this new proceeding. The new code outlined who could be potential parties to constitutional controversies, who could stand as interested third parties, which officials could represent the president in proceedings, what information filings must contain, deadlines for litigant responses, and so on—very little space was left for SCJN interpretation or any type of court-led entrepreneurial behavior to control the litigation flow (Vargas, 1996).

In addition, the 1994 reforms failed to provide the SCJN with the ability to institute more wide-ranging institutional changes affecting its relations with lower courts. The SCJN has only limited ability to avoid rulings in substantive matters or to devolve powers to other courts. Although caseload has historically been one of the greatest problems facing the SCJN, the 1994 reforms did not increase the court's ability to restrict its docket in constitutional issues. This only came about in 1999, following an additional set of reforms that allowed the SCJN to delegate certain cases to the collegiate circuit courts, and only then if the case did not entail important constitutional issues. As a result, even after the 1999 reforms, the SCJN receives approximately 3,000 cases per year. It must hear and decide each case unless the subject matter falls within one of the areas in which delegation is permitted (Zamora, 2004, p. 193). What reforms are made continue to be made primarily at the behest of the federal legislative branch. When in 2000 activists led by former justice Góngora Pimentel presented Congress with a package of reforms meant to refine the amparo law, Congress rejected the reforms (Concha Cantú, 2006, p. 382, fn. 19).

The 1994 reforms recognized and reinforced a decade-long trend in declining PRI dominance. The rise of a more competitive party environment suggests the possibility of a more active court during this period. As will be seen, however, this did not happen. Instead, the SCJN continued to be constrained by a highly articulated constitutional and procedural framework governing the courts. Although the SCJN's formal institutional independence was greatly strengthened by the reforms, little change occurred in terms of the level of flexibility of procedural rules. This restricted the court's ability to become a selective enforcer of international human rights in the post-reform era, meaning that at times it was subject to unwanted and damaging attention. The SCJN's low to moderate exposure to international law influences, the concentration of power in and concomitant political attention to the court at the expense of a public support orientation, and the inflexible procedural environment combined to produce a post-reform judiciary characterized by minimal attempts to enforce human rights and, at times, the SCJN's outright rejection of any such role in the constitutional structure. It is to the court's role in specific issue areas of international human rights that I now turn.

Subcase 1: Impunity

In the subcases, I test the theory that the low to moderate level of international embeddedness, limited public support orientation, and constrained procedural environment prevented the SCJN from acting as an effective enforcer of international human rights or increasing its role over time. The selection of subcases for Mexico was based on the theoretical expectation that the number of court cases is not directly reflective of the societal potential for court-based enforcement efforts. This is particularly important in a case such as Mexico, where political actors have often preconditioned court access on factors (such as electoral insurance for the party itself) that are not directly related to the demand for human rights enforcement. As such, a review of reports from the U.S. Department of State, United Nations, and human-rights NGOs was critical in determining the areas of greatest potential demand for litigation. The review of these documents indicated consistent allegations of impunity for violations by state agents for human rights violations in the overlapping areas of extrajudicial killings, torture, and disappearances of civilians. During the 20-year period of review, this appeared in 18 of the 20 years.

The ongoing relevance of this issue is not unexpected, given the decades-long struggle in Mexico between government forces and insurgent movements fueled by the drug trade. Allegations of impunity have much earlier roots, however, beginning in the *guerra sucia*, or "Dirty War" of the 1960s and

1970s.[49] During this period, government forces engaged in violent repression of political opponents, resulting in 645 disappearances, 99 extrajudicial killings, and at least 2,000 victims of torture.[50] It was during this period that the infamous October 1968 Tlatelolco and June 1971 Jueves de Corpus student massacres occurred in Mexico City.[51]

Abuses resumed in the 1990s with the armed uprisings among Mexico's southern states. In 1994, the Zapatista uprising led to allegations of widespread human rights violations and impunity on the part of the military (Human Rights Watch, 1994). In 1995, civilians on their way to a protest were detained outside of the town of Aguas Blancas, Guerrero, and 17 were killed when police opened fire on the group. Mexico's National Human Rights Commission (CNDH)[52] concluded at least one of the individuals was the victim of an extrajudicial killing (Human Rights Watch, 1995). In 1996, military and state police were accused of torture, extrajudicial killings, and disappearances in Guerrero, Oaxaca, Sinaloa, and Chihuahua (Human Rights Watch, 1997). Violence continued in 1997, with 45 civilians massacred in Acteal, Chiapas. Although the attack was carried out by civilians, it was alleged that they had received their arms from the military (Human Rights Watch, 1998, 1999). In Jalisco, the theft of a soldier's weapon resulted in retaliatory torture and murder of 20 civilians by the military; the soldiers were prosecuted in military tribunals (Human Rights Watch, 1999). That year also saw allegations against the military of extrajudicial killings of 11 people in Guerrero (Human Rights Watch, 1999).

These abuses have been exacerbated by the country's decades-old fight against illicit drug trafficking to the United States. Beginning in the late 1960s but intensifying during the 1980s, Mexico's anti-trafficking efforts resulted in increased prosecutions in Mexico and extraditions to the United States. This, in turn, resulted in increased levels of violence associated with cartel competition within Mexico. By the mid-2000s, extreme levels of violence had led to an increase in the size and funding of the military and state police, as well as infringement of constitutional rights in those areas where the military operates (Lindau, 2011). The pattern of impunity, then, covers three related but distinct periods: the Dirty War (1960s–1970s), the rural uprisings (1990s), and more recent drug-related violence (2000s).

Given the nature of the underlying human rights violations, it is not surprising that the problem of impunity is widespread but not well documented. The country's post-WWII political settlement left Mexico as one of the few Latin American states not subject to repeated military interference in politics, but at the expense of a military whose operations were not subject to civilian oversight and transparency (Camp, 1992; Concha Cantú, 2006). Moreover, Mexico lacks a national or interstate system to document abuses such as disappearances. Only recently has the federal government created a database of allegations of disappearances; the information, compiled by the federal prosecutor's office, was very quickly criticized by human rights organizations as being woefully inaccurate or incomplete.[53] According to Human Rights Watch, the military prosecutor's office claims to have opened 3,671 investigations into human rights violations against civilians during the recent drug war; fewer than 15 of these investigations resulted in conviction.[54]

In dealing with these issues, the SCJN might be expected to draw on any of the numerous treaties to which Mexico is a party and which deal with military-civilian relations, international criminal law, and impunity. At the global level, protections are included in the ICCPR, but Mexico is also party to numerous regional treaties covering these areas of international law. The legal environment, then, was amenable to enforcement of international human rights. Despite this, the SCJN proved an inhospitable environment for human rights adjudication throughout most of the period of inquiry, adopting enhanced enforcement measures only after political actors again reformed the legal and institutional environment in the late 2000s.

Investigation: Avoid and Retreat

The SCJN's early efforts to require some level of responsibility on the part of state actors were relatively ineffectual. The concentration of review powers in the court made it the focus of human rights enforcement efforts, but the rigid procedural environment rendered the court unable to effectively expand its powers to match the demands placed upon it. Ultimately, this would lead to the SCJN's retreat from its minimal enforcement efforts.

The first attempt at exercising some form of oversight came in 1996 and dealt with contemporary events: the previous year's massacre in Aguas Blancas. Following the massacre, human rights groups and the human rights secretary of the main opposition party, the Partido Revolucionario Democratico (PRD), petitioned the CNDH to investigate. In its investigation, the CNDH determined that grave violations had occurred; it also recommended the appointment of a special prosecutor, a restructuring of security forces in the state, and the dismissal or suspension of numerous officials.[55] At this point, a human rights NGO petitioned the SCJN to use its investigatory powers in the Aguas Blancas matter.

The special investigatory powers to which the NGO referred were those granted in Article 97 of the constitution. Under this article, the SCJN was empowered to investigate "an act or acts that constitute a grave violation of individual guarantees" found in the constitution.[56] This historical grant was envisioned as an emergency power to be used in the event of national collapse or a state of affairs resulting in widespread rights violations. The investigatory function had been within the SCJN's mandate since the initial adoption of the constitution. Despite this, the court had exercised the power only once in its nearly 80-year history.[57]

Presented with the opportunity to use its power, the SCJN waffled. Now 2 years into its reform era, the court was severely hampered by two institutional constraints: first, the exercise of the investigatory power was limited by a lack of clarity over who could request an investigation; second, the SCJN would find its powers constrained by a limited jurisdictional grant.

First, unlike the amparo suit, no regulatory law provided a legal framework for the constitutional grant of judicial authority. This proved to be an obstacle for a judiciary still mired in civil law training and accustomed to strict adherence to statutory provisions. The court at first refused to conduct any investigation, noting that the petitioner did not have proper standing. Moreover, another constitutionally authorized actor (the CNDH) was already investigating the matter. With regard to standing, the constitutional text provided only that the SCJN could initiate an investigation "when it deems it necessary or when requested by the Federal Executive or one of the Houses of Congress of the Union, or a governor of a State."[58] A minority of the court argued that although the petitioner did not fall within the ambit of Article 97, the SJCN could nonetheless take note of the request and act ex officio based on the language allowing the court to act "when it deems it necessary."[59] A majority resisted this approach, however, instead interpreting this clause as restrictive in nature and allowing only the three government actors named in Article 97 to request an investigation.

This attempt to avoid an investigation ultimately failed when political pressure drove the president to request an investigation. Even without a regulatory framework, the constitution clearly designated the executive branch as one party that could request that the court act. By early 1996, President Zedillo was coming under intense political pressure to address the human rights situation in the country. As a result, on March 4 his administration filed paperwork with the SCJN requesting that it exercise its investigatory function.[60] In a public session on March 5, the court's plenary chamber accepted the petition and voted 10-to-1 in favor of exercising its Article 97 powers.

The investigation concluded that there had indeed been "grave violations" of individual rights under the constitution. The court went so far as to name specific state officials in the state of Guerrero who were responsible for these violations. It determined that it would send reports to Congress, the president, and the attorney general so that they could take appropriate actions. Charged with this information, the attorney general concluded that no federal abuses had occurred, and that the case was, therefore, properly within the jurisdiction of the Guerrero state authorities (Morineau, 1997).

At this point, the SCJN's participation ended. This was the direct result of the second constraint faced by the court: a lack of jurisdiction. The SCJN had historically interpreted the constitutional language as granting investigatory powers only, with the court receiving no jurisdiction over the breaches and no power to proclaim sentences. The purpose of the investigation was to restore the rule of law, not by exercising jurisdiction and passing judgments but by acting as an instructive body (Carpizo, 2011).[61] In short, the court could offer findings but not remedies.

This was clearly problematic in a human rights investigation. The SCJN had already concluded that rights violations had occurred. Without the ability to exercise jurisdiction, however, it could not translate these findings into penal proceedings. Indeed, one court finding in particular reveals the extent to which the SCJN was hampered by the inflexible procedural environment: With no statutory procedures governing delivery of its final report, the SCJN was not even sure to whom the court should send its findings. It solved this problem by referencing an adjacent constitutional provision dealing with electoral disputes. That provision ordered the court to provide a report to "competent organs."[62] One of the *tesis* (rulings of law)[63] adopted by the court in the Aguas Blancas matter thus related exclusively to dissemination of its findings.

The SCJN's findings did not, however, lead to any convictions, calling into question the efficacy of the court. This put the SCJN in a precarious position: the court represented a potential institutional focal point for activists and for public concern over rights abuses, but one unable to address flexibly its findings by crafting politically acceptable rulings. Under these less-than-optimal conditions, the SCJN used what little flexibility it did have to engage in prospective retrenchment. In effect, the SCJN undertook to increase its discretion to reject future difficult cases and thereby remove itself from the political spotlight.

First, the SCJN promulgated rulings that would allow it to avoid exercising this politically contentious form of investigation. In its vote to investigate Aguas Blancas, the court took the opportunity to vote unanimously that exercising this power was discretionary—even when requested by the executive.[64] This desire to limit the court's exposure to criticism and adverse political interactions can be seen in subsequent rulings as well. Having ruled in 1996 that the investigatory function was discretionary, the SCJN in a subsequent ruling found that it was not bound to provide reasons for any refusal to exercise this function.[65]

Second, the SCJN crafted a blanket rule that would allow it to refrain from exercising any ongoing oversight of rights violations. It did this by distinguishing the constitutional and legal frameworks governing the amparo suit and the investigatory function. The amparo law provided "the procedural instruments by which the Supreme Court and, in general, amparo courts, are legally able to achieve compliance with the terms of amparo sentences."[66] As such, any oversight of amparo claims would occur within the amparo framework. The investigatory power would be treated as an entirely distinct function of the court, and any attempt to use it as a means of overseeing and ensuring compliance with amparo sentences would be rejected.

These interpretive stances would allow the SCJN to avoid becoming involved in other situations where it might be forced to recognize widespread rights violations but lack the capacity to act. The inefficacy of the court in the matter of Aguas Blancas would serve as a warning for years to come. Indeed, those opposed to exercising this power would continue to cite it as a cautionary tale for the next decade.[67] It would take that long before the court would accept another petition to exercise this function. In the interim, the SCJN experienced sustained pressure to exercise the power, receiving petitions at a much higher rate than before the 1994 reforms, as outlined in Figure 14.

The failure to use its power was understandable in the era of PRI dominance, when a judiciary lacking independence might not be expected to exercise institutional prerogatives in opposition to the government. Following the reforms of 1994, however, expectations for the court were higher, and the judiciary no longer operated in a party environment fully dominated by the PRI. After 1998, the former ruling party no longer had a majority in Congress, and in 2000 it lost the presidency. Given this change, the SCJN found itself in a much less restrictive political environment when it was again

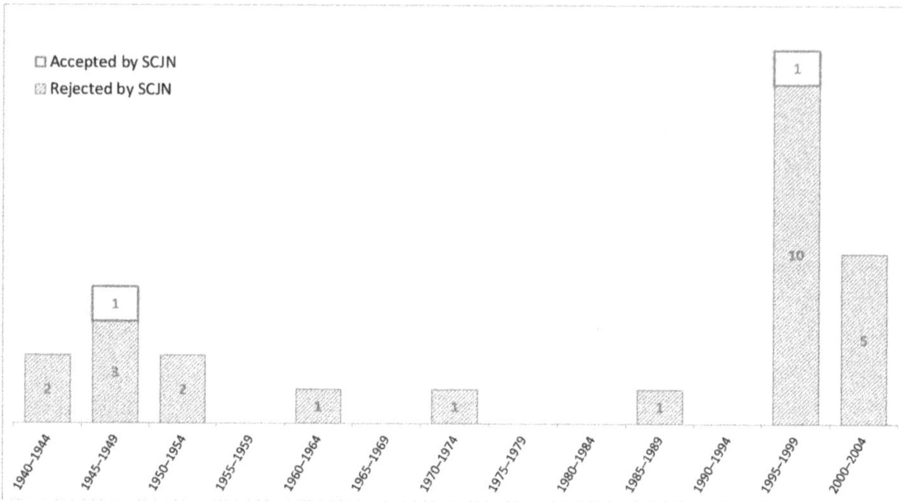

Figure 14. Petitions for the Mexican Supreme Court of Justice of the Nation to Exercise Its Investigatory Function, 1940–2005.

presented with opportunities to exercise the investigatory function. By the mid-2000s, faced with ongoing calls to use its investigatory powers, the SCJN reconsidered its earlier reluctance. Despite this newfound willingness, the court would find its efforts impeded by the same procedural restrictions it had encountered in 1996.

The opportunity arose in a series of cases dealing with human rights, many of which again dealt directly with impunity. The first, in 2006, dealt with the detention of the journalist Lydia Cacho. The court was criticized when it found no rights violations (Colli Ek, 2012). In two separate undertakings, the SCJN investigated military abuses in 2006—in Atenco (in Mexico State) and in Oaxaca. In the Atenco case, the court found no state liability for the abuses, and NGOs criticized the court both for dismissing allegations against state officials and for failing to observe international obligations.[68] In Oaxaca, however, the SCJN found the state governor guilty of violations of individual rights. The outcome was the same as for Aguas Blancas: the transmission of a report to political leaders with no further judicial involvement.[69]

It was a fourth case, unrelated to military impunity, that would sound the death knell for the SCJN's attempt to expand its role. On June 5, 2009, a fire in a day care center in Hermosillo, Sonora, claimed the lives of nearly 50 children. Within a month, the parents petitioned the SCJN to exercise its Article

97 investigatory powers. The court originally noted that the parents did not have standing, but in an unorthodox exercise in openness the SCJN accepted the case on the motion of the court's own justices—in contravention to the procedures it followed in the Aguas Blancas case a decade earlier. The SCJN expressed confidence in "the constitutional role that the Supreme Court has in the new democratic system" and that the power of investigation "allows one to see this Supreme Court as a supreme guarantor clad in the highest constitutional, political, and moral authority."[70] Despite this lofty language, the SCJN found itself bound by the same institutional limitations, namely its lack of jurisdiction. As a result, the court again suffered a loss of legitimacy. While noting "grave violations," the SCJN did not hold any individuals responsible for the act, leading NGOs, members of the public, and even one former justice to question the effectiveness of the court.[71]

The inability of the SCJN to deal effectively with human rights issues ultimately led the members of the court to support a transfer of its investigatory authority to a distinct institution outside the federal judiciary. The lack of a jurisdictional grant, they argued, was incompatible with the new role of the SCJN as a constitutional body. The investigation of national tragedies without the ability to address them meaningfully left the SCJN at the center of numerous emotional debates that ultimately served only to damage the court's reputation. The members of the court asked that political reforms either restrict access to the SCJN or remove the power entirely (Carpizo, 2011). The political branches responded by transferring the investigatory powers to the CNDH.

The SCJN was unable to successfully avoid human rights cases altogether due to its central role in a concentrated review structure. At the same time, it was unable to expand its power because of the extremely rigid, politically determined limits on its procedural environment and jurisdictional grant. The court found itself unable to balance the public against political actors, but it also found itself unable to pivot away from the public gaze. As a result, the investigatory function ultimately resulted in the court's loss of prestige and diminution of its institutional power.

Convictions: The Marginal Court

The investigatory function demonstrated the SCJN's limited maneuverability in an elite-oriented judicial system. A parallel set of cases indicate the degree to which the court was able to render meaningful decisions enforcing international human rights, but only to the extent that political actors were willing to pursue these claims. The court itself was procedurally incapable of providing broad-based rights-affirming outcomes that might enhance its public support orientation. The result in the 2000s was a decade that saw the SCJN increasingly willing to engage the issue of military impunity, but with limited results.

The court's activity was preceded by increased political moves toward compliance with international human rights law standards. In 2001, the CNDH completed its investigation into human rights violations during the Dirty War. Because the CNDH lacked prosecutorial powers, its president forwarded the report to the executive branch under incoming president Vicente Fox. Fox responded by appointing a special prosecutor, Ignacio Carrillo Prieto, to examine allegations of military involvement in disappearances during Mexico's Dirty War.[72]

This domestic attention to past crimes was accompanied by a renewed emphasis on human rights at the international level. In 2002, Mexico ratified the Convention on the Non-Applicability of Statutory Limitations to War Crimes and Crimes Against Humanity (CNASL) after a delay of more than 30 years.[73] In addition, Mexico had previously ratified the Convention Against Torture and Other Cruel, Inhuman or Degrading Treatment or Punishment (CAT) and in 2002 filed a declaration for the first time accepting that treaty's Article 22 procedure for individual complaints. This was accompanied by the country's signature in 2003 and ratification in 2005 of the CAT optional protocol establishing a system of inspections of detention centers. Mexico also ratified the ICCPR's optional protocol, accepting that instrument's individual complaint procedure.

All of these changes suggested an increasing level of embedded internationalism for the legal system. It was in this environment that the SCJN took its first concrete steps against impunity, yet these steps again came at the instigation of government actors outside the judiciary. The SCJN's first opportunity came in 2003, when the national attorney general attempted to bring charges against past officials for Dirty War–era crimes.[74] The attorney general brought the first of these cases in a district court in Nuevo León seeking the prosecution of Luis de la Barreda, ex-head of the Federal Security Directorate; Miguel Nazar Haro, head of the paramilitary force Brigada Blanca; and state judicial agent Juventino Ramos Cisneros. All three men were implicated in the 1975 disappearance of the human rights activist Jesús Piedra Ibarra. The district court found that the prosecution was barred by the statute of limitations.

At this point the attorney general filed an appeal with the SCJN, and the first chamber agreed to take the case sitting as a criminal appeals body.[75] The SCJN overruled the lower court, finding that the statute of limitations on forced disappearances did not begin to toll when the person went missing, but rather when the person reappeared or was remanded before the proper authorities.[76] The majority opinion ruled that the disappearance constituted a continuing rights violation. This interpretation brought Mexico into compliance with international law standards and the findings of other courts throughout Latin America. It also opened the way for prosecutions at the highest levels of government.

Such a politically charged case arrived at the SCJN in 2005. The case arose out of President Luis Echeverría's alleged ordering of the repression of student protests in the 1971 Jueves de Corpus massacre that likewise occurred during Mexico's Dirty War. After receiving allegations that government officials had been involved in the repression, the Special Prosecutor's Office for Social and Political Movements of the Past (FEMOSPP) ordered an investigation in 2002.[77] FEMOSPP brought charges in 2004 in Mexico City district court against former president Echeverría and 10 other officials, alleging that their actions constituted genocidal acts. On July 24 of that year, the district court determined that the prosecution of the 1971 events was barred by Mexico's 30-year statute of limitations.[78] The decision was appealed to the circuit court, but the SCJN interceded and heard the case directly.[79]

On appeal, the prosecution argued on various grounds that under international law the statute of limitations could not be applied to a claim of genocide. The SCJN's first chamber recognized that Mexico was bound by the CNASL but determined that the bar on statutes of limitation only applied to cases arising after Mexico's 2002 ratification of the CNASL. (Mexico's ratification of that treaty included an interpretive declaration indicating that the treaty would not be held to apply to crimes committed prior to the treaty's entry into force vis-à-vis Mexico.) As a result, the court had to rely on the constitution for pre-2002 violations, which did not allow for ex post facto application of laws.[80]

Under this analysis, the genocide claim would be barred. The SCJN issued a subsequent ruling dealing with the prosecutor's additional arguments, however, and this time found in favor of the prosecution. The court determined that the statute of limitations applied, but that it was tolled while accused individuals held official positions that entitled them to immunity from prosecution. This meant that the statute of limitations for former president

Echeverría and his interior secretary, Mario Moya Palencia, did not begin to run until they left office in 1976, allowing charges to proceed upon remand to the lower court.[81]

Although these rulings opened up the possibility of prosecutions at the highest levels of government, the effects were ultimately limited. In the Echeverría case, the SCJN's reliance on domestic law meant that only two individuals could be charged; the remaining nine implicated in the investigation had left office early enough that the statute of limitations had run out. Just as important, because the SCJN chose to sit as an appeals tribunal (rather than as a court of first instance), prosecutions were held in lower courts. As a result, many of the accused ultimately avoided conviction when lower-court judges found in favor of defendants.[82] As long as the SCJN was reliant on government officials for determining which cases it heard, its role would be limited.

Political Reform: Toward an Outward-Looking Court

An opening for the court to increase its role would have to wait until the introduction of another round of constitutional reforms. The constitutional reforms of 2011 incorporated pro homine language that increased the SCJN's interpretive flexibility such that the court could base rulings on international human rights norms and not just those direct grants of rights found in the constitution. The pattern of strict SCJN adherence to textual requirements finally began to change as the court received and exercised greater latitude to interpret international law, yet the extent of these changes would again be limited by the restrictive nature of the court's procedural environment.

The SCJN began to test the use of this new power in July 2011. In a landmark decision, the court exercised its jurisdiction to determine the judiciary's obligations vis-à-vis rulings of the Inter-American Court of Human Rights (IACHR). The importance of the IACHR as an alternative venue had been growing in the previous decade. After Mexico's acceptance of the international court's jurisdiction in December 1998, the IACHR rendered several opinions against the country dealing with impunity for human rights abuses. These cases are summarized in Table 7.

In these cases, the IACHR ordered Mexico to conduct investigations into the alleged crimes in the ordinary court system. It also ordered Mexico to make legislative and constitutional changes in order to bring the country's military code of justice into line with international standards, including the

Table 7. Opinions of the Inter-American Court of Human Rights Involving Mexico and Impunity

Case (Short Title)	Date of Violation	Date of Ruling	Type of Violation
Radilla Pacheco v Mexico	Aug. 1974	Nov. 2009	Forced disappearance
Fernández Ortega et al. v Mexico	Mar. 2002	Aug. 2010	Rape and torture by state agents and military; failure to investigate; improper use of military forum
Rosendo-Cantú and Other v Mexico	Feb. 2002	Aug. 2010	Rape and torture by state agents and military; failure to investigate; improper use of military forum
Cabrera García and Montiel-Flores v Mexico	May 1999	Nov. 2010	Torture, detention by military, lack of adequate investigation into torture; use of military courts in a human rights investigation and trial

American Convention on Human Rights, and to provide an effective means for civilians to contest military jurisdiction as a means of overcoming impunity.[83] For most of the decade, however, Mexico failed to comply with these rulings. Not until after the constitutional changes of 2011 did the judiciary become an active participant in enforcing these decisions.

It should be noted that, prior to 2011, the SCJN had held that international treaties were subservient to the constitution and that their relation to statute was unclear. The 2011 constitutional reforms provided a political and legal opening for the SCJN by elevating the importance of human rights in the constitutional framework.[84] The SCJN asserted its jurisdiction over these issues in an unprecedented way—by turning directly to the IACHR's jurisprudence. The SCJN, in effect, presented itself with a question: What obligations did the federal judiciary have in ensuring compliance with IACHR rulings? It answered this question in a two-step process.

First, the court in 2010 charged itself with answering the question of what process should govern IACHR enforcement. The plenary chamber exercised jurisdiction over this question by referring to a paragraph in what is known as the organic law that regulates the federal judiciary, or LOPJF.[85] This law consists of 251 articles outlining the jurisdiction of the federal courts and the procedures by which they operate. Section 2, Article 10, of the LOPJF describes in detail the jurisdictional grant to the SCJN's plenary chamber, including amparo suits and constitutional controversies. The section is generally restrictive in nature, specifying which types of cases cannot be delegated to individual chambers and must instead be heard by the full court. Paragraph XI, however, provided that the plenary chamber could hear "any other matter within the competence of the Supreme Court of Justice which does not correspond to the separate chambers." In short, it did not represent a separate jurisdictional grant, but rather designated the plenary as the appropriate venue for cases over which the SCJN already had jurisdiction but which had not been devolved to an individual chamber.

The SCJN used this paragraph, however, to assert jurisdiction and provide a forum for the court to expound on the role of the judiciary in enforcing international human rights. The SCJN used as a point of reference the IACHR's *Radilla Pacheco v Mexico* ruling, a case arising from the Dirty War. In a lengthy ruling, three justices concluded that there was no appropriate framework in which the SCJN could consider the question, as no formal notification process existed between the IACHR and the domestic judiciary—an interpretation consistent with the long-standing traditions of formalism in the Mexican judiciary. The majority, however, took a different approach. They voted that the SCJN could proceed motu proprio (of its own volition, or sua sponte) to comply with the IACHR ruling—even without coordinating with the other branches of government.[86]

Second, the SCJN followed this 2010 determination with a July 2011 ruling on the handling of the *Radilla Pacheco* case. The court began by referencing the president's 1999 decree recognizing the IACHR's contentious jurisdiction. On the basis of this recognition, the SCJN determined, Mexico had an obligation to ensure compliance with the IACHR's rulings in *Radilla Pacheco*. The SCJN also recognized that it faced a conundrum: the IACHR ruling required constitutional and legal changes. The SCJN stated that it could not enact those changes, for that would be encroaching on the power of the political branches. At the same time, this did not absolve the judiciary of its obligations. To resolve this contradiction, the court simply reinterpreted the military code such that military jurisdiction could not be extended to any case involving a human rights violation.[87] In the case before the court, this meant that *Radilla Pacheco* could not be referred to military courts, but also that all future cases would have to apply the new rules. It also ordered all federal courts to notify the SCJN of any relevant cases so that the latter could assume jurisdiction, given the importance and significance of this issue.[88]

The SCJN also used this same case to extend the applicability of international human rights law to future cases, as well as to extend the reach of international law throughout the domestic court system. It did so by adopting conventionality control as a feature of diffuse judicial review.[89] Under this form of judicial review, courts are required to apply human rights laws and norms found in treaties ("conventions"). The IACHR had established diffuse conventionality control as a treaty obligation through a series of cases beginning in 2006.[90] In subsequent cases, the IACHR had ordered Mexico to exercise conventionality control: first in a 2009 case arising from forced disappearance[91] and again in a 2010 torture case.[92]

The SCJN's ruling in this area was particularly sweeping. The court determined that all judges in the country must apply human rights contained both in the constitution and in federal judicial precedent. They were also ordered to enforce all human rights contained in treaties to which Mexico was a party. Lastly, they were required to enforce binding rulings of the IACHR. This final element is the most expansive: the SCJN determined that Mexican judges would be bound not just by rulings in cases to which Mexico was a party but also by those IACHR precedents set forth in cases to which Mexico was not a party.[93]

The SCJN did this by relying extensively on the reforms to the constitution that had just taken effect. The court stated that the expanded pro homine principle now included in Article 1 of the constitution required "all authorities in the country" to safeguard human rights, meaning that the lower courts were empowered to take on an expanded role.[94] Importantly for the theory examined here, the procedural environment conditioned the manner in which these changes came about. The SCJN noted that its competence in this matter depended on the absence of a legal structure governing compliance with IACHR rulings. In the face of such an absence, the court was empowered to act.[95]

It did not go beyond the procedural limits set, however, by the political branches. Instead, it recognized and validated conventionality control only to the extent that it did not overtly counteract the SCJN's role as the only court politically enabled to annul laws: "While judges may not make a general pronouncement of invalidity or expel from the legal order those norms they consider contrary to human rights contained in the Constitution or treaties . . . they are obligated to stop applying those inferior norms, giving preference to those contained in the Constitution or applicable treaties."[96] The language is striking for a court system with such a strong civil law history: the offending legal norms are to be considered "inferior" in the analysis. The practical effect, however, is in line with guidelines set by political actors: lower courts must consider international law in their decision-making, but their decisions will still enjoy only inter partes effect, limiting the immediate impact and protecting the central court's role as the primary political actor in the judicial system.

The ruling was well received by human rights organizations and court watchers more broadly domestically and internationally.[97] Little attention was paid, however, to the fact that the SCJN's inflexible, politically determined institutional environment greatly reduced the ruling's effect. In particular, the groundbreaking ruling did not create binding precedent, since it did not meet the strictly regulated requirements of jurisprudence through repetition or contradiction (appeal). Because no case was being prosecuted before the courts, the SCJN's opinion on *Radilla Pacheco* amounted to instructions to its own chambers and to the lower courts on how to handle future cases should they arise.

Despite not having created binding precedent, however, these interpretations have begun to permeate the judicial system. On August 12, 2011, a lower court determined that the prosecution of soldiers for the alleged rape of two indigenous women—Inés Fernández Ortega and Valentina Rosendo Cantú, whose cases were heard by the IACHR (see Table 7)—could no longer proceed in the military courts because these crimes represented human rights violations against civilians. The SCJN also began the slow process of creating binding precedent. On August 10 and 21, 2012, the court handed down two rulings in which it found Article 57, section 2, of the military code to be unconstitutional, requiring the cases to be transferred from military to civilian jurisdiction.[98] Still, this did not meet the five-repetition requirement for binding precedent, which continued to hamper any court-centered reform strategy.

At the same time, the lack of procedural flexibility prevented further engagement with this issue. Mexican authorities have still not investigated the alleged detention and torture of two environmentalists, Teodoro Cabrera García and Rodolfo Montiel-Flores, whose cases were also heard by the IACHR (see Table 7). For this reason, it would appear that the courts are indeed willing to apply conventionality in those cases already at bar, but that they otherwise lack the procedural tools to ensure compliance by otherwise intransigent officials. Consequently, any further progress would have to come from the political branches. In 2014, the Senate and the Chamber of Deputies finally approved a reformed code of military justice.[99] The revised code removed from military jurisdiction any cases involving civilians as victims.

This shows the limited role of the SCJN. On the one hand, meaningful changes still rely on political actors. On the other hand, the court's role must be recognized in catalyzing that action. An increasingly embedded level of international human rights made the SCJN more sensitive to this area of human rights obligations. A procedural lacuna allowed it to finally pivot in such a way as to use international law to enhance its own legitimacy in a manner not possible in earlier cases.

Subcase 2: Indigenous Rights

This pattern of increasingly embedded internationalism, coupled with a procedural opening, can be seen as well in the area of indigenous rights. The review of human rights reports indicated that indigenous rights represented an additional legal area with widespread and ongoing abuses. In part, these abuses were related to the question of impunity. Many of the allegations of torture, disappearances, and extrajudicial killings were made by or on behalf of indigenous individuals and groups. Indigenous communities are concentrated in the southern and central states of Mexico, overlapping with insurgent and drug-related violence and often closely related to these phenomena.[100] The types of abuses noted by the reports, however, extended beyond this class of rights violations, focusing instead on internationally recognized rights such as language and cultural rights, preconsultation for development projects, and other issues relating to autonomy for indigenous communities.

The ongoing importance of these issues is to be expected, given the size of Mexico's indigenous population. Mexico has one of the largest indigenous populations of any country both in terms of raw numbers (10,688,535) and as a percentage (11%) of total national population (Ramirez, 2006, pp. 150–151).[101] When cases related to indigenous groups (qua groups)[102] entered the court system, they historically were under the rubric of other rights, such as land tenure (Ansolabehere, 2010, p. 99).

A lack of court activity is not due to a lack of justiciable rights or standards at the level of international human rights law. To be sure, indigenous rights at the international level represent a relatively recent phenomenon. Decolonization of the Americas primarily entailed a transfer of authority to Creole populations. When 150 years later human rights were recognized as part of the UN system, the drafters of the UN Charter likewise were careful to define self-determination rights in ways that excluded indigenous peoples' autonomy claims. International tribunals followed this practice, excluding these subnational groups on the basis of their lack of standing. In short, native peoples' rights were historically considered to be an exclusively national consideration (Reisman, 1995).

International law has nevertheless taken halting steps over the past several decades to define indigenous rights following sustained efforts of indigenous rights advocacy groups (Brysk, 2000). The first codification came in 1957, when the International Labour Organization adopted the Indigenous and Tribal Populations Convention (No. 107). Convention No. 107 reflected the assumption that indigenous groups would eventually be integrated into their states' dominant sociocultural groups, and, as such, the instrument encouraged broad development goals.[103]

This integrationist approach was abandoned in the 1980s when the ILO replaced Convention No. 107 with Convention No. 169, focusing on "peoples" rather than "populations" and recognizing indigenous groups as permanent societies (Swepston, 1990). This was followed in 2007 by the UN General Assembly's adoption of the UN Declaration on the Rights of Indigenous Peoples (UNDRIP), which collected in one document the many rights provisions of other declarations and treaties and applied them to the context of indigenous peoples.[104] ILO Convention No. 169 is a legally binding instrument, and Mexico ratified the treaty in 1990.[105] The UNDRIP is nonbinding but has influenced the interpretation of statutes and rights adjudication in numerous countries and by international organizations (Pulitano, 2012). As a result the SCJN today has had numerous sources of international human rights law on which to draw when enforcing and interpreting indigenous rights claims.

The first cases dealing with indigenous rights did not reach the SCJN, however, until much later than these international developments—7 years after the domestic political reforms of 1994. In the intervening years, indigenous rights activists primarily attempted to achieve their goals through nonjudicial means. Indigenous rights during this period were seen primarily through the lens of the Zapatista uprising in the state of Chiapas. The Mexican government concluded the San Andrés Accords with the Zapatistas in 1996, recognizing the group's demands for increased local autonomy and democratization. By 2001, those accords had not been implemented, and as a result the Zapatistas organized an historic march on Mexico City. This direct-action effort was followed by President Fox's 2001 proposal to implement the

San Andrés Accords through a package of five constitutional reforms. Congress passed the reform package in 2001, but only after major changes that watered down provisions granting greater autonomy to indigenous communities (Yashar, 2005, pp. 25–26, 296).[106]

It was at this juncture that the SCJN became implicated in the struggle over indigenous rights. The constitutional changes became official with publication in the government gazette in August 2001, and numerous indigenous communities, in concert with local state organs, immediately brought constitutional claims challenging the reforms. Although the amendments passed, they were rejected by all of the southern states with sizable indigenous populations; as many as 320 towns and organizations challenged the reforms on the grounds that they did not follow the proper procedures for amending the Mexican constitution. The groups also argued that the reforms did not conform to international standards, including a requirement for prior consultation with indigenous groups (Carbonell, 2003). The controversial nature of the reforms, along with the longstanding concern over the Zapatista uprising, put the SCJN at the center of an intensely political issue.[107] The spike in the number and percentage of cases involving international law–based constitutional controversies entering the SCJN's docket as a result of these 2001 filings can be seen in Figure 15.

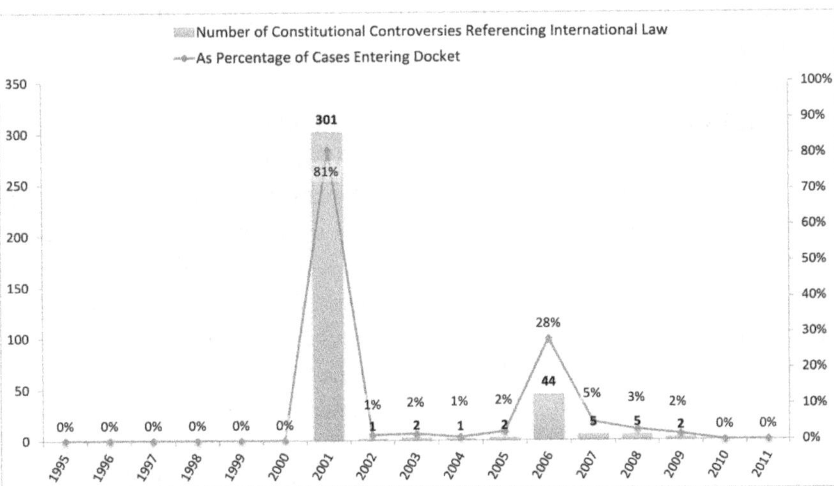

Figure 15. Prevalence of Constitutional Controversies Based in International Law on the Docket of the Mexican Supreme Court of Justice of the Nation, 1995–2011.

The SCJN never reached the merits of the claims. Instead, the court determined this to be a nonjusticiable dispute. In an opinion replete with constitutional and legislative history, the SCJN explained that the reforms of 1994 and the designation of the court as a constitutional tribunal had as its core purpose the protection of the federal system. Under that scheme, the constitutional controversy was designed to allow the individual governmental units listed in Article 105 of the constitution (the federal government, the states, municipalities) to challenge encroachments on their respective areas of power within the federal structure and to allow the organs of state to maintain a balance of powers. It was not designed to allow challenges against these individual units when they acted in tandem as a special constitutional reform entity.

The court was criticized for its failure to reach the merits of the claim.[108] Although the SCJN did not offer a substantive ruling, it did, however, take this opportunity to hand down two *tesis* that developed points of law relating to the constitutional amendment process. It should be noted that the court designated these two *tesis* as *jurisprudencia*, despite the court's insistence that the case at hand was not a justiciable constitutional controversy.[109]

In the first of these, the SCJN determined that the procedure for amending and adding to the constitution was itself not subject to constitutional review. The individual state institutions of Congress, the individual states, and the electoral organs operating together constituted a special reform body of the constitution. Operating in this manner, they were more than their individual parts, and as such they exercised a sovereign function that could not be subjected to external control.[110]

The SCJN reinforced this conclusion in a second *tesis*. This time the court explicitly found that it was not empowered to hear this type of claim. In particular, the court noted that section 105 of the constitution, from which the SCJN derived its jurisdictional grant, provided for only a limited set of constitutional controversies. Constitutional controversies were limited to cases that policed the boundaries of federalism and the division of powers between state organs. A state organ could not use this type of claim to impugn a constitutional reform.[111] Whereas the reform apparatus was an expression of the people acting as sovereign, the courts and other political units were mere creations of that grander sovereign entity. As such, the created unit (the SCJN) could not question the actions of the creator. The practical result was the court's removal of itself from the constitutional reform process.[112] Unlike the Colombian Constitutional Court, the SCJN would not take the opportunity to articulate an international law–informed *bloque de constitucionalidad* for constitutional amendments.

This nonintervention marked the high period of court activity on indigenous rights for another decade. It should be noted that the lack of court activity over the subsequent decade cannot be attributed to a lack of substantive rights in the constitution. On the contrary (and despite activists' claims that the constitutional reforms did not go far enough to implement the San Andrés Accords), the constitutional reforms indicated a meaningful change in the state's recognition of substantive indigenous rights. The text of the constitution was changed to recognize the "pluricultural" nature of the Mexican state, "originally based in its indigenous populations."[113] Beyond this rhetorical change, much of the new constitutional language was inspired by ILO Convention No. 169 (Carbonell, 2003; González Galván, 2003b). The changes included a definition of indigenous groups based on self-identification and a list of the minimal contents to be included in any recognition of autonomy, balancing this with the need for national unity (Giménez, 2014). The reform granted substantive rights, including control over socioeconomic and political organization, separate legal apparatuses and electoral mechanisms, protection of language and cultural identity, and priority use of land and natural resources. It also marked the first time that collective rights, and not just the rights of individuals, were included in the constitution.[114]

The substantive shift was clear. Yet indigenous rights claims did not become a normal part of the SCJN's docket, and according to one commentator these constitutional changes became yet another reform effort that was completely forgotten.[115] Why did this occur? The reason can be found in the court's inability to fashion procedural tools to accompany the new substantive rights. Under the Mexican constitutional system, the creation of necessary procedural instruments resides with political actors. Despite this, no such changes were forthcoming. Collective causes of action to enforce the newly recognized collective rights did not arrive for another decade, after Congress implemented another set of constitutional and legal reforms that finally brought procedural tools in line with substantive rights.

The first change was an additional amendment to constitutional Article 17 in 2010 that provided for the possibility of collective causes of action. Like in earlier reforms, however, the constitutional changes were not accompanied by the necessary secondary legislation (Olaiz-González & Bosco López, 2011). Without accompanying legislation, the courts would be unable to adjudicate these rights, because the "current procedural paradigms, in many aspects, [would] be insufficient and even contrary to the spirit of collective actions and procedures."[116] It would take another year and a further round of constitutional amendments and statutory revisions before the courts were truly empowered to act in this field.

Congress finally amended the necessary procedural laws to allow for collective actions in 2011, a decade after the 2001 constitutional reforms. Collective actions were permitted, however, in only a limited set of subject matter areas: consumer protection, environmental protection, financial services, and antitrust issues.[117] The focus was clearly on areas relating to commercial transactions and economic development. No mention was made of indigenous groups or other ascriptive minorities.

The use of collective actions for indigenous rights claims did not become a viable alternative until additional constitutional reforms were made in 2011. These reforms undertook substantial revisions to those articles of the constitution dealing with human rights and likewise envisioned a reform of the procedures governing amparo suits.[118] Like all previous constitutional reforms, those of 2011 required extensive secondary legislation in order for the reforms' ends to be fully realized. This was particularly true with regard to the amparo suit, as the extremely rigid institutional environment prevented the SCJN from taking the initiative in expanding access to the court.

One important potential area of change was the creation of collective amparo suits. Before the reforms, the Mexican constitution referred to "individuals" as rights holders. The revised constitutional provisions referred to the "person," opening up the possibility that legal persons and not just natural persons would be able to use the courts to affirm their rights. This, in turn, suggested the possibility of collective legal persons, such as indigenous groups, gaining access to the courts. The concept of collective legal persons is one that the courts had failed to develop in the period leading up to the reform (Carbonell, 2014, p. 276). The legislative reforms were themselves slow in coming, however, and this delay highlights the intensely politicized nature of procedural rules in the Mexican legal system. The reforms were completed only after what has been described as a "tortuous" process of repeated exchanges of the legislation between the Chamber of Deputies and Senate (Carbonell, 2014, p. 270). Congress finally passed procedural reform allowing for collective amparo suits in 2013, nearly 2 years after the relevant constitutional reform and more than a decade after constitutional reforms first expanded indigenous rights.

The result again underscores the judiciary's reliance on political branches for meaningful reform to the procedural environment. The 2013 changes were accompanied by a noticeable uptake in the number of court cases and *tesis* determined by the SCJN. In the entire period 2002 through 2012, the SCJN issued only 26 *tesis* dealing with indigenous rights, an average of only 2.4 per year. In 2013, the first year of the new legislation, the SCJN issued 13 such *tesis*—a fivefold increase.

Although the full impact of procedural reform has yet to be realized, members of the judiciary made clear that they see this as a potential opening for increased indigenous rights litigation. In a presentation on April 15, 2013, SCJN President Juan Silva Meza recognized that the *pro homine*[119] principle adopted in the 2011 constitutional reforms would require the SCJN to enforce group rights: "In the case of indigenous peoples [the *pro homine* principle] has a clear collective dimension."[120] Likewise when speaking of the reformed amparo law, Silva Meza said that the "amparo suit also becomes an appropriate instrument for the procedural defense of collective rights recognized by the national and international legal framework relating to indigenous peoples."[121]

In coming years, the substantive reforms—combined with new, legislatively created procedural tools—offer the possibility of a much more robust SCJN-focused rights-enforcement strategy. It seems clear that the court is willing to use these new tools to protect indigenous rights, but it is also clear that the court's protection of these rights follows the lead of the political branches, due to the latter's ability and willingness to control the necessary procedures that govern rights adjudication. Although the SCJN is able to protect substantive rights today, its ability to do so in the future will depend equally on its ability to overcome its reliance on procedural tools dictated by political branches.

Indigenous claims are international claims in the most basic sense: they call into question the nation-state's claim to exclusive jurisdiction over its territory and people. Even as the Mexican government has increasingly constitutionalized indigenous rights, however, the ability of indigenous groups to exercise these rights has been limited by the procedural restrictiveness of the Mexican judicial system. As Ansolabehere notes, the Mexican constitutional framework "recognizes group rights outside the judicial sphere, but those rights are not easily exercised as individual rights by members of the ethnic group in question" (2010, p. 101). This is an accurate description of indigenous rights adjudication, but access at any one point in time does not fully capture the dynamic between political actors, the court, and litigants. Rather, the *inflexibility* of the institutional environment prevents the SCJN itself from adapting to changing societal needs as concepts of substantive rights evolve. In other court systems (for example in Colombia), a flexible institutional environment has allowed the high court to fashion procedural tools that allow for greater court enforcement of indigenous rights. This has not been possible in Mexico, where even basic procedural reforms are under the control of the legislator. As demonstrated by the case of indigenous rights in Mexico, even the clearest substantive right cannot be enforced in a high court that lacks the flexibility to match procedural tools to substantive claims.

Linking Theory to the Subcases

A low to moderate degree of embedded internationalism, a limited public support orientation, and an inflexible procedural environment characterize the SCJN. My theory postulates that such a high court may be amenable to claims based on international human rights law, but that the legal legitimacy of its rulings will not be significantly determined by international human rights law. Moreover, the opportunities to hear and rule on these claims will be constrained by political actors' easy monitoring of the judiciary. As a result, the court may serve as a check on the government at the margins of policy, but an elite orientation and general procedural inflexibility should result in only weak potential for a court-initiated expansion of its role over time. On the one hand, the court will be unable to avoid cases that call into question its legitimacy or threaten its institutional strength; on the other, procedural inflexibility will prevent it from expanding rights adjudication into areas that would empower actors that could support the court in politically difficult cases. An examination of the SCJN's activity and institutional outputs indicates general conformity with these theoretical expectations.

In the area of impunity, the inflexible procedural environment interacted with the lack of a public support orientation to limit the SCJN's role. Although during the 1990s and early 2000s the court managed to develop precedents by which it avoided launching investigatory commissions, the court's unique role in the political system prevented it from completely avoiding demands for action. Citizens could not turn to other courts in hopes of receiving structural rulings that might protect their rights; after all, the strict legislative control over amparo proceedings meant those suits would have only inter partes effect. By the mid-2000s, the SCJN found itself in the position of receiving submissions and then producing unsatisfactory results. Rather than enhancing the court's powers, these incidents resulted in decreased legitimacy for the

SCJN. This became evident when the SCJN lobbied the legislature to reform the process so that the court would not be responsible for further investigations into such politically salient issues. Ultimately, the SCJN's inability to control its own procedural environment meant that it had little choice but to support a reduction in its own institutional strength through the transfer of its investigatory powers to a separate institution, the CNDH.

These same factors likewise reveal limitations in the SCJN's ability to hold government actors accountable. In cases brought against Dirty War–era violations, the court brought Mexico into compliance with international human rights standards governing statutes of limitation, but these rulings in individual cases did not result in broad-based prosecutions. Unlike more flexible courts, the SCJN was unable to establish ongoing commissions that could empower litigants other than government prosecutors. A similar logic explains the constraints faced by the SCJN in its ruling limiting the use of military tribunals. Although the IACHR ruled against Mexico as early as 2009, the SCJN did not take meaningful action until the government itself initiated reforms in 2011 that broadened the scope of international human rights protection. In this instance, the SCJN ruled that the judiciary was responsible for implementing IACHR rulings, and the SCJN accordingly limited the use of military tribunals. Its ability to do so was only possible given a procedural lacuna—the lack of a legal framework governing the federal judiciary's interaction with IACHR rulings. The force of the SCJN's ruling was again limited, however, by preexisting procedural conditions set out by political branches.

Congruence with theoretical expectations is also apparent in the area of indigenous rights. Although Mexico undertook reforms to increase internationally recognized indigenous rights in the constitution, the SCJN failed to act as a meaningful enforcer of these rights, either at the time of reform or subsequent to their adoption. At the time of reform, the court rejected challenges based on the strict delineation of constitutional controversies in the Mexican judicial system. The constitutional controversy, originally created by the PRI as a targeted means of ensuring the court would act as an arbiter of disputes between federal entities, was found by the court to be of limited use in the later claims brought by indigenous groups.

The indigenous rights subcase likewise affirms the theoretical prediction that a court operating in a restrictive procedural environment will have limited opportunities to expand its role over time. In the years following President Fox's 2001 package of constitutional reforms, no great increase was apparent in the court's indigenous rights docket. This is despite the reforms' incorporation of a broad array of indigenous peoples' rights. Instead, any increase in indigenous rights litigation did not come until after the political branches undertook further reforms in 2011 and 2013, finally matching procedural forms to substantive rights. The SCJN itself was not a major player in this transformation, as it continued to be constrained by a procedural environment dominated by the political branches.

In both subcases, the institutional constraints faced by the SCJN greatly limited its immediate effectiveness and the growth of its institutional strength over time. The SCJN was able to rule in favor of international human rights in individual cases, such as those dealing with Dirty War rights violations, but the effects have been limited. Nor has the court been effective in expanding its role over time. Only when political actors reformed the constitution or expanded the panoply of procedural tools did rights litigation increase. The court itself was generally incapable of initiating these processes, as predicted by the theory.

Conclusion

The Mexican case demonstrates that a court's likelihood of serving as an enforcement mechanism for international law depends on more than the ratification of treaties and political support for judicial independence broadly writ. Although the 1994 reforms to the SCJN increased that court's independence and its role as constitutional arbiter, this did not lead to any profound change in its treatment of international law. Although the court took tentative steps in this direction, its role was limited by the factors considered here.

Like independent courts in the other cases examined in this project, the SCJN has the ability to rely on international human rights law in its decisions. It has been less likely to do so, however, given the superficial embeddedness of international human rights law. The constitution throughout the period of study suggested the possibility of treaties serving as a source of binding law, but it did not require such treatment. Nor did the majority of justices themselves have high exposure to international influences. Overall, this neither predisposed the court to being a leader in human rights enforcement nor provided an overtly hostile venue for rights enforcement efforts. Instead, the court was unlikely to venture beyond the confines of the domestic constitution, except in those instances when international obligations clearly required more—as in the area of impunity—or when the political branches themselves indicated a willingness to go further—as in the area of indigenous groups' procedural rights.

International embeddedness alone does not account for the court's output. Rather, it helps explain the court's decision-making in those situations in which opportunities for rights enforcement were available. The availability of those opportunities is explained by the two remaining variables: a limited public support orientation and the SCJN's lack of procedural flexibility. The limited public support orientation of the court system rendered the SCJN the subject of ongoing monitoring by political actors. The 1994 reforms themselves were a targeted project meant to secure the PRI's continued access to the political process. Later reforms in 1996 (granting the court jurisdiction over electoral laws) and in 2001 (expanding indigenous rights) were likewise politically targeted efforts. Over time, this has resulted in increased visibility for the court and expectations that it act more forcefully in the policy arena, but without the tools to do so. The court continues to operate while considering only one dimension: the concern of political actors. It has been hampered in its ability to orient itself toward international law or the public.

Moreover, the reforms have done little to transform the extremely rigid procedural environment in which the SCJN operates. As a result, the heightened focus on the court has not resulted in enhanced rights enforcement over time. Instead, it has resulted in the court's conducting human rights investigations, ruling on prosecutions, and considering indigenous rights claims in an environment where substantive rights outrun procedural mechanisms. Interestingly, the historical unwillingness to investigate rights violations has elsewhere been attributed to procedural vagueness. According to one commentator, the court has had to overcome "one of the greatest historical limits to its labor, the lack of regulation" (Suárez Ávila, 2012, p. 247). On the contrary, the evidence presented here suggests that the few times the SCJN was able to act effectively was when it managed to overcome its extremely dense, rigid procedural environment, finding procedural lacunae and transforming these into rights-affirming opportunities.

These opportunities, however, have been limited. The SCJN did not begin to assert its role as an international human rights enforcer until after political actors undertook additional reforms in 2011 and 2013, more deeply embedding international law and expanding the procedural mechanisms available to enforce it. These reforms both elevated the importance of international human rights in the Mexican constitutional framework and increased the likelihood that the amparo suit would be an effective means of protecting individual and collective human rights. The innovation of these procedural tools, however, was again a legislative project. This calls into question the ability of the SCJN to continue to serve as a rights lock-in mechanism were the political winds to shift yet again. As long as political actors tightly regulate the procedural environment, it will be they, rather than the court, who are able to control the flow of litigation. Only if the newly empowered SCJN uses the current period of widened access to increase the number of stakeholders in the judicial process—to orient itself toward the public—will the Mexican high court solidify its role as a long-term enforcer of international human rights law.

CHAPTER 6

Conclusions

When do domestic courts in transitional regimes entrench international human rights law? This question has been of ongoing concern to both international-relations researchers and scholars of comparative politics. In this project, I have drawn on the literature of both groups to develop a new theory of domestic court behavior. The theory treats courts as strategic actors, but strategic actors whose decision-making is necessarily bound up with questions of legal and institutional legitimacy.

In doing so I find that courts are active participants in their institutional development and that, therefore, the following assertions hold true: (1) The willingness of courts to supply rights adjudication is not uniformly reflective of the potential demand for litigation. (2) Courts that enjoy a flexible institutional environment do not treat procedural rules as fixed; instead, court access, adjudication, and remedies are epiphenomena of the courts' strategic legitimacy concerns. (3) This flexibility allows courts to avoid potentially institution-damaging backlash, increasing the likelihood that they will successfully maintain or expand their enforcement role over time. (4) The ability of a court to engage in this selective rights enforcement behavior is enhanced by a support orientation that provides greater opportunities for a high court to balance public concerns against political considerations. (5) These processes also depend on whether there is a link between a court's legitimacy and international law concerns; where there is a strong link, the likelihood of judicial enforcement of international human rights law increases, even absent treaty ratification.

Each of these five claims finds support in the individual case studies, but the logic of each claim becomes much clearer by examining the case studies alongside one another. In particular, I revisit next each of the three main independent variables explored throughout this project: the domestic high court's international embeddedness, the degree to which the court is oriented toward the public, and the level of procedural flexibility enjoyed by the court. For each variable, I draw on evidence simultaneously from across the cases and subcases; doing so reveals important variation and lends further support to the five claims just put forth. Of course, although I analyze each of the three variables in turn, there is no simple one-to-one correspondence between each variable and each of the five claims. Rather, the independent variables interact in meaningful, dynamic ways: a court that is sensitive to international human rights considerations may be unable to adequately incorporate the substance of those laws because of a lack of flexibility; an elite orientation may constrain an otherwise procedurally flexible court's ability to alter the locus of review. By revisiting the case studies in tandem, I am able to demonstrate how each variable operates across cases, how variables interact with one another, and how this ultimately leads to the five main claims I have outlined.

Embedded Internationalism

Courts that are sensitive to international law because of their institutional standing and professional considerations are the most likely to enforce international human rights obligations. This rather uncontroversial statement leads to a more provocative finding of this project: the linkage between embedded internationalism and rights enforcement occurs even in the absence of treaty ratification. Though the ratification of individual treaties is not dispositive of individual enforcement efforts, however, constitutionalization of those same rights does improve the likelihood that a court will rule against the government. Indeed, when a court finds a commitment to international human rights law in the constitution, the court is likely to consider protection of international human rights law to be intricately bound up with the court's own role in the political system. Constitutionalization, however, does not end with the integration of a legal norm by political actors; it is enhanced by the international credentials of the judicial actors themselves. In that sense, embeddedness is not just about the constitutional document but also about the attitudes of those hearing the case, as these actors may be primed by their professional development to see international law as legitimacy enhancing. In such situations, the court may find ways to incorporate international human rights law to which the state, through its elected political institutions, has not yet formally committed itself. When constitutionalization is paired with a commitment to international law, moreover, the likelihood that the court will rule against the government is further enhanced. Embedded internationalism allows the court to build its legitimacy by drawing on international legal principles to fill domestic legal gaps, as the domestic political settlement is itself seen as informed by international human rights.

Although scholars have called attention to courts' potential to serve as enforcement mechanisms for human rights commitments in democracies, the case studies indicate the contingent nature of any such outcome. Courts may indeed serve as venues for rights articulation and contestation over policy agendas. Yet they only assume this role in limited circumstances that have little to do with the binding nature of the treaty itself. When a state is bound by treaty law to comply, the court often has the ability to restrict its docket in ways that maintain a ruling's legal legitimacy while avoiding political backlash against the court. This was seen in the Colombian Constitutional Court's handling of the *falsos positivos* cases. Alternatively, as seen in the South African case, a high court may make selective use of legal fictions, such as the distinction between self-executing and non-self-executing treaties, to give differential domestic effect to treaties that are, from the standpoint of international law, equally binding on the state.

Likewise, even when treaty ratification is followed by legislative incorporation, this does not always serve as an effective means of binding future governments. Where international law is incorporated directly by legislation, courts have been willing to permit subsequent governmental changes to that legislation. In doing so, they give effect to the traditional principle that though international law may bind a state internationally, a state may derogate domestically without judicial recourse. In short, domestic courts often treat international law as a juridical Schrödinger's cat: international law simultaneously binds and does *not* bind. This can be seen clearly in the Mexican case, in which the Supreme Court of Justice of the Nation regularly interpreted treaties as a source of domestic law, but as a source without the necessary status to override federal statutes.

Treaty ratification is, therefore, seldom a *sufficient* condition for domestic court enforcement—but neither is it a *necessary* condition. As shown by the behavior of high courts in all three states, when a court is considering a generally recognized human right, it often resorts to international legal standards that would not be considered binding on the state under international law principles of treaty ratification or accession. In Colombia, the CCC is exceedingly receptive to international law principles, incorporating

UN declarations and guiding principles into its jurisprudence. The South African Constitutional Court has done so to a lesser extent, at times citing treaties such as the ICESCR in its interpretations, despite South Africa's not having completed ratification at the time of a ruling. Only the Mexican court, with its historically superficial level of internationalism, has been relatively immune to this process.

In contrast to treaty ratification, constitutionalization increases the ability of a domestic court to resist legislative or executive backsliding on human rights. When an international law principle has been incorporated into the constitution (even without direct ratification of the treaty from which that principle derives), courts tend to take this as a serious commitment to the domestic political community. As a result, any policy deviation may be seen not just as reneging on an international commitment but also as reneging on the domestic political settlement. For a court such as the SACC, the constitution serves as an important indicator of what is acceptable and demanded of domestic institutions in the reform era. To the Mexican SCJN, the changes of 2011 confirm the society's desire to move beyond the previous era of ambivalence (or even hostility) toward foreign legal influences. The SCJN's implementation of the *pro homine* principle occurred not because of new treaty ratifications or domestic incorporation but because the high court began to see these rights as constitutive of a broader rights-affirming normative environment that the court was charged with protecting.

Constitutionalization matters for rhetorical purposes as well. When rights advocates seek to use courts to challenge government action, exclusive reliance on international law can be problematic.[1] When the Treatment Action Campaign in South Africa demanded compliance with human rights law and broader access to antiretroviral drugs for people with HIV or AIDS, for example, government officials, including the president, were quick to claim that the group was supported by foreigners opposed to African National Congress rule.[2] The court ultimately rejected this framing, in part because TAC was able to make reference to the Final Constitution's inclusion of health rights. Indeed, the appeal to nationalism was undermined by the ANC's own role in expanding the range of international human rights principles entrenched in the Final Constitution (Heywood, 2005).

This leads to a final point: though constitutional protections can bind in ways that treaty law alone cannot, constitutional protections are at their strongest when buttressed by international law. Except for those institutions situated in the rapidly diminishing number of states where parliamentary supremacy is still recognized, courts look first to the constitution when judging the validity of new legislation or executive action. The old adage—quoted often by South African judges in reference to the Apartheid era—that they merely "apply the law as it is," is simply no longer tenable as a rule-of-law precept. The constitution, understood as a Kelsenian compact above normal laws, binds meaningfully in a way that international law alone seldom does. When a court interprets a constitution to embody elements of international human rights, however, the constitution no longer stands alone as a backstop against legislative and executive action. Instead, courts in states with constitutions heavily imbued by international human rights law increasingly treat international law itself as part of the constitutional matrix.

This is the case even where the government has the electoral wherewithal to overcome procedural obstacles to constitutional change. In such situations, courts increasingly treat international law as a further measure against which to judge proposed constitutional amendments. Use of this international measuring stick is more likely where the members of the court themselves have been trained in international law or see enforcement of international human rights norms as intrinsic to their professional identity. This is most readily apparent in the Colombian case, where the desire to imbue all aspects of governmental activity with international human rights considerations is part of the state's transformation from an *estado de derecho* to an *estado social de derecho*. Thus, the *bloque de constitucionalidad* may even require constitutional amendments to conform to international law obligations.

To be sure, ratification matters. Contrary to many scholarly accounts, however, it matters not because it serves as an independent legal source that individual litigants can use to counter majoritarian desires, but because treaty ratification operates as an indicator of the societal bargain the high court must enforce to ensure its ongoing institutional legitimacy in the domestic political arena. Overall the case studies support the claim that *embedded internationalism is more predictive of judicial enforcement of international human rights law than is state ratification (claim 5).*

Public Support Orientation

Support orientation describes the audiences on which a court relies for institutional support. It takes into consideration both the degree to which various courts throughout the judicial system are empowered to review government action (or inaction) and whether, as a practical matter, this power is available to the broad public or confined to a small number of elite actors. The importance of diffuse adjudicatory power and accessibility to that power is well-documented, both in the international and domestic court literatures, and the findings here build on and extend these analyses. The importance of a public orientation is reflected in the varied degree of societal-court engagement seen across the states in this study.

The diffuse adjudicatory environment in Colombia has afforded individuals relatively quick and inexpensive adjudication of their rights without stringent procedural burdens. As a result, citizens from all socioeconomic groups and all regions of the state have been able to challenge government policies, and courts throughout the state have been able to rule on government action or inaction. Consequently, the CCC is not the only court that politicians must monitor, and litigants enjoy multiple points of entry to the court system. The CCC benefits further by being able to take the most contentious issues off of its agenda while focusing resources on cases with broad public relevance. Once the CCC accepted oversight of the internally displaced persons issue, it employed a broad range of remedial procedures to effectuate its ruling, engaging various sectors of society and benefiting from the increased rights consciousness of Colombian society. The court is able to leverage public concern to offer meaningful rights-protecting rulings in cases that might otherwise invite political backlash.

The importance of a public support orientation is highlighted by its absence in South Africa. Although both the CCC and the SACC enjoy a high degree of latitude over their access procedures, only the CCC has been able to both open and close its doors to the public; the SACC has been constrained to swing the door in exactly one direction: shut. The CCC was well attuned to public concerns and, therefore, able to craft its agenda in a way that answered broad-based demands for rights enforcement. In contrast, the vast majority of South Africans lack the necessary resources to wage sustained litigation through multiple layers of appeals. More importantly, the broad public has been supportive of the ANC at the ballot box, making it less likely that the SACC could balance public support against elite monitoring. As a result, an elite-oriented court with little public engagement found that docket control was a blunt filtering mechanism. In such a constrained setting, the SACC has embarked on a prudent course: it has limited the number of cases it hears across all issue areas, minimizing the likelihood of conflict.

This also helps explain the two courts' differing approaches to remedies. The CCC has enjoyed a ready supply of litigants in a rights-imbued culture, providing it with a broad base of support. Consequently, it could expand its efforts to include monitoring and follow-up. The SACC, meanwhile, stands in elite disconnect from the larger South African population. Instead, the population identifies with the dominant political party, and the legal system does not play an important role in the lives of everyday citizens. In such an environment, the SACC has avoided follow-up litigation and structural rulings, instead building institutional legitimacy through rights-affirming decisions that entail little subsequent monitoring by the court.

Compare this with the situation of Mexico's SCJN. A cursory appraisal would suggest a court similarly situated to the CCC. The broad availability of the amparo suit should provide the SCJN with a steady supply of information on the demand for human rights enforcement throughout the country, similar to that seen in the Colombian cases. On closer inspection, however, this similarity gives way to an important distinction: Mexican litigants' opportunities to use the amparo have been curtailed by an inflexible procedural environment primarily determined not by the high court but by elected officials. As a result, citizens have had limited opportunities to bring claims challenging the general applicability of laws for noncompliance with human rights obligations. Similar restrictions have limited group standing to bring claims. Taken together, a court initially designed to support political actors has been unable to effect a reorientation toward the public. This has left the Mexican SCJN with little ability to cultivate a support constituency among the broader human rights–seeking public. Meanwhile, successive court reforms have heightened the political nature of the high court, preventing it from successfully avoiding legitimacy-damaging cases and (until recently) investigatory commissions. For these reasons, the SCJN has enjoyed few opportunities to balance public concerns against the potential of political backlash, placing the high court in the most precarious position: its central role in the court system increases societal expectations, but it lacks the resources to follow through on these demands.

This analysis provides support for two claims. First, the differing outcomes across cases support the claim that *a public support orientation will provide greater opportunities for the high court to avoid political backlash by balancing public concerns against political considerations (claim 4).* The Colombian court was able to draw on broad public access to selectively engage issues and draw more litigants into the courtroom to support court-based enforcement.

The lack of such broad access prevented the South African court from drawing on the public in a similar manner. The Mexican court enjoyed only moderate access that was constrained by political actors' formulation of important procedural rules, meaning that it was unable to forge ongoing linkages to the public that would enable it to balance against political considerations.

The case studies also strongly support the claim that *the supply of rights adjudication is not directly reflective of the potential demand for litigation (claim 1)*. The CCC selectively restricted the supply of adjudication, whereas the SACC constrained the supply across the broad scope of issue areas. The Mexican SCJN likewise failed to offer consistent judicial recourse across issue areas where a demand for court enforcement was evident. These outcomes are explained more fully by incorporating the final variable in the theory: procedural flexibility.

Procedural Flexibility

The case studies provide ample support for the claim that *when a court enjoys a flexible procedural environment, procedural rules will be epiphenomena of the court's strategic legitimacy concerns (claim 2)*. This can be most clearly seen in the Colombian case. The CCC faced the possibility of strong political backlash in the extrajudicial execution cases, and as a result it constricted court access in a way not seen in the cases of internally displaced persons. Rather than accepting appeals in line with the court's role as rights protector, it allowed these cases to be removed from its docket by limiting the number of tutela appeals, affirming changes in victims' rights to court access, and ultimately endorsing retrenchment that shifted military trials to separate institutions. Alternatively, the CCC greatly expanded access to the court when it engaged the IDP issue. It required follow-up reports under continuing orders, and when it lacked expertise it deputized NGOs to collect information and act as government watchdogs. This innovation even extended to metaprocedures such as those governing ratification and incorporation of international human rights law. The CCC was quite willing to embark on novel interpretations that gave binding weight to everything from regional court rulings to UN declarations. International law's deep embeddedness in the Colombian constitutional framework encouraged the CCC to overcome the textual lack of specificity on individual rights, and the court used its flexibility to find novel ways of drawing on international legal principles.

In South Africa, the SACC likewise used its procedural flexibility to further its legitimacy concerns. Although the Final Constitution offered a broad grant of direct litigant access to the high court, the SACC severely restricted this access in order to avoid taking an oversight role in otherwise contentious cases. It also used this flexibility to craft limited remedies that reinforced the court's legitimacy as an enforcer of international human rights law without unnecessarily antagonizing government actors. At the same time, it engaged in a more limited form of the metaprocedural manipulation seen in the Colombian case. The SACC was willing to embark on considerations of international treaty law, such as the ICESCR, that had not been incorporated into domestic law at the time of decisions. When broad interpretations of treaty law would have been detrimental to the court's institutional concerns, however, it flexibly interpreted concepts such as "self-executing" in ways that avoided political confrontations.

Both of these courts likewise demonstrate the ways in which procedural flexibility interacts with the other variables considered in this project. The public support orientation of the CCC provided that court with a selection of issues to draw cases from and a wide range of potential follow-up actors. This allowed the CCC to draw on a flexible procedural environment to engage and further cultivate those resources. The lack of this public support orientation in South Africa meant that the SACC's flexibility was predetermined to operate in one direction only: further constriction of adjudicatory supply. Both the Colombian and South African situations lend further support to the claim that *the supply of rights adjudication is not directly reflective of the potential demand for litigation (claim 1)*. Instead, supply is reflective of court institutional concerns. Indeed, the Colombian case suggests the possibility that the willingness of the high court to supply adjudication has the potential to stimulate further demand in an iterative process.

The most constrained court in terms of flexibility was Mexico's SCJN. The importance of procedural flexibility is perhaps best revealed by comparing the outcome there with the outcome in Colombia. Both states are participants in the inter-American system of rights protection, and they share similar treaty obligations and regional institutional frameworks. Citizens of both states have also had recourse to seemingly analogous court-access provisions, in the form of the Mexican amparo suit and the Colombian tutela. (Indeed, the tutela is itself a derivative of the amparo.) Both the Colombian and Mexican judiciaries underwent reform at a period of democratic transition marked by insurgency and political violence.[3] What differed, however, was the form that constitutional and judicial rehabilitation would take. In Colombia, the establishment of a new constitutional court resulted in a new judicial actor not bound by decades of the extreme procedural rigidity common to civil law systems. The tutela was itself a new procedural tool, and the CCC's procedures were left to the court to develop in its case law. In contrast, the Mexican SCJN was not a new court and thus inherited a procedural environment characterized by extreme rigidity in the form of a politically determined amparo law and procedural restrictions embedded in the constitution itself.

As a result, the SCJN found itself without adequate tools with which to alter procedures in line with its strategic legitimacy concerns. This is seen perhaps most clearly in the SCJN's inability to overcome restrictions in its use of the investigatory function. In that subcase, the rigid procedural environment meant the court was unable to further a rights agenda and even struggled to determine how to report its findings, let alone act on them. To be sure, even in the Mexican case, the SCJN was able to take advantage of a few instances of flexibility to enhance its legitimacy. In its consideration of the Inter-American Court of Human Rights rulings, for example, the lack of any clear procedural structure linking the domestic judiciary to the regional system provided an opening for the SCJN to engage in procedural innovation.

The Mexican case also provides support for the claim that *a flexible procedural environment increases the likelihood that a court will successfully maintain or expand its enforcement role over time (claim 3)*. When the SCJN was presented with an opening, it was able to seize that opportunity in a way that potentially expanded its enforcement role over time. The SCJN also demonstrates the converse, however: lack of flexibility inhibits this process. The court was unwilling to engage international legal principles unless and until elected officials not only articulated human rights norms but also provided the court with the necessary procedural tools to effectuate them.

This contrasts with the much more successful expansion of the high court's role in both Colombia and South Africa. In Colombia, this took the form of creating new institutional and procedural tools through which to engage litigants, NGOs, and international organizations. The CCC also systematically expanded the degree to which it could call on international law principles to legitimate its power. In doing so, it cultivated an internationally informed, legalized rights culture that has allowed it to address increasingly contentious issues over time. Although less dramatic in its approach, the SACC has also used its flexible procedural environment to lay the groundwork for increased rights adjudication. It has used remedies that limited the immediate impact on the South African government but has ruled in ways that further entrench international human rights in the domestic legal system. It has also reiterated that the common law—an area of law completely within the court's cognizance—must be developed in line with international human rights law principles. The SACC has undoubtedly taken a gradualist approach, but it is an approach that has gradually moved South Africa in the direction of compliance with human rights obligations.

The cases here demonstrate the importance of a flexible procedural environment. When a court enjoys a flexible environment, it is able to deal with difficult issues in a nuanced fashion. This will undoubtedly lead, at times, to less-than-satisfying outcomes for human rights activists or victims of abuses. The longer-term trend, however, should be positive as the high court is able to pick and choose its battles. These courts may even become conduits for implementation of human rights principles that political actors have been unable or unwilling to enact, as seen in the Colombian case and to a lesser extent in South Africa. A flexible procedural environment allows a high court to engage in the art of the possible.

In contrast, procedural rigidity results in a court bound to follow the law as the executive and legislature define it. Such a court lacks the ability to follow developing trends in international jurisprudence on its own initiative. Instead, it must await political actors' decision to implement these reforms domestically. More importantly, this rigidity indicates the court will be unlikely to continue to act as a rights enforcement venue once political winds change. Procedurally inflexible courts may at first appear to act as *lock-in* mechanisms, but they do so only in *lockstep* with political leaders, and without the ability to promote or preserve international human rights when those political leaders are not already leaning toward compliance.

Implications

This examination of domestic courts expands our understanding of their role as enforcers of international human rights law in several ways. First, I leverage case studies to better explain variation in human rights enforcement. I look at two distinct legal issues in each of three states, revealing variation both across and within states. Previous international law and international relations scholarship has focused on issues of compliance across multiple states but has done so in specific issue areas and often without considering the motivations of domestic court actors. The comparative judicial politics literature, in contrast, has dealt extensively with domestic court systems, but often at the expense of comparing across regional legal systems. This study examines variation across states while simultaneously considering variation that occurs within individual court systems. In doing so, it develops a richer theoretical framework that better explains judicial enforcement patterns both across states and within states across issue areas.

Second, this project increases our understanding of international human rights enforcement by treating judicial actors as entrepreneurs. Extant theories have focused on variations in treaty ratification patterns, the strategies of domestic or international activists, or the form, content, and articulation of individual human rights norms. In these theories, courts sometimes play key roles as enforcement sites, but they are generally passive institutions that receive and adjudicate others' claims. Such theories treat the courts themselves as merely instrumental. In contrast to these extant theories, I show that courts are active participants in the process of rights enforcement. While politicians, activists, and citizens undoubtedly do attempt to use courts instrumentally, courts themselves are more than passive recipients of litigant claims. Courts' treatment of individual cases transforms legal and policy outcomes in those same individual cases but also over the long term. Judges act in ways that create opportunities for themselves and for human rights enforcement by crafting procedures and forging new autonomies.

Lastly, the theory presented here moves beyond the debate over whether law is either purely nonpolitical or simply another field for politics. To be sure, courts act strategically, but they also take into consideration the potential costs to their legitimacy of overtly politicized legal interpretations. A court's failure to treat the law as a unique deliberative field would undermine the court's own claim to legitimacy in the democratic system. As a result, a court's strategic behavior is informed by legal normativity, and political considerations from one point in time create path dependencies that shape the role of courts as venues of rights enforcement in later periods. My theory takes into account this hybrid nature of the law. In doing so, it is better able to address variation in state compliance with human rights obligations by examining how courts are both bound by the law but also able to shape it strategically at key moments of doctrinal development.

This project also speaks to normative questions about the role of courts in democratic societies. High courts are often seen as countermajoritarian institutions. International law has likewise been criticized as intrinsically antidemocratic. And yet throughout the late twentieth century, the rapid expansion of international law coincided with an ongoing spread of court power. If critics are correct, then these two trends, taken together, represent a profound undermining of democratic principles. This project argues for the opposite conclusion. As others have demonstrated, purportedly antidemocratic international institutions can actually enhance domestic processes of democratic deliberation (Keohane et al., 2009). Likewise, domestic courts can act as necessary counterweights to majoritarian excesses. As such, domestic courts play a critical pro-democracy role by embedding international human rights.

In short, the rise of independent domestic judiciaries and an ever-expanding web of international human rights obligations do not together signal the death of domestic democratic autonomy. At the same time, courts do not offer a straight path to democratic consolidation in newly democratic states, nor an easy way to protect liberalism's gains in times of democratic backsliding—they are, after all, just one institution in a constellation of institutions. Domestic courts can offer a venue for enforcement of international human rights obligations, but only if they are able to engage these issues in ways that take into consideration political realities and conform the demands of international law to domestic contingencies. The rights-protective role of courts in the domestic policy sphere is potentially robust, but it is unlikely to endure where court rulings deviate greatly from the demands of both political elites and the broad public.

How effective courts are in threading this needle depends on several variables. Does their legitimacy rely to some extent on a faithful reading of international human rights law? Does the level of public participation in the court system provide opportunities to learn about and engage the public's demand for rights enforcement? And, most importantly, does the court enjoy a level of procedural flexibility that allows it to selectively engage politically difficult questions of law and policy? Courts with favorable institutional settings can serve as domestic compliance mechanisms for international human rights obligations at specific moments, entrenching international law over the long term. In doing so, the most successful courts will balance public concerns, political considerations, and the institutional needs of the court itself, leading to improved human rights outcomes. Where courts fail to balance these considerations, however, they risk their institutional independence, their legitimacy, and ultimately their ability to protect international human rights.

APPENDIX 1

Transitional States

Transitional states are states that registered at least 6 on the Polity IV scale (a measure of democracy) for at least 1 year during the period 1975–2000 but which did not consistently rank at a polity score of 8 or higher for the entire period.

Argentina
Armenia
Bangladesh
Belarus
Benin
Bolivia
Botswana
Brazil
Bulgaria
Cape Verde
Chile
Colombia
Croatia
Czech Republic
Dominican Republic
Ecuador
El Salvador
Estonia
Fiji
Gambia
Ghana
Guatemala
Guyana
Haiti
Honduras
Hungary
India
Indonesia
Korea, South
Latvia
Lesotho
Lithuania
Macedonia
Madagascar
Malawi
Mali
Mexico
Moldova
Mongolia
Montenegro
Namibia
Nepal
Nicaragua
Niger

Nigeria
Pakistan
Panama
Paraguay
Peru
Philippines
Poland
Portugal
Romania
Russia
Senegal
Serbia
Slovak Republic
Slovenia
Solomon Islands
South Africa
Spain
Sri Lanka
Sudan
Taiwan
Thailand
Turkey
Ukraine
Uruguay
Venezuela
Zambia

APPENDIX 2

Major International Human Rights Treaty Ratifications

Colombia

Convention against Torture and Other Cruel Inhuman or Degrading Treatment or Punishment: signed April 10, 1985; ratified December 8, 1987; accepted inquiry procedure.

International Covenant on Civil and Political Rights: signed December 21, 1966; ratified October 29, 1969; accepted individual complaint procedure.

Second Optional Protocol to the International Covenant on Civil and Political Rights aiming to the abolition of the death penalty: acceded August 5, 1997.

Convention for the Protection of All Persons from Enforced Disappearance: signed September 27, 2007; ratified July 11, 2012; accepted inquiry procedure.

Convention on the Elimination of All Forms of Discrimination against Women: signed July 17, 1980; ratified January 19, 1982; accepted individual complaint procedure January 23, 2007.

International Convention on the Elimination of All Forms of Racial Discrimination: signed March 23, 1967; ratified September 2, 1981.

International Covenant on Economic, Social and Cultural Rights: signed December 21, 1966; ratified October 29, 1969.

International Convention on the Protection of the Rights of All Migrant Workers and Members of Their Families: acceded May 24, 1995.

Convention on the Rights of the Child: signed January 26, 1990; ratified January 28, 1991.

Optional Protocol to the Convention on the Rights of the Child on the involvement of children in armed conflict: signed September 6, 2000; ratified May 25, 2005.

Optional Protocol to the Convention on the Rights of the Child on the Sale of Children, Child Prostitution and Child Pornography: signed September 6, 2000; ratified November 11, 2003.

Convention on the Rights of Persons with Disabilities: signed March 30, 2007; ratified May 10, 2011.

Mexico

Convention against Torture and Other Cruel Inhuman or Degrading Treatment or Punishment: signed March 18, 1985; ratified January 23, 1986; accepted individual complaint procedure March 15, 2002; accepted inquiry procedure.

Optional Protocol of the Convention against Torture: signed September 23, 2003; ratified April 11, 2005.

International Covenant on Civil and Political Rights: acceded March 23, 1981; accepted individual complaint procedure March 15, 2002.

Second Optional Protocol to the International Covenant on Civil and Political Rights aiming to the abolition of the death penalty: acceded September 26, 2007.

Convention for the Protection of All Persons from Enforced Disappearance: signed February 6, 2007; ratified March 18, 2008; accepted inquiry procedure.

Convention on the Elimination of All Forms of Discrimination against Women: signed July 17, 1980; ratified March 23, 1981; accepted individual complaint procedure March 15, 2002; accepted inquiry procedure March 15, 2002.

International Convention on the Elimination of All Forms of Racial Discrimination: signed November 1, 1966; ratified February 20, 1975; accepted individual complaint procedure March 15, 2002.

International Covenant on Economic, Social and Cultural Rights: acceded March 23, 1981.

International Convention on the Protection of the Rights of All Migrant Workers and Members of Their Families: signed May 22, 1991; ratified March 8, 1999; accepted individual complaint procedure.

Convention on the Rights of the Child: signed January 26, 1990; ratified September 21, 1990.

Optional Protocol to the Convention on the Rights of the Child on the involvement of children in armed conflict: signed September 7, 2000; ratified March 15, 2002.

Optional Protocol to the Convention on the Rights of the Child on the Sale of Children, Child Prostitution and Child Pornography: signed September 7, 2000; ratified March 15, 2002.

Convention on the Rights of Persons with Disabilities: signed March 30, 2007; ratified December 17, 2007; accepted individual complaint procedure; accepted inquiry procedure.

South Africa

Convention against Torture and Other Cruel Inhuman or Degrading Treatment or Punishment: signed January 29, 1993; ratified December 10, 1998; accepted individual complaint procedure; accepted inquiry procedure.

Optional Protocol of the Convention against Torture: signed September 20, 2006.

International Covenant on Civil and Political Rights: signed October 3, 1994; ratified December 10, 1998; accepted individual complaint procedure August 28, 2002.

Second Optional Protocol to the International Covenant on Civil and Political Rights aiming to the abolition of the death penalty: acceded August 22, 2002.

Convention on the Elimination of All Forms of Discrimination against Women: signed January 29, 1993; ratified December 15, 1995; accepted individual complaint procedure October 18, 2005; accepted inquiry procedure October 18, 2005.

International Convention on the Elimination of All Forms of Racial Discrimination: signed October 3, 1994; ratified December 10, 1998; accepted individual complaint procedure.

International Covenant on Economic, Social and Cultural Rights: signed October 3, 1994; ratified January 12, 2015.

Convention on the Rights of the Child: signed January 29, 1993; ratified June 16, 1995.

Optional Protocol to the Convention on the Rights of the Child on the involvement of children in armed conflict: signed February 8, 2002; ratified September 24, 2009.

Optional Protocol to the Convention on the Rights of the Child on the Sale of Children, Child Prostitution and Child Pornography: acceded June 30, 2003.

Convention on the Rights of Persons with Disabilities: signed March 30, 2007; ratified November 30, 2007; accepted individual complaint procedure; accepted inquiry procedure.

NOTES

Chapter 1

1. This project draws on the definitions of hard and soft law used by Abbott and Snidal (2000). In particular, the notion of soft law indicates those areas of law that "are weakened along one or more dimensions of obligation, precision, and delegation." (p. 422)

2. As such, these constructivist and sociological accounts can be seen as part of a long theoretical tradition in international relations that treat global norms and shared ideas as constituting both the world political system and the actors operating within that system (Boli-Bennett & Meyer, 1978; Wendt, 1992).

3. Legal scholars operating in this tradition have attempted to create a constructivist methodology that would allow for falsifiable hypotheses regarding domestic internalization of global legal norms (Goodman & Jinks, 2003, 2004). In general, however, these attempts have not explained when domestic courts are receptive to litigation attempts that draw on international legal rules.

4. Ginsburg does not explicitly address enforcement mechanisms within the domestic realm, focusing instead on the greater likelihood of new democracies to take the step of referencing international law in the state's foundational legal document. The role of domestic courts is not clearly delineated, though he does address judicial review of governmental policy elsewhere. See, e.g., Ginsburg (2003).

5. Transitional states for the period 1975–2000, inclusive, are defined as those with a polity score of at least 6 for 1 year but that did not have a score of 8 or higher consistently during this period. This allows for consistency with the literature and with the Polity IV definition of democracy (Marshall et al., 2009). A complete list of these states is included in Appendix 1.

Chapter 2

1. Abuse of discretion does not necessarily mean a court or an individual justice is acting with caprice, with malice, or in a corrupt manner. It might simply mean that the actor in question based a legal decision on factors that it was not lawfully empowered to consider (Fallon, 2005, p. 1819).

2. An example from the American context provides some clarity. When the U.S. Supreme Court decided *Bush v Gore*, 531 U.S. 98 (2000), the Gore supporters might have agreed that the ruling should be obeyed, even though they disagreed with the

decision. In that situation, the ruling might have reflected the court's *authoritative* legitimacy, but it might have nevertheless lacked *substantive* (or *content*) validity. Meanwhile, lawyers, a more particularized audience, may have argued over the Supreme Court's specific interpretation of the Equal Protection Clause and Title 3, Section 5 of the U.S. Code. This disagreement among lawyers reflects the ruling's contested *legal* legitimacy.

3. Judicial hierarchies can function as learning systems in terms of the creation, articulation, and dissemination of legal doctrine (Gewirtzman, 2011). Here, I suggest that the judicial hierarchy may also serve as a source of information beyond legal doctrine, providing information on the salience of various legal issues.

4. "Horizontal effect" refers broadly to court enforcement of public law protections to private actors—e.g., the application of anti–race-discrimination protections to private business owners.

5. Similarly, Cichowski (2004) explores the use of Article 234 (the current designation of the former Article 177) to expand European governance of women's rights.

6. *Marbury v. Madison*, 5 U.S. (1 Cr.) 137 (1803).

7. The period of review varied by country so as to coincide with the timing of its court reform. For Colombia, I reviewed materials from 1991 through 2010; for Mexico, from 1994 through 2013; and for South Africa, from 1993 through 2012.

8. Unless otherwise noted, all translations throughout the case studies are the author's own.

9. Gauri and Brinks (2008, p. 9), for example, find that claims against the government represent a minority of judicial attempts to enforce socioeconomic rights.

Chapter 3

1. As of 2011, the internally displaced population was estimated at anywhere between 3.9 million and 5.3 million, or between 8% and 11% of the Colombian population. Internal Displacement Monitoring Centre, *Global Overview 2011: People Internally Displaced by Conflict and Violence* (April 2012).

2. The Supreme Court preceded the CCC as the primary judicial body exercising oversight in the domestic political system. The 1991 constitution allocates judicial powers to a national system composed of the Supreme Court (Articles 234–235), the Council of State (Articles 236–238), the Constitutional Court (Articles 239–245), the Prosecutor General (Articles 249–253), the Superior Judicial Council (Articles 254–257), and various tribunals with special jurisdiction, such as indigenous peoples' tribunals (Articles 246–248).

3. Hereinafter referred to simply as the "tutela."

4. This diversity of interests was, paradoxically, the result of low turnout (roughly one-quarter of eligible voters) in elections to the representative assembly that drafted the new constitution. As a result of this low turnout, 40% of the representatives were from outside the traditionally dominant Liberal and Conservative parties (Schor, 2009, p. 185).

5. Political Constitution of Colombia (1991), Art. 214(2).

6. Political Constitution of Colombia (1991), Art. 214(6).

7. Decree 2591 (1991), Art. 4: "Interpretation of rights under the tutela: Rights protected by the tutela action will be interpreted in conformity with international human rights treaties ratified by Colombia."

8. "The constitutionality block consists of those rules and principles that, without formally appearing in the text of the Constitution, are used as control parameters of the constitutionality of laws, because they have been normatively integrated into the Constitution, in various ways and by mandate of the Constitution. They are thus true principles and rules of constitutional weight, that is, they are rules at the constitutional level" (Colombian Constitutional Court, Decision C-225/95 [May 18, 1995]).

9. Occasional irregularities in this pattern occur due to retirements and temporary replacements. A "court zero" was also temporarily in operation following the constituent assembly and until the first selections could be confirmed by the Senate.

10. This section will focus on the widespread nature of the tutela writ. The section on procedural flexibility will explore how the tutela's popularity provides the CCC with leverage to choose from among a wide array of issue areas.

11. Political Constitution of Colombia (1991), Art. 214(6).

12. Political Constitution of Colombia (1991), Art. 278(5).

13. Political Constitution of Colombia (1991), Art. 173 and 239.

14. Maria Isabel Rueda, "La tutela: entre dios y el diablo," *La semana*, January 13, 1992, http://www.semana.com/opinion/articulo/la-tutela-entre-dios-el-diablo/16693-3.

15. The Supreme Court's resistance to the tutela will be discussed in more detail in the section on extrajudicial executions. In summary, the Supreme Court resisted the use of the tutela by citizens to challenge before constitutional law judges what these citizens argued were unconstitutional rulings by the Supreme Court.

16. "La tutela pasó el año," *La semana*, December 21, 1992, http://www.semana.com/especiales/articulo/la-tutela-paso-ano/18872-3.

17. See, e.g., Colombian Constitutional Court, Decision T-426/92 (June 24, 1992): "Although the Constitution does not establish a right to subsistence it can be inferred from the rights to life, health, work and care or social security. The person requires a minimum of material elements to survive. The consecration of fundamental rights in the Constitution seeks to guarantee economic and spiritual conditions necessary for the dignity of the human person and the free development of his personality. In interpreting restrictively the scope of the right to subsistence the judge ignored the importance of the tutela application in respect of social security rights and the welfare of the elderly, in the special circumstances of the applicant."

18. Political Constitution of Colombia (1991), Art. 214(6).

19. These two rebel groups are known by their Spanish-language acronyms: the Revolutionary Armed Forces of Colombia (Fuerzas Armadas Revolucionarias de Colombia) and the National Liberation Army (Ejército de Liberación Nacional).

20. United Nations Office for the Coordination of Humanitarian Affairs, *Boletín humanitario mensual—Colombia*, no. 15, April 30, 2013, http://reliefweb.int/sites/reliefweb.int/files/resources/Boletin_Mensual_Abril_2013_ES.pdf.

21. Departamento Administrativo Nacional de Estadística, Dirección de Censos y Demografía, *Colombia, una nación multicultural* (May 2007), p. 3, http://www.dane.gov.co/files/censo2005/etnia/sys/colombia_nacion.pdf.

22. Internal Displacement Monitoring Centre, *Colombia: Property Restitution in Sight but Integration Still Distant* (December 29, 2011).

23. The tutelas were combined into a single case by the third review chamber, composed of Manuel José Cepeda Espinosa, Jaime Córdoba Triviño, and Rodrigo Escobar Gil.

24. The registry is generally known by its Spanish-language acronym, RUPD (Registro Único de Población Desplazada). The RUPD came into being following Presidential Decree 290 of 1999, which established the right of displaced persons to be registered with the state. Decree 290 of 1999 (February 17), Diario Oficial No. 43.507, de 22 de febrero de 1999.

25. UN Economic and Social Council, Commission on Human Rights, 54th Session, *Report of the Representative of the Secretary-General, Mr. Francis M. Deng, Submitted Pursuant to Commission Resolution 1997/39. Addendum. Guiding Principles on Internal Displacement*, E/CN.4/1998/53/Add.2 (February 11, 1998).

26. Law 387 of 1997 (July 18), Diario Oficial No. 43.091, de 24 de julio de 1997.

27. El Sistema Nacional de Atención Integral a la Población Desplazada.

28. Colombian Constitutional Court, Decision T-025/04, Appendix 3 (June 17, 2004).

29. Colombian Constitutional Court, Decision T-025/04, §§10–10.2.9 (June 17, 2004).

30. Individual orders are available on the CCC's website for the continuing chamber, http://www.corteconstitucional.gov.co/T-025-04/.

31. Colombian Constitutional Court, Order 185/04 (December 10, 2004).

32. Colombian Constitutional Court, Order 176/05 (August 29, 2005).

33. Colombian Constitutional Court, Order 177/05 (August 29, 2005).

34. Colombian Constitutional Court, Order 116/08 (May 13, 2008).

35. Colombian Constitutional Court, Order 200/07 (August 13, 2007).

36. Colombian Constitutional Court, Order 237/08 (September 19, 2008).

37. Colombian Constitutional Court, Order 251/08 (October 6, 2008).

38. Colombian Constitutional Court, Order 004/09 (January 26, 2009).

39. Colombian Constitutional Court, Order 005/09 (January 26, 2009).

40. Colombian Constitutional Court, Order 006/09 (January 26, 2009).

41. Decree 250 of 2005 (February 7), Diario Oficial No. 45.816, de 8 de febrero de 2005.

42. Law 1190 of 2008 (April 30), Diario Oficial No. 46.976, de 30 de abril de 2008.

43. The special chamber consisted of Luis Ernesto Vargas Silva (president), Nilson Pinilla Pinilla, and Luis Guillermo Guerrero Pérez.

44. Colombian Constitutional Court, Order 178/05 (August 29, 2005), Appendix: "The Court also considered it necessary to rely on the evaluation of human rights

organizations and displaced persons who have participated in the monitoring of judgment T-025 of 2004 on the adequacy of the measures taken by the various agencies responsible for comprehensive care of the displaced population to comply with the ruling in that case to overcome the state of unconstitutionality."

45. See, e.g., Colombian Constitutional Court, Order 109/07 (April 5, 2007), Par. 9, 15.

46. See, e.g., Colombian Constitutional Court, Order 176/05 (August 29, 2005): "Orders relating to the budgetary effort required to implement policies dealing with the displaced population, in accordance with judgment T-025 of 2004," Appendix, paragraphs 15 and 18.8.

47. Figure 9 reproduces and reports accounting done by CODHES. Consultoría para los Derechos Humanos y el Desplazamiento (CODHES), "De la seguridad a la prosperidad democrática en medio del conflicto," *CODHES Informa: Boletín de la Consultoría para los Derechos Humanos y el Desplazamiento CODHES*, no. 78, September 19, 2011.

48. The number of IDPs continued to grow for several more years, despite the signing of a peace agreement between the Colombian government and the FARC, the main insurgency group. United Nations High Commissioner for Refugees (UNHCR), "Briefing Notes: Forced Displacement Growing in Colombia Despite Peace Agreement," March 10, 2017, https://www.unhcr.org/news/briefing/2017/3/58c26e114/forced-displacement-growing-colombia-despite-peace-agreement.html. In addition, the demobilization of FARC guerillas has in many rural areas caused a power vacuum, resulting in further displacement. UNHCR, *Global Report 2017*, http://reporting.unhcr.org/sites/default/files/gr2017/pdf/GR2017_English_Full_lowres.pdf. The peace agreement between the government and the FARC is explored in more depth in the second subcase.

49. In retrospect, the CCC's calculation may have had an even wider effect than it anticipated. As one court watcher has noted, the ruling "may have contributed to changing public perception of the urgency and gravity of forced displacement in Colombia, or it may have legitimized the claims and reinforced the negotiating power of human rights NGOs and international human rights agencies that had been pressuring the Colombian government to do more for the IDPs" (Rodríguez-Raga, 2011, p. 1678).

50. "Sala especial de Seguimiento a la Sentencia T-025 de 2004," http://www.corteconstitucional.gov.co/T-025-04/.

51. Presidential figures and CCJ estimates are reported in Alston (2010, pp. 9–11).

52. These figures are reported by the Office of the Public Prosecutor to the CCC in the tutela review case T-318 (2011), a tutela filing seeking protection in relation to the extrajudicial killing of the petitioner's relative.

53. Inter-American Commission on Human Rights, "Annex to the Press Release Issued at the Close of the 147th Session," Organization of American States (OAS) website, April 5, 2013, http://www.oas.org/en/iachr/media_center/PReleases/2013/023A.asp.

54. The NGO in question was the Federación Internacional de Derechos Humanos. Melodie Arian, "Complaints of Extrajudicial Executions in Colombia," *Human Rights Brief*,

March 24, 2013, http://hrbrief.org/2013/03/complaints-of-extrajudicial-executions-in-colombia-2/.

55. National Security Statute, Decree No. 1923 of September 6, 1978 (Martz, 1997, p. 190).

56. Political Constitution of Colombia (1991), Art. 221.

57. Political Constitution of Colombia (1991), Art. 91.

58. Colombian Constitutional Court, Decision C-141/95 (March 29, 1995).

59. The revised language now appears as, "Such Courts or Tribunals will be made up of members of the Public Force in active service or in retirement." Political Constitution of Colombia (1991, as amended by Legislative Act 2 of 1995), Art. 221.

60. Colombian Constitutional Court, Decision C-358/97 (August 5, 1997).

61. U.S. Department of State, Bureau of Democracy, Human Rights, and Labor, *2001 Country Reports on Human Rights Practices: Colombia*, March 4, 2002, https://2009-2017.state.gov/j/drl/rls/hrrpt/2001/wha/8326.htm.

62. Mauricio Martínez, "Los conflictos entre las altas Cortes," *UN periódico*, *113*(5), July 2008, http://historico.unperiodico.unal.edu.co/Ediciones/113/05.html.

63. Decree 1382 of 2000 (July 12, 2000). Colombia, Diario Oficial No. 44.082, del 14 de julio de 2000.

64. As explored in preceding paragraphs, the 1991 constitution treated military tribunals and ordinary prosecutions separately. Article 221 governs prosecution of active military before military tribunals for crimes related to their military service, whereas Article 250 governs civilian cases. As such, the 2002 reforms to Article 250 would come into play in those instances where a civilian court asserted jurisdiction.

65. The case was a constitutionality challenge to Law 600 of 2000, the then-current criminal procedure law. Specifically, the court stated that Article 137 of the law was constitutional insofar as it would be read to include a right to truth and justice. Colombian Constitutional Court, Decision C-228/02 (April 3, 2002).

66. The revised article states that "the law will fix the terms according to which victims can intervene in criminal proceedings and restorative justice mechanisms" ("la ley fijará los términos en que podrán intervenir las víctimas en el proceso penal y los mecanismos de justicia restaurativa"). Political Constitution of Colombia (1991, as amended by Legislative Act 3 of 2002), Art. 250.

67. Law 906 of 2004 (August 31), Diario Oficial No. 45.678, de 1 de septiembre de 2004.

68. Law 906 of 2004, Arts. 11 and 132–37.

69. Colombian Constitutional Court, Decision C-454/06 (June 7, 2006). Specifically, the challengers argued that Articles 11, 132–136, and 357 of the 2004 Criminal Procedure Law were unconstitutional. Due to insufficiencies in the pleadings, the court limited itself to consideration of Articles 135 and 357. Decision C-454/06, §VI.C., ¶27.

70. Decision C-454/06, §VI.D., ¶¶29–40.

71. Decision C-454/06, §VI.D., ¶¶48–59.

72. Decision C-454/06, §VI.D., ¶¶61–70.

73. Specifically, the court stated that "it is clear that this constitutional regime of the tutela action . . . cannot be interfered with by the legislator with the goal of restricting its scope." In the original, "es claro que ese régimen constitucional de la acción de tutela . . . no puede ser interferido por el legislador con miras a restringir su ámbito de aplicación." Decision C-591/05, §V.C.3.a., ¶13.

74. In the original, "recurso sencillo, efectivo y breve de protección efectiva de los derechos fundamentales[.]" Decision C-591/05, §V.C.3.d., ¶31.

75. Decision C-591/05, §V.C.3.d., ¶32.

76. Decision C-591/05, §V.C.3.b., ¶24.

77. Decision C-591/05, §V.C.3.b., ¶24.b.

78. Simon Romero, "Colombia Lists Civilian Killings in Guerrilla Toll," *New York Times*, October 29, 2008, http://www.nytimes.com/2008/10/30/world/americas/30colombia.html.

79. Because the peace process has played out after the conclusion of this case study's 20-year time frame, the analysis here is limited. For the more detailed examination on which this draws, see Kendall (2020).

80. "Landmark Day for Colombia as Government, FARC Sign Definitive Peace Deal," *LatinNews Daily*, August 25, 2016.

81. República de Colombia, Registraduría Nacional del Estado Civil, Boletín Nacional 53, Plebiscito 2 octubre 2016, https://elecciones.registraduria.gov.co/pre_plebis_2016/99PL/DPLZZZZZZZZZZZZZZZZZ_L1.htm. Of course, it should also be noted that turnout was low, at just over 37%.

82. "Colombia: Santos Moves Ahead Without Support of 'No' Camp," *LatinNews*, Weekly Report, November 24, 2016.

83. Final Agreement for Ending the Conflict and Building a Stable and Lasting Peace (the "Final Agreement"), Part 5, November 24, 2016.

84. Final Agreement, 5.1.2, §II, ¶32.

85. Sentencia C-579/13, §§6.4.1 and 8.2.1; Sentencia C-577/14, §§5.2, 6.2.3, 7.1.1, and 7.1.2.

86. Final Agreement, 5.1.2, §II, ¶52.

87. CODHES, "De la seguridad a la prosperidad democrática en medio del conflicto," p. 5.

88. Human Rights Department, Ministry of National Defense, Republic of Colombia, *Commitment and Transparency: A Report on the Comprehensive Policy for Human Rights and International Humanitarian Law at the Ministry of National Defense* (2009), p. 13.

Chapter 4

Note to epigraph: *S v Mhlungu and Others* (CCT25/94) [1995] ZACC 4; 1995 (3) SA 867; 1995 (7) BCLR 793 (CC) (June 8, 1995), Kriegler concurrence at ¶138.

1. Constitution of the Republic of South Africa Act, No. 200 of 1993 (the "Interim Constitution").

2. Interim Constitution, Schedule 4.

3. Constitution of the Republic of South Africa Act, No. 108 of 1996, as adopted on May 8, 1996, and amended on October 11, 1996, by the Constitutional Assembly (the "Final Constitution").

4. Final Constitution, Chapter 2.

5. Final Constitution, §39(1)(b).

6. Final Constitution, §39(1)(c).

7. Interim Constitution, §231(3).

8. Final Constitution, §231(4).

9. See *Certification of the Constitution of the Republic of South Africa*, 1996 (10) BCLR 1253 (CC) (the *First Certification Case*), ¶¶50–103; *Certification of the Amended Text of the Constitution of the Republic of South Africa*, 1997 (1) BCLR 1 (CC) (the *Second Certification Case*), ¶¶17–21.

10. *S v Makwanyane and Another*, 1995 (6) BCLR 665 (CC).

11. Final Constitution, §233.

12. Final Constitution, §232.

13. Interim Constitution, §4; Final Constitution, §2.

14. Final Constitution, §§2 and 237.

15. *First Certification Case* at ¶¶482–483.

16. *First Certification Case* at ¶¶86–88.

17. *Second Certification Case.*

18. Under the Final Constitution, §167(3)(c): "The Constitutional Court . . . makes the final decision whether a matter is a constitutional matter or whether an issue is connected with a decision on a constitutional matter."

19. The court has stated, "There is only one system of law. It is shaped by the Constitution which is the supreme law, and all law, including the common law, derives its force from the Constitution and is subject to constitutional control." *Pharmaceutical Manufacturers Association of South Africa and Another: In re Ex Parte President of the Republic of South Africa and Others*, 2000 (3) BCLR 241 (CC), at ¶44.

20. For a more in-depth discussion of the SACC's recognition as an apex court, see Mtshaulana (2001).

21. Act to Amend the Constitution of the Republic of South Africa, 1996, No. 34 of 2001, Gazette No. 22853, November 21, 2001, §11.

22. Final Constitution, §167(5); Constitutional Court Complementary Act Amendment Act, No. 79 of 1997, Gazette No. 18495, December 5, 1997.

23. Final Constitution, §167(4)(d).

24. Final Constitution, §79(4).

25. Such a request requires the assent of one third of all members of the assembly. Final Constitution, §80(2)(a).

26. Interim Constitution, §§98(2)(d) and 98(9).

27. *In re: Gauteng School Education Bill of 1995*, 1996 (4) BCLR 537 (CC).

28. *In re: National Education Policy Bill No 83 of 1995*, 1996 (4) BCLR 518 (CC).

29. Even then, the Final Constitution requires that the law remain in force unless the SACC determines the suit has a reasonable likelihood of succeeding on the merits. In addition, the constitution provides the court with the ability to sanction abusive use of this tool; where the court determines a suit was without merit, it can order the applicant to pay all costs of the suit. Final Constitution, §80(3).

30. Final Constitution, §167(3)(c).

31. Final Constitution, §167(6). Emphasis is mine.

32. Constitutional Court Complementary Act Amendment Act, No. 79 of 1997, Gazette No. 18495, December 5, 1997.

33. In comparison, the U.S. Supreme Court is governed by the Federal Rules of Civil Procedure, which are subject to congressional approval prior to final adoption (Staszak, 2010).

34. See section "Moderately Embedded Internationalism."

35. Compiled using electoral data from the Electoral Commission of South Africa.

36. The exceptions are protections found in the Bill of Rights or a limited number of areas dealing with provincial powers. In these matters, at least six of the country's nine provinces must affirm the amendment. Final Constitution, §§74(2) and (3). The constitution also allows for a two-thirds override vote in the National Assembly for passage of legislation affecting provincial powers without assent by the National Council of Provinces. Final Constitution, §§76(1)(e), (i), and (j); §76(5)(b)(ii). Of course, during those years the ANC also controlled seven of nine provincial legislatures.

37. A list of what the SACC considers to be its "landmark" cases is available on the court's website at https://www.concourt.org.za/index.php/23-history-of-the-court/landmark-cases/90-landmark-cases.

38. I deal with the issue of direct access here, as opposed to in my discussions of the individual subcases, as the limitation on access applies across substantive legal areas. I deal with questions of adjudication and remedies in the individual subcases, as the SACC's treatment varies by issue area.

39. Information compiled using court data available from the website of the SACC, http://www.constitutionalcourt.org.za/uhtbin/cgisirsi/0/0/x/503/9. Cases are included based on the year of the court's decision, not the year in which they first appeared on the court's docket.

40. Final Constitution, §167(5).

41. Final Constitution, §7(2).

42. Indeed, the Final Constitution made a move beyond second-generation rights to include third-generation group rights in the form of cultural, religious, and linguistic protections. See Final Constitution, §§30–31.

43. The objectors were the South African Institute of Race Relations, the Free Market Foundation, and the Gauteng Association of Chambers of Commerce and Industry. *First Certification Case*, Appendix: Summary of Objections and Submissions, pp. 282–283.

44. *First Certification Case* at ¶77.

45. Final Constitution, §27.

46. In addition to the Universal Declaration of Human Rights, the ICCPR, and the ICESCR, the International Bill of Human Rights also includes two optional protocols to the ICCPR, one establishing an individual complaint procedure and one aiming to abolish the death penalty. See "Fact Sheet No.2 (Rev.1), The International Bill of Human Right," Office of the High Commissioner for Human Rights, http://www.ohchr.org/Documents/Publications/FactSheet2Rev.1en.pdf. Like the ICCPR, the ICESCR is buttressed by an optional protocol that establishes an individual complaint procedure. The ICESCR optional protocol is only open for ratification to states that have ratified the ICESCR; as such, South Africa was not yet eligible during the first two decades following the transition from Apartheid. See Optional Protocol to the International Covenant on Economic, Social and Cultural Rights, Art. 17, §1.

47. Although the government reiterated its intention to ratify the ICESCR in 2012, this was after the time of the cases decided in this section. See Statement on Cabinet Meeting of 10 October 2012, §2.1, https://www.gov.za/statement-cabinet-meeting-10-october-2012.

48. See, e.g., *Makwanyane.*

49. African Charter on Human and Peoples' Rights (Banjul Charter).

50. *TAC 2*, 2002 (10) BCLR 1033 (CC). An accompanying temporary order, *Minister of Health and Others v Treatment Action Campaign and Others (No 1)*, or *TAC 1*, required enforcement of a previous High Court order directing the government to make nevirapine available where medically indicated at pilot sights already established by the government. *TAC 1*, 2002 (10) BCLR 1075 (CC).

51. *TAC 2* at ¶1.

52. *TAC 2* at ¶3.

53. *TAC 2* at fn. 3.

54. *TAC 2* at ¶2.

55. *Treatment Action Campaign and Others v Minister of Health and Others*, Case No. 21182/2001 (High Court of South Africa, Transvaal Provincial Division) (*TAC HC*), Order at ¶¶1–2.

56. *TAC HC*, Order at ¶¶4–8.

57. *TAC 2* at ¶135(2).

58. *TAC 2* at ¶135(3).

59. *TAC 2* at ¶129.

60. *Government of the Republic of South Africa and Others v Grootboom*, 2000 (11) BCLR 1169 (CC).

61. *Grootboom* at ¶¶29–30.

62. *Grootboom* at ¶45.

63. *Grootboom* at ¶26, citing Final Constitution, §39, and *Makwanyane.*

64. The Final Constitution mandates that the Human Rights Commission monitor socioeconomic rights in the country (Heyns & Viljoen, 2001, p. 503).

65. *Grootboom* at ¶37.

66. This approach differed from the court below, which felt comfortable instructing the government that providing "tents, portable latrines and a regular supply of water (albeit transported) would constitute the bare minimum" (*Grootboom* at ¶4).

67. *Grootboom* at ¶33.

68. *Grootboom* at ¶99.

69. *TAC 2* at ¶35.

70. *TAC 2* at ¶34.

71. *TAC v Minister of Health/MECS*, March 11, 2002 (Execution Order) [2002] ZAGPHC 3, at ¶19.

72. *TAC 2* at ¶9.

73. *TAC 2* at ¶20.

74. *TAC 2* at ¶123.

75. *TAC 2* at ¶20.

76. *TAC 2*, citing Final Constitution, §§38 and 172(1)(a).

77. *TAC 2* at ¶104.

78. *TAC 2* at ¶129.

79. *TAC 2* at ¶135.

80. *TAC HC*.

81. The World Bank currently categorizes Botswana, Namibia, and South Africa as upper-middle-income countries. Namibia, however, has significantly fewer resources in terms of GDP. For the 15-year period of 1997–2011, Namibia's per capita GDP never exceeded 75% of that of South Africa. World DataBank Africa Development Indicators, http://data.worldbank.org/data-catalog/africa-development-indicators.

82. South Africans in this respect have been subject to the same economic and structural limitations in rights enforcement that have been documented in previous studies of cause lawyering. Galanter (1974) provides an early foray into the importance of structural constraints. Epp (1998) provides the classic comparative account of the structural foundations of legal mobilization.

83. See, e.g., the cabinet meeting statement of April 17, 2002, wherein the government noted, "In conducting this campaign, government's starting point is based on the premise that HIV causes AIDS."

84. Advertisement accompanying the cabinet meeting statement of February 21, 2002.

85. Cabinet meeting statement, April 30, 2002.

86. The 2003 statement, for example, cites a need to "continue the awareness campaign with regards to AIDS."

87. Statement of the National Executive Committee on the Occasion of the 95th Anniversary of the ANC, January 8, 2007, http://www.anc.org.za/list.php?t=January%208th%20Statements.

88. *Mazibuko and Others v City of Johannesburg and Others*, 2010 (3) BCLR 239 (CC).

89. International Covenant on Civil and Political Rights (ICCPR), Art. 7.

90. ICCPR, Art. 14.

91. ICCPR, Art. 9.

92. ICCPR, Art. 2(3).

93. Interim Constitution, Chapter 3, §§7–35.

94. Final Constitution, Chapter 2, §§7–39.

95. *Azanian Peoples Organization (AZAPO) and Others v President of the Republic of South Africa and Others*, 1996 (8) BCLR 1015 (CC).

96. Promotion of National Unity and Reconciliation Act, No. 34 of 1995, Gazette No. 16579, July 26, 1995.

97. The act mandated that any offender who had been granted amnesty could not be held liable either criminally or civilly for the acts in question. Nor could the government or any other organization be held vicariously liable for the acts for which amnesty had been granted. Promotion of National Unity and Reconciliation Act, §20(7)(a).

98. *AZAPO* at ¶8.

99. *AZAPO* at ¶25.

100. *AZAPO* at ¶19.

101. *AZAPO* at ¶24.

102. *AZAPO* at ¶26. The transformation into domestic legislation would not occur for another decade (Du Plessis, 2013).

103. *AZAPO* at ¶27.

104. *AZAPO* at ¶¶22–24. In this analysis, the court analogized South Africa to states such as Argentina, Chile, and El Salvador, all of which had chosen amnesty as part of the process of democratic consolidation.

105. *S v Williams and Others*, 1995 (7) BCLR 861 (CC).

106. Criminal Procedure Act, No. 51 of 1977, §294.

107. *Williams* at ¶21.

108. South Africa signed the ICCPR in October 1994 but did not ratify it until 1998.

109. *Williams* at ¶23.

110. South Africa signed the Convention Against Torture in 1983 but did not ratify it until 1998.

111. South Africa signed the Convention on the Rights of the Child in January 1993 but did not ratify it until June 16, 1995.

112. *Williams* at ¶¶50–53.

113. *Williams* at ¶96.

114. Abolition of Corporal Punishment Act, No. 33 of 1997, Gazette No. 18256, September 5 1997.

115. The section "Moderately Embedded Internationalism" describes the adoption of the "self-executing" language in the Final Constitution, §231(4).

116. Little progress has been made in refining this definition in the following decades. See, e.g., Paust (1988); Sloss (1999). The importation of the doctrine into the South African context has been no less confounding for legal scholars. See Dugard (2011, pp. 56–60).

117. The SACC consolidated the cases in *President of the Republic of South Africa and Others v Quagliani, President of the Republic of South Africa and Others v Van Rooyen and Another; Goodwin v Director-General, Department of Justice and Constitutional Development and Others*, 2009 (4) BCLR 345 (CC); hereafter *Goodwin/Quagliani*.

118. *Goodwin/Quagliani* at ¶¶4–6.

119. *Goodwin/Quagliani* at ¶¶41-46.

120. *Claassen v Minister of Justice and Constitutional Development*, [2010] 4 All SA 197 (WCC) (December 8, 2009).

121. The text states, "Anyone who has been the victim of unlawful arrest or detention shall have an enforceable right to compensation." ICCPR, Art. 9(5).

122. *Claassen* at ¶21.

123. *Claassen* at ¶¶36–39.

124. Final Constitution, §8(3)(a).

125. *Carmichele v Minister of Safety and Security*, 2001 (10) BCLR 995 (CC).

126. *Carmichele* at ¶36.

127. *Carmichele* at ¶73 referring to the National Prosecuting Authority Act, No. 32 of 1998, Gazette No. 19021, 3 July 1998.

128. *Carmichele* at ¶62.

129. *Carmichele* at ¶62, fn. 67.

130. *Carmichele* at ¶84.

131. *Government of the Republic of Zimbabwe v Fick and Others*, 2013 (10) BCLR 1103 (CC).

132. *Zimbabwe* at ¶30.

133. *Zimbabwe* at ¶¶51–69.

134. *Zealand v Minister for Justice and Constitutional Development and Another*, 2008 (6) BCLR 601 (CC).

135. *Zealand* at ¶53. The protections are found in Final Constitution, §12(1)(a).

136. *Zealand* at ¶55.

137. *Zealand* at ¶¶ 30 and 52.

138. *Fose v Minister of Safety and Security*, 1997 (7) BCLR 851.

139. *Fose* at ¶¶ 70–72.

140. Hirschl (2007) and Meierhenrich (2008) have made compatible arguments about the enabling role of law and courts in transitional regimes.

141. Iain Currie, quoted in "Nine Years Under the Kgotla Tree," *Mail and Guardian*, May 3, 2004 (online edition), http://mg.co.za/article/2004-05-03-nine-years-under-the-kgotla-tree.

Chapter 5

Note to epigraph: *Solicitud de ejercicio de la facultad de investigación 1/2009*, minority vote of Mariano Azuela Güitrón, Guillermo Ortiz Mayagoytia, and Sergio Salvador Aguirre Anguiano, at pp. 5–6.

1. Mexico and Argentina were the only Latin American countries to undergo significant reform without adopting a new constitution. Both states undertook their reforms in 1994 (Uprimny, 2011).

2. The Mexican Constitution of 1917 was adopted at the close of the Mexican Revolution. It is alternatively referred to as the Fundamental Law or the Carta Magna.

3. The Mexican constitution has been amended 239 times, with amendments in 80 of the 101 years since its adoption. Any references to the constitution will, therefore, include the year in square brackets where necessary in order to avoid ambiguity (e.g., Const. Art. 94 [1994]). No year is indicated when the constitutional provision was consistent throughout the 20-year period of this study. A complete list of amendments is available on the website of the Mexican Chamber of Deputies, http://www.diputados.gob.mx/LeyesBiblio/ref/cpeum.htm.

4. See also Finkel (2005) and Ríos-Figueroa (2007).

5. Const. Art. 94 and 96 [1994]. Other judges in the federal judiciary were to be appointed by a new Federal Judicial Council, without the direct involvement of the president or Senate. Const. Art. 97 [1994]. For more on this court reform and earlier twentieth-century court reforms, see Domingo (2000).

6. Vargas (1995) 1995 provides an extensive overview of constitutional changes occurring in the years up to and including 1994. Vargas (1996) provides additional detail on the 1994 court reforms.

7. UN Department of Public Information, News and Media Division, "Selection Committee Announces 2013 Winners of United Nations Human Rights Prize," press release HR/5164, December 5, 2013, http://www.un.org/News/Press/docs/2013/hr5164.doc.htm.

8. SCJN jurisprudence is divided into "epochs" (*épocas*). The first through fourth epochs are considered *no aplicable* (nonapplicable or nonbinding), as they cover the prerevolution years. Binding jurisprudence begins with the fifth epoch, which coincides with the establishment of the new constitution in 1917 (Guerrero Lara, 1982). The ninth epoch began in 1995 and ended in September 2012. The tenth epoch began in October 2012 and continued through the final years examined here. The *Semanario Judicial de la Federación* (*Federation Judicial Weekly*) serves as the equivalent of an official court reporter.

9. The language of Article 133 has not changed since 1934.

10. Tercer Tribunal Colegiado en Materia Administrativa del Primer Circuito. Amparo en revisión 256/81. C. H. Boehringer Sohn. 9 de julio de 1981. Unanimidad de votos. Ponente: Genaro David Góngora Pimentel. Amparo en revisión 269/81. José Ernesto Matsumoto Matsuy. 14 de julio de 1981. Unanimidad de votos. Ponente: Samuel Hernández Viazcán. Amparo en revisión 160/81. National Research Development Corporation. 16 de julio de 1981. Unanimidad de votos. Ponente: Sergio Hugo Chapital Gutiérrez.

11. Tercer Tribunal Colegiado en Materia Administrativa del Primer Circuito. Amparo en revisión 256/81. C. H. Boehring Sohn. 9 de julio de 1981. Unanimidad de votos. Ponente: Genaro David Góngora Pimentel.

12. Amparo en revisión 2069/91. Manuel García Martínez. 30 de junio de 1992. Mayoría de quince votos. Ponente: Victoria Adato Green. Secretario: Sergio Pallares y Lara.

13. Amparo en revisión 1475/98. Sindicato Nacional de Controladores de Tránsito Aéreo. 11 de mayo de 1999. Unanimidad de diez votos. Ausente: José Vicente Aguinaco Alemán. Ponente: Humberto Román Palacios. Secretario: Antonio Espinoza Rangel.

14. Amparo en revisión 1475/98. Sindicato Nacional de Controladores de Tránsito Aéreo. 11 de mayo de 1999. Unanimidad de diez votos. Ausente: José Vicente Aguinaco Alemán. Ponente: Humberto Román Palacios. Secretario: Antonio Espinoza Rangel.

15. Participación de la Señora Ministra Olga Sánchez Cordero de García Villegas, en el Congreso Internacional para Apoyar la Armonización de las Legislaciones Locales con los Instrumentos Internacionales en Materia de Derechos Humanos de las Mujeres, Organizado por la Subscretaría para Temas Globales de la Secretaría de Relaciones Exteriores, el 29 de Abril de 2004, en la Sala Magna de la Cancillería, en la Ciudad de México, https://web.archive.org/web/20150413091231/https://www.scjn.gob.mx/conocelacorte/ministra/LA%20APLICACION%20DE%20LOS%20INSTRUMENTOS%20INTERNACIONALES%20DXS%20DE%20LA%20MUJER.pdf.

16. La Constitución y los Tratados Internacionales. Un Acercamiento a la Interpretación Judicial de la Jerarquía de las Normas y la Aplicación de los Tratados en la Legislación Nacional, https://web.archive.org/web/20120617111315/https://www.scjn.gob.mx/conocelacorte/ministra/LA%20CONSTITUCION%20Y%20LOS%20TRATADOS%20INTERNACIONALES%201103.pdf.

17. Diario Oficial, 10 de junio 2011.

18. Chapter 1 of the Mexican constitution includes 29 articles covering human rights and guarantees of those rights.

19. The name of the suit derives from the Spanish word *amparar*, meaning "to protect." The amparo suit is also the progenitor of the Colombian tutela action explored in Chapter 3 of this book. The amparo will be examined more closely in the sections that follow on the Mexican court system's support orientation and flexibility.

20. The amparo is not available when the violation is at the hands of a private party. Const. Art. 107(II).

21. Const. Art. 107(I) [2011].

22. Const. Art 105(2)(g) [2011].

23. The biographies of current justices are available at both the SCJN website (www.scjn.gob.mx) and the website of the Federal Judicial Counsel (www.cjf.gob.mx). The biography of one justice, Juventino Castro y Castro, was not available on these official sites, so reference is made to Camp (2011).

24. The federal court system exhibits a familiar hierarchical structure: initial claims are heard in the district courts (los Juzgados de Distrito); appeals are carried to the circuit courts (los Tribunales Colegiados y Unitarios de Circuito); and final pronouncements of law are made in the Supreme Court of Justice of the Nation (la Suprema Corte de Justicia de la Nación). Additional judicial institutions outside the three-tiered

hierarchy include the Electoral Tribunal (el Tribunal Electoral) and the Federal Judicial Council (el Consejo de la Judicatura Federal). Const. Art. 94.

25. This is referred to as the "Otero formulation," after Mariano Otero, the original promoter of the amparo suit at the national level (Zamora, 2004, p. 25).

26. The Spanish word *jurisprudencia* should not be confused with the English word "jurisprudence." Although the latter refers to legal theory, the Mexican term refers specifically to binding judicial precedent (Vargas, 2009).

27. For example, although the 1994 reforms increased SCJN justices' decisional insulation from political actors, each justice is appointed for a single 15-year term. This provides the possibility that during any individual president's *sexenio* (single 6-year term), that president will have the opportunity to replace several justices.

28. Zamora (2004) also notes that the SCJN is more likely to influence state law for practical (in addition to legal) reasons: the high court widely disseminates its decisions in both physical and electronic format (p. 85, fn. 29).

29. Const. Art. 105(I).

30. This type of claim requires 33% of either chamber of Congress or the state legislature in question. The claim also has to be brought within 30 days of a new law's passage. Const. Art. 105(II) [1994].

31. Under such circumstances, a supermajority of 8 of the 11 justices is required for the ruling to have general effects. In other cases, the ruling is binding only on the parties to the dispute. Const. Art. 105(I).

32. Const. Art. 107(IX).

33. Const. Art. 105(V) [1994].

34. Const. Art. 105(II) [1996].

35. Const. Art 29 at ¶5 [2011].

36. Const. Art. 107(II) at ¶2 [2011].

37. Const. Art. 107(II) at ¶3 [2011].

38. Ugalde (2001) and other scholars use the term "meta-constitutional" to describe these party-based powers in order to distinguish them from the ex officio powers derived from the constitutional text.

39. *Diario Oficial de la Federación*, Vol. 184, No. 41 (February 19, 1951), and corrections in Vol. 185, No. 12 (March 14, 1951).

40. Ch. 6, "The Judicial System," in Zamora (2004). For a more historical perspective, see Butte's (1974) analysis of the evolution of the Mexican courts' use of precedent and *jurisprudencia* in the pre-reform era.

41. These data were compiled using information available on the website of Mexico's National Electoral Institute, www.ine.mx/portal/site/ifev2/Elecciones.

42. The Mexican legislature consists of two houses, a lower chamber (the Chamber of Deputies) and an upper chamber (the Senate). The Chamber of Deputies comprises 500 deputies elected every 3 years through a combination of single-district, first-past-the-post elections (300 seats) and proportional representation at the regional level (200 seats). The Senate consists of 128 members elected for 6-year terms in a mixed

system of party ballots at the district level and national proportional representation. This system is the consequence of an ongoing series of reforms over several decades that originally guaranteed one party would hold a majority of seats. This system was eventually reformed to ensure continued opposition-party participation in the electoral system (Molinar Horcasitas & Weldon, 2001; Weldon, 2001). The electoral requirements are outlined in Const. Arts. 50–54 and 56, and amendments to the constitution are controlled by Const. Art. 135.

43. The members of the judiciary were not involved in the process, which is perhaps not surprising given that the entire SCJN bench of 25 justices was dismissed and replaced with 11 new justices under new appointment procedures. See Commission on Human Rights Report on Mexico, Independence of the Judiciary, January 24, 2002, E/CN.4/2002/72/Add.1 at ¶13.

44. Const. Art. 107. By way of comparison, the other states examined in this project exhibit much less textual formality. The Colombian tutela system is outlined in Columbia's constitution in just seven paragraphs, totaling under 250 words (Political Constitution of Colombia [1991], Art. 86; Art. 241, ¶9; Art. 282, ¶3). South Africa's Final Constitution is even more reticent when dealing with court procedures and courts' adjudication of citizens' claims, containing just two paragraphs totaling approximately 75 words (§167[6] and §171). This has allowed these states' respective constitutional courts much more leeway in determining how and when to engage—or avoid—litigants.

45. Const. Art. 107(II) ¶3 [2011].

46. Const. Art. 107(X) ¶1.

47. Const. Art. 107(XII) ¶2.

48. Ley de amparo, reglamentaria de los artículos 103 y 107 de la Constitución política de los Estados Unidos Mexicanos.

49. Although the Dirty War is generally considered to have occurred during the 1960s and 1970s, additional human rights violations, including disappearances, continued into the 1980s. See Fiscalia Especial para Movimientos Sociales y Políticos del Pasado, *Informe Histórico a la Sociedad Mexicana: 2006* (Special Prosecutor for Past Social and Political Movements, *Historical Report to Mexican Society: 2006*). (Report on file with author.)

50. U.S. Department of State, Bureau of Democracy, Human Rights, and Labor, *2006 Country Reports on Human Rights Practices: Mexico*, March 6, 2007, https://2009-2017.state.gov/j/drl/rls/hrrpt/2006/78898.htm.

51. U.S. Department of State, Bureau of Democracy, Human Rights, and Labor, 2002 Country Reports on Human Rights Practices: Mexico, March 31, 2003, https://2009-2017.state.gov/j/drl/rls/hrrpt/2002/18338.htm.

52. The National Human Rights Commission is known by its Spanish-language acronym, CNDH (Comisión Nacional de los Derechos Humanos).

53. See, e.g., Human Rights Watch, "Mexico: Build Accurate Database of Disappeared," November 12, 2013, http://www.hrw.org/news/2013/11/12/mexico-build-accurate-database-disappeared; Maureen Meyer and Clay Boggs, "One Year into

Mexican President Enrique Peña Nieto's Administration," Washington Office on Latin America, November, 27, 2013, http://www.wola.org/commentary/one_year_into_the_enrique_pena_nieto_administration.

54. Human Rights Watch, *Neither Rights Nor Security: Killings, Torture, and Disappearances in Mexico's "War on Drugs"*, November 2011, p. 10, http://www.hrw.org/sites/default/files/reports/mexico1111webwcover_0.pdf.

55. Comisión Nacional de los Derechos Humanos (CNDH), Recomendación 104/1995, México, D.F., 14 de agosto de 1995.

56. Const. Art. 97 ¶2 [pre–2011].

57. The only prior use had been an investigation into deaths of 40 protestors at the hands of the military in Guanajuato in 1946.

58. Const. Art. 97 ¶2 [pre-2011].

59. Expediente "Varios" 451/95.

60. Solicitud numero 3/96 relativa a la peticion del presidente de la republica para que se ejerza la facultad prevista en el segundo parrafo del articulo 97 constitucional, May 4, 1996. (Document on file with author.)

61. Reyes Reyes (2003) expounds on the origins of this power, arguing that its creation was inspired by international fact-finding commissions, such as those which investigated the 1898 *Maine* incident and border disputes between France and Germany. In any event, his analysis accepts that this SCJN power was envisioned as purely fact-finding and nonjurisdictional.

62. Const. Art. 97 ¶3 [pre-2011].

63. The SCJN offers *tesis*—rulings on precise points of law—when it decides cases. An isolated *tesis* must be reiterated in five separate rulings to allow for jurisprudencia through repetition.

64. The court held: "By unanimous vote of eleven it is resolved that the exercise of the investigatory function conferred on the Supreme Court of Justice of the Nation by paragraph 2 of Article 97 of the Constitution is discretional." Solicitud numero 3/96 relativa a la petición del presidente de la republica para que se ejerza la facultad prevista en el segundo párrafo del articulo 97 constitucional, May 4, 1996. (Document on file with author.)

65. Tesis 193781, *Semanario Judicial de la Federación y su Gaceta*, Novena Época, p. 10 (Tesis P. XLVII/99).

66. Tesis 199251, *Semanario Judicial de la Federación y su Gaceta*, Novena Época, p. 655 (Tesis P. XLIV/97).

67. In a 2009 case (which the court ultimately accepted), the minority noted the inefficacy of the Aguas Blancas investigation, stating that despite having "confirmed the existence of close range shooting deaths of residents of Guerrero . . . as of this date [August 6, 2009] we have none of those involved in prison." Ruling on the request to exercise the investigatory function of August 6, 2009 (Facultad de Investigación 1/2009), minority opinion of Justices Güitron, Ortiz Mayagoitia, and Aguirre Anguiano, at 7.

68. See, e.g., Amnesty International, "Mexican Supreme Court's Resolution on Atenco—The Route to Justice?," AMR 41/008/2009, February 17, 2009,http://www.amnesty.org/en/library/info/AMR41/008/2009/en.

69. See Jesús Aranda, "Violó Ulises Ruiz garantías individuales durante el conflicto en Oaxaca: SCJN," *La jornada*, October 15, 2009, http://www.jornada.unam.mx/2009/10/15/index.php?section=politica&article=014n1pol.

70. See Ruling on the request to exercise the investigatory function of August 6, 2009 (Facultad de Investigación 1/2009), at 11.

71. Trans-Border Institute, *Justice in Mexico New Report*, June 2010, pp. 15–16, http://catcher.sandiego.edu/items/peacestudies/june2010.pdf.

72. President Fox created the Special Prosecutor's Office for Social and Political Movements of the Past, known by its Spanish acronym (FEMOSPP) in 2001. FEMOSPP conducted an exhaustive investigation based on government archives and interviews with individuals affected by the events of the Dirty War.

73. United Nations, *Treaty Series*, Vol. 754, p. 73. Mexico signed the treaty in 1969 but only ratified the treaty in 2002.

74. The attorney general was Rafael Macedo de la Concha. The FEMOSPP was in the office of the Procuraduría Nacional de la República.

75. Carlos Avilés Allende, "En noviembre, fallo de la Corte sobre 'guerra sucia,'" *El universal*, October 2, 2003, http://www.eluniversal.com.mx/nacion/102690.html.

76. *Recurso de Apelación Extraordinaria 1/2003*, in *La Retroactividad en el Delito de Desaparición Forzada de Personas y la Prescripción Ilegal de la Libertad*, Decisiones Relevantes de la Suprema Corte de Justica de la Nación 20, Mexico City, 2007.

77. Averiguación Previa # A.P. PGR/FEMOSPP/011/2002.

78. Although "period of prescription" is more commonly used in civil law jurisdictions such as Mexico and is a more faithful translation of the Spanish-language term *prescripción*, I use the term "statute of limitations" here for conformity with other English-language writing on this topic.

79. Solicitud de facultad de atracción 8/2004–PS; Expediente Relativo al Recurso de Apelación Atraído 1/2004–PS.

80. Const. Art. 14.

81. Suprema Corte de Justicia de la Nación, "Prescripción del delito de genocidio (Halconazo)," *Crónicas: Serie de Crónicas de asuntos relevantes del Pleno y las Salas de la Suprema Corte de Justicia de la Nación*, 2006.

82. De la Barreda died in June 2008, never having been imprisoned. "Murió Luis de la Barreda, ex titular de la disuelta Dirección Federal de Seguridad," *La jornada*, June 10, 2008, http://www.jornada.unam.mx/2008/06/10/index.php?section=politica&article=018n1pol. Nazar Haro also avoided serving prison time; he died in February 2012. "Nazar y la Brigada Blanca," *La jornada*, February 3, 2012, http://www.lajornadaguerrero.com.mx/2012/02/03/index.php?section=opinion&article=002a1soc.

83. Case of Radilla Pacheco v. Mexico. Preliminary Objections, Merits, Reparations, and Costs. Judgment of November 23, 2009. Inter-American Court of Human Rights

Series C No. 209, at §XII. Case of Fernández Ortega et al. v. Mexico. Preliminary Objection, Merits, Reparations, and Costs. Judgment of August 30, 2010. Inter-American Court of Human Rights Series C No. 215, at ¶308. Case of Rosendo-Cantú and other v. Mexico. Preliminary Objection, Merits, Reparations, and Costs. Judgment of August 31, 2010. Inter-American Court of Human Rights Series C No. 216, at ¶295. Case of Cabrera García and Montiel-Flores v. Mexico. Preliminary Objection, Merits, Reparations, and Legal Costs. Judgment of November 26, 2010. Inter-American Court of Human Rights Series C No. 220, at ¶274.

84. See section "Superficial Internationalism" earlier in the chapter.

85. Ley orgánica del poder judicial de la federación.

86. Expediente 489/2010, pp. 43–44.

87. Expediente 912/2010, ¶¶38-45.

88. Expediente 912/2010, ¶¶45 and 55. The SCJN retained the power of "attraction"—meaning it could assert jurisdiction over those cases it considered of importance and significance to the nation.

89. Expediente 912/2010, ¶¶ 22–36.

90. The IACHR adopted this standard for the first time in the case of a failure to prosecute the alleged perpetrators of an extrajudicial execution in Chile. *Case of Almonacid-Arellano et al v Chile*, Preliminary Objections, Merits, Reparations, and Costs, Judgment of September 26, 2006, Series C No. 154 at ¶124.

91. *Radilla Pacheco v Mexico*, at ¶339.

92. *Cabrera García*, at ¶225. For an extensive overview of the development and implications of this doctrine, see Concurring Opinion of Ad Hoc Judge Eduardo Ferrer Mac-Gregor Poisot Regarding the Judgment of the Inter-American Court of Human Rights in the *Case of Cabrera García and Montiel-Flores v Mexico*, November 26, 2010.

93. Expediente 912/2010, ¶ 31.

94. Expediente 912/2010, ¶¶26–36.

95. Expediente 912/2010, ¶10.

96. Expediente 912/2010, ¶29.

97. See, e.g., Washington Office on Latin America, *Mexico's Supreme Court Decides to End Military Jurisdiction for Soldiers Who Commit Human Rights* Violations, 13 July 2011, available at http://www.wola.org/commentary/mexico_s_supreme_court_decides_to_end_military_jurisdiction_for_soldiers_who_commit_human and Tracy Wilkinson, *Mexico High Court Rules Civilian Courts Should Handle Alleged Military Abuses*, Los Angeles Times, 13 July 2011, available at http://articles.latimes.com/2011/jul/13/world/la-fg-mexico-military-trials-20110713.

98. Suprema Corte, 38/2012 de agosto, 133/2012 de agosto.

99. "Mexico Lawmakers OK Civilian Courts for Soldiers," *Washington Post*, April 30, 2014.

100. Eighty percent of Mexico's indigenous population live in the southern states of Campeche, Chiapas, Guerrero, Hidalgo, Oaxaca, Puebla, Quintana Roo, Tabasco, Tlaxcala, Veracruz, and Yucatán (Ramirez, 2006, p. 151).

101. The definition of indigeneity is subjective. The numbers here are relatively conservative, as Ramirez (2006) bases this on whether or not an indigenous language is spoken in the home. Other measures, such as self-identification as indigenous, put the number much higher. For example, when the Mexican government added a question on self-identification to the 2015 intercensal survey, more than 21% of the population identified as indigenous. See Instituto Nacional de los Pueblos Indígenas, Numeralia indígena 2015, available for download at: https://gob.mx/inpi/articulos/indicadores-socioeconomicos-de-los-pueblos-indigenas-de-mexico-2015-116128.

102. I note this only to distinguish cases dealing with an individual indigenous person's claim, such as those found in the section in this chapter dealing with military impunity. The identification of an individual as a member of an indigenous group undoubtedly relates to many forms of rights infringement or persecution, but in this section I deal exclusively with those claims brought on behalf of indigenous groups as collective entities to which rights appertain.

103. See "C107—Indigenous and tribal populations convention, 1957 (no. 107)," International Labour Organization, https://www.ilo.org/dyn/normlex/en/f?p=NORMLEXPUB:12100:0::NO::P12100_ILO_CODE:C107.

104. United Nations, "General Assembly Adopts Declaration on Rights of Indigenous Peoples," press release GA/10612, September 13, 2007, https://press.un.org/en/2007/ga10612.doc.htm.

105. Mexico ratified ILO Convention No. 107 on June 1, 1959. It renounced the convention on September 5, 1990, in conjunction with its ratification of ILO Convention No. 169 the same day.

106. The reforms were widely condemned by activists as failing to adequately address issues of indigenous autonomy. "Press Attacks MPs over Indian Law," BBC News, May 2, 2001, http://news.bbc.co.uk/2/hi/world/monitoring/media_reports/1307411.stm.

107. "Mexican Supreme Court Rejects Challenges to Indian Rights Law," *New York Times*, September 7, 2002, http://www.nytimes.com/2002/09/07/world/mexican-supreme-court-rejects-challenges-to-indian-rights-law.html.

108. See, e.g., González Galván (2003a); González Galván (2003b).

109. Binding *jurisprudencia* can indeed result from constitutional controversies. The court rules, however, do not provide for how binding *jurisprudencia* could result from a decision *not to rule on* a constitutional controversy, nor did the SCJN explore this issue.

110. Semanario Judicial de la Federación y su Gaceta, Novena Época, Tomo XVI, septiembre de 2002, página 1136, Pleno, tesis P./J. 39/2002.

111. Semanario Judicial de la Federación y su Gaceta, Novena Época, Tomo XVI, septiembre de 2002, página 997, Pleno, tesis P./J. 40/2002.

112. The type of controversy was important because an Article 105 constitutional controversy would have allowed the court to offer a ruling with general binding effect. Carbonell (2002) suggests that an action of unconstitutionality, the other form of action that would allow for general effects, would also be considered inappropriate under the

court's analysis, rendering constitutional amendments a "zone of immunity" for state actors (Carbonell, 2002, p. 148). This conclusion seems reasonable, given the court's unwillingness to examine the procedural correctness of legislative acts more generally. (See Ejecutoria CC 82/2001 at p. 31, quoting Jurisprudencia P./J. 129/2001, wherein the court, sitting in plenary session, found that it was only empowered to determine the constitutionality of the final published law, not the individual steps which led to that law's publication.) This leaves only the amparo, an action whose inter partes effects are of questionable value as a means of challenging constitutional amendments.

113. Const. Art. 2, 2001.

114. Const. Art. 2(A), 2001.

115. Carbonell (2014) writes that the reforms of 2001 "parece estar completamente sepultada en el olvido" (p. 294).

116. Dictamen de las Comisiones Unidas de Puntos Constitucionales, de Gobernación y de Estudios Legislativos, respecto a la iniciativa que adiciona el artículo 17 de la Constitución Política de los Estados Unidos Mexicanos, en materia de acciones colectivas, del 3 de diciembre de 2009, p. 9., quoted in Olaiz-González & Bosco López (2011, pp. 175–176).

117. Diario Oficial, 30 de agosto de 2011.

118. Diario Oficial, 10 de junio de 2011. The changes relating to domestication of international law are examined in the section "Superficial Internationalism" earlier in this chapter. These were part of the same set of constitutional reforms examined in the subcase on impunity.

119. The SCJN refers to this alternatively as the "pro persona" principle.

120. Dirección General de Comunicación y Vinculación Social de la Suprema Corte de Justicia de la Nación, *Protocolo de actuación para quienes imparten justicia en casos que involucren derechos de personas, comunidades y pueblos indígenas*, 2014. Video of presentation available at http://www.sitios.scjn.gob.mx/videoteca/reproduccion/474/Protocolo%20de%20actuación%20para%20quienes%20imparten%20justicia%20en%20casos%20que%20involucren%20derechos%20de%20personas%2C%20comunidades%20y%20pueblos%20ind%C3%ADgenas. The remarks come approximately thirty-five minutes into the presentation.

121. Dirección General de Comunicación y Vinculación Social de la Suprema Corte de Justicia de la Nación, *Protocolo de actuación para quienes imparten justicia en casos que involucren derechos de personas, comunidades y pueblos indígenas*, 2014.

Chapter 6

1. See Knop (2000) on the role of domestic courts in the particularization and justification of international law for domestic audiences. Maveety and Grosskopf (2004) suggest a distinct role for high courts as legitimating conduits for international law.

2. A cabinet statement in March 2002, for example, revealed the extent to which the government viewed the debate as one of South African exceptionalism by emphasizing "the renewed campaign[,] particularly in some international media around this issue, directed against government in general and the President in particular." Statement on

Cabinet meeting of 6 March 2002, https://www.gcis.gov.za/content/newsroom/media-releases/cabinet-statements/statement-cabinet-meeting-6-march-2002.

3. In Colombia, this took the form of the FARC and the assassination of presidential candidates Bernardo Jaramillo and Carlos Pizarro. In Mexico, similar unrest was found in the Zapatista uprising in the state of Chiapas, and reform was likewise punctuated by the assassination of PRI presidential candidate Luis Donaldo Colossio and the majority leader of Congress, Jose Francisco Ruiz Massieu. Both states had also spent numerous years under executive-ordered states of emergency.

REFERENCES

Abbott, K. W., & Snidal, D. (2000). Hard and soft law in international governance. *International Organization*, *54*(3), 421–456. https://doi.org/10.1162/002081800551280

Ackerman, B. (1997). The rise of world constitutionalism. *Virginia Law Review*, *83*, 771–798.

Alston, P. (2010). *Report of the Special Rapporteur on extrajudicial, summary or arbitrary executions* (A/HRC/14/24/Add.2). Office of the United Nations High Commissioner for Human Rights.

Alter, K. J. (2013). *The new terrain of international law: Courts, politics, rights*. Princeton University Press. http://public.eblib.com/choice/publicfullrecord.aspx?p=1414125

Alter, K. J., & Helfer, L. R. (2009). The Andean Tribunal of Justice and its interlocutors: Understanding preliminary reference patterns in the Andean community. *New York University Journal of International Law and Politics*, *41*, 871–929.

Ansolabehere, K. (2010). More power, more rights? The Supreme Court and society in Mexico. In J. Couso, A. Huneeus, & R. Sieder (Eds.), *Cultures of legality judicialization and political activism in Latin America* (pp. 78–111). Cambridge University Press.

Barron, P., Pillay, Y., Doherty, T., Sherman, G., Jackson, D., Bhardwaj, S., Robinson, P., & Goga, A. (2013). Eliminating mother-to-child HIV transmission in South Africa. *Bulletin of the World Health Organization*, *91*(1), 1–80.

Benvenisti, E., & Downs, G. W. (2009). National courts, domestic democracy, and the evolution of international law. *European Journal of International Law*, *20*(1), 59–72. https://doi.org/10.1093/ejil/chp004.

Berat, L. (2005). The Constitutional Court of South Africa and jurisdictional questions: In the interest of justice? *International Journal of Constitutional Law*, *3*(1), 39–76. https://doi.org/10.1093/icon/moi003

Berger, J. (2008). Litigating for social justice in post-Apartheid South Africa. In V. Gauri & D. M. Brinks (Eds.), *Courting social justice: Judicial enforcement of social and economic rights in the developing world* (pp. 38–99). Cambridge University Press.

Berger, J. M., & Kapczynski, A. (2009). The story of the TAC case: The potential and limits of socio-economic rights litigation in South Africa. In D. Hurwitz & M. L. Satterthwaite (Eds.), *Human rights advocacy stories* (pp. 69–107). Foundation Press; Thomson/West.

Bickel, A. M. (1986). *The least dangerous branch: The Supreme Court at the bar of politics*. Yale University Press.

Bilchitz, D. (2003). Towards a reasonable approach to the minimum core: Laying the foundations for future socio-economic rights jurisprudence. *South African Journal on Human Rights*, *19*(1), 1–26. https://doi.org/10.1080/19962126.2003.11865170

Bishop, M. (2008). Remedies. In S. Woolman, T. Roux, & M. Bishop (Eds.), *Constitutional law of South Africa* (2nd ed., §§ 9.1–9.8). Juta.

Bodansky, D. (2015). Legal realism and its discontents. *Leiden Journal of International Law; Cambridge*, *28*(2), 267–281. http://dx.doi.org.ezproxy.ups.edu/10.1017/S0922156515000072

Boli-Bennett, J., & Meyer, J. W. (1978). The ideology of childhood and the state: Rules distinguishing children in national constitutions, 1870–1970. *American Sociological Review*, *43*(6), 797–812. https://doi.org/10.2307/2094622

Borgen, C. J. (2007). Transnational tribunals and the transmission of norms: The hegemony of process. *George Washington International Law Review*, *39*, 685–764.

Bradford, A., & Posner, E. A. (2011). Universal exceptionalism in international law. *Harvard International Law Journal*, *52*(1), 1–54.

Brewer-Carías, A. R. (2008). *Constitutional protection of human rights in Latin America: A comparative study of amparo proceedings*. Cambridge University Press.

Brysk, A. (2000). *From tribal village to global village: Indian rights and international relations in Latin America*. Stanford University Press.

Burley, A.-M., & Mattli, W. (1993). Europe before the Court: A political theory of legal integration. *International Organization*, *47*(1), 41–76. https://doi.org/10.1017/S0020818300004707

Butte, W. L. (1974). Stare decisis, doctrine, and jurisprudence in Mexico and elsewhere. In J. Dainow (Ed.), *The role of judicial decisions and doctrine in civil law and in mixed jurisdictions* (pp. 311–330). Louisiana State University Press.

Cameron, C. M. (2002). Judicial independence: How can you tell it when you see it? And, who cares? In S. B. Burbank & B. Friedman (Eds.), *Judicial independence at the crossroads: An interdisciplinary approach* (pp. 134–147). Sage Publications.

Camp, R. A. (1992). *Generals in the Palacio: The military in modern Mexico*. Oxford University Press.

Camp, R. A. (2011). *Mexican political biographies, 1935–2009* (4th ed.). University of Texas Press.

Carbonell, M. (2002). Epílogo: La reforma indígena y la Suprema Corte. In M. Carbonell & K. Pérez Portilla (Eds.), *Comentarios a la reforma constitucional en materia indígena* (pp. 145–149). Universidad Nacional Autónoma de México.

Carbonell, M. (2003). La reforma constitucional en materia indígena. Un primer acercamiento. In Tribunal Electoral del Poder Judicial de la Federación (México), *Derechos indígenas y elecciones* (pp. 50–69). Tribunal Electoral del Poder Judicial de la Federación.

Carbonell, M. (2014). Tres grandes reformas: Derechos humanos, justicia penal y acceso a la información. In M. A. Casar & I. Marván (Eds.), *Reformar sin mayorías. La dinámica del cambio constitucional en México: 1997–2012* (pp. 130–222). Santillana Ediciones.

Carpizo, J. (2011). ¿Es acertada la probable transferencia de la función de investigación de la Suprema Corte a la Comisión Nacional de los Derechos Humanos? In M. Carbonell & P. Salazar (Eds.), *La reforma constitucional de derechos humanos: Un nuevo paradigma* (pp. 313–337). Universidad Nacional Autónoma de México.

Carrubba, C. J. (2009). A model of the endogenous development of judicial institutions in federal and international systems. *Journal of Politics, 71*(01), 55–69. https://doi.org/10.1017/S002238160809004X

Cepeda-Espinosa, M. J. (2004). Judicial activism in a violent context: The origin, role, and impact of the Colombian Constitutional Court. *Washington University Global Studies Law Review, 3*(4), 529–700.

Cepeda-Espinosa, M. J. (2009). The constitutional protection of IDPs in Colombia. In R. Arango Rivadeneira (Ed.), *Judicial protection of internally displaced persons: The Colombian experience* (pp. 1–48). Brookings Institution—University of Bern, Project on Internal Displacement.

Chayes, A. (1976). The role of the judge in public law litigation. *Harvard Law Review, 89*(7), 1281–1316. https://doi.org/10.2307/1340256

Chigwedere, P., Seage, G. R., Gruskin, S., Lee, T.-H., & Essex, M. (2008). Estimating the lost benefits of antiretroviral drug use in South Africa. *JAIDS Journal of Acquired Immune Deficiency Syndromes, 49*(4), 410–415. https://doi.org/10.1097/QAI.0b013e31818a6cd5

Cichowski, R. A. (2004). Women's rights, the European Court, and supranational constitutionalism. *Law and Society Review, 38*(3), 489–512. https://doi.org/10.1111/j.0023-9216.2004.00055.x

Cichowski, R. A. (2006). Courts, rights, and democratic participation. *Comparative Political Studies, 39*(1), 50–75. https://doi.org/10.1177/0010414005283217

Cichowski, R. A., & Stone Sweet, A. (2006). Participation, representative democracy, and the courts. In B. E. Cain, R. J. Dalton, & S. E. Scarrow (Eds.), *Democracy transformed? Expanding political opportunities in advanced industrial democracies* (pp. 192–220). Oxford University Press.

Cifuentes Muñoz, E. (2002). Jurisdicción constitucional en Colombia. *Ius et Praxis, 8*(1), 283–317. https://doi.org/10.4067/S0718-00122002000100015

Colli Ek, V. M. (2012). Improving human rights in Mexico: Constitutional reforms, international standards, and new requirements for judges. *Human Rights Brief, 20*(1), 7–14.

Concha Cantú, H. A. (2006). The justice system: judiciary, military, and human rights. In L. Randall (Ed.), *Changing structure of Mexico: Political, social, and economic prospects* (2nd ed., pp. 361–383). M. E. Sharpe.

Cope, K. L., & Creamer, C. D. (2016). Disaggregating the human rights treaty regime. *Virginia Journal of International Law, 56*, 459.

Cope, K. L., Creamer, C. D., & Versteeg, M. (2019). Empirical studies of human rights law. *Annual Review of Law and Social Science, 15*(1), 155–182. https://doi.org/10.1146/annurev-lawsocsci-101317-031123

Cross, F. B. (2010). Judicial independence. In K. E. Whittington, R. D. Kelemen, & G. A. Caldeira (Eds.), *The Oxford handbook of law and politics* (pp. 557–575). Oxford University Press.

Dahl, R. A. (1957). Decision-making in a democracy: The Supreme Court as a national policy-maker. *Journal of Public Law, 6*(2), 279–295.

de Wet, E. (1996). *The constitutional enforceability of economic and social rights: The meaning of the German constitutional model for South Africa.* Buttersworth Publishers.

Delaney, E. F. (2016). Analyzing avoidance: Judicial strategy in comparative perspective. *Duke Law Journal, 66*(1), 1–67.

Dixon, R., & Issacharoff, S. (2016). Living to fight another day: Judicial deferral in defense of democracy. *Wisconsin Law Review, 2016*(4), 683–731. https://doi.org/10.2139/ssrn.2726045

Dixon, R., & Landau, D. (2015). Transnational constitutionalism and a limited doctrine of unconstitutional constitutional amendment. *International Journal of Constitutional Law, 13*(3), 606–638. https://doi.org/10.1093/icon/mov039

Domingo, P. (2000). Judicial independence: The politics of the Supreme Court in Mexico. *Journal of Latin American Studies, 32*(3), 705–735. https://doi.org/10.1017/S0022216X00005885

Du Plessis, M. (2013). The Geneva conventions and South African law (Institute for Security Studies Policy brief *43*).

Dugard, J. (2006). Court of first instance? Towards a pro-poor jurisdiction for the South African Constitutional Court. *South African Journal on Human Rights, 22*(2), 261–282. https://doi.org/10.1080/19962126.2006.11864890

Dugard, J. (2011). *International law: A South African perspective.* Juta.

Dugard, J. (2013). Courts and structural poverty in South Africa: To what extent has the Constitutional Court expanded access and remedies to the poor? In D. B. Maldonado (Ed.), *Constitutionalism of the Global South: The activist tribunals of India, South Africa, and Colombia* (pp. 293–327). Cambridge University Press.

Elkins, Z., Ginsburg, T., & Simmons, B. A. (2013). Getting to rights: Treaty ratification, constitutional convergence, and human rights practice. *Harvard International Law Journal, 54*(1), 61–95.

Epp, C. R. (1998). *The rights revolution: Lawyers, activists, and supreme courts in comparative perspective.* University of Chicago Press.

Epstein, L., Knight, J., & Martin, A. D. (2001). The Supreme Court as a strategic national policymaker. *Emory Law Journal, 50*, 583.

Epstein, L., Knight, J., & Shvetsova, O. (2001). The role of constitutional courts in the establishment and maintenance of democratic systems of government. *Law & Society Review, 35*(1), 117–164. https://doi.org/10.2307/3185388

Fallon, R. H. (2005). Legitimacy and the Constitution. *Harvard Law Review, 118*(6), 1787–1853.

Fassin, D., & Schneider, H. (2003). The politics of AIDS in South Africa: Beyond the controversies. *BMJ, 326*(7387), 495–497. https://doi.org/10.1136/bmj.326.7387.495

Felstiner, W. L. F., Abel, R. L., & Sarat, A. (1980). The emergence and transformation of disputes: Naming, blaming, claiming. . . . *Law & Society Review, 15(3/4)*, 631–654. https://doi.org/10.2307/3053505

Ferejohn, J. (2002). Judicializing politics, politicizing law. *Law and Contemporary Problems, 65*(3), 41–68. https://doi.org/10.2307/1192402

Finkel, J. (2003). Supreme Court decisions on electoral rules after Mexico's 1994 judicial reform: An empowered court. *Journal of Latin American Studies, 35*(4), 777–799. https://doi.org/10.1017/S0022216X03006989

Finkel, J. (2005). Judicial reform as insurance policy: Mexico in the 1990s. *Latin American Politics and Society, 47*(1), 87–113. https://doi.org/10.1111/j.1548-2456.2005.tb00302.x

Finnemore, M. (1996). *National interests in international society*. Cornell University Press.

Finnemore, M., & Sikkink, K. (1998). International norm dynamics and political change. *International Organization, 52*(4), 887–917. https://doi.org/10.1162/002081898550789

Fiss, O. M. (1993). The right degree of independence. In I. Stotzky (Ed.), *Transition to democracy in Latin America: The role of the judiciary*. Westview Press.

Fix-Fierro, H. (2003). Judicial reform in Mexico: What next? In E. Jensen & T. Heller (Eds.), *Beyond common knowledge: Empirical approaches to the rule of law* (pp. 240–289). Stanford Law and Politics.

Galanter, M. (1974). Why the "haves" come out ahead: Speculations on the limits of legal change. *Law & Society Review, 9*(1), 95–160.

Garavito, R. G., & Franco, D. R. (2010). *Cortes y cambio social: Cómo la Corte Constitucional transformó el desplazamiento forzado en Colombia*. Centro de Estudios de Derecho, Justicia y Sociedad, Dejusticia.

Gauri, V., & Brinks, D. M. (Eds.). (2008). *Courting social justice: Judicial enforcement of social and economic rights in the developing world*. Cambridge University Press. https://doi.org/10.1017/CBO9780511511240

George, A. L., & Bennett, A. (2005). *Case studies and theory development in the social sciences*. MIT Press.

Gewirtzman, D. (2011). Lower court constitutionalism: Circuit court discretion in a complex adaptive system. *American University Law Review, 61*(3), 457–522.

Gibson, J. L. (2008). The evolving legitimacy of the South African Constitutional Court. In F. Du Bois & A. Du Bois-Pedain (Eds.), *Justice and reconciliation in post-Apartheid South Africa* (pp. 229–266). Cambridge University Press.

Gibson, J. L. (2012). *Electing judges: The surprising effects of campaigning on judicial legitimacy*. University of Chicago Press.

Gibson, J. L., & Caldeira, G. A. (1995). The legitimacy of transnational legal institutions: Compliance, support, and the European Court of Justice. *American Journal of Political Science, 39*(2), 459–489. https://doi.org/10.2307/2111621

Gibson, J. L., & Caldeira, G. A. (2003). Defenders of democracy? Legitimacy, popular acceptance, and the South African Constitutional Court. *Journal of Politics*, *65*(1), 1–30. https://doi.org/10.1111/1468-2508.t01-1-00001

Gibson, J. L., Caldeira, G. A., & Baird, V. A. (1998). On the legitimacy of national high courts. *American Political Science Review*, *92*(2), 343–358. https://doi.org/10.2307/2585668

Giménez, F. P. (2014). Las reformas en materia de derechos fundamentales. In M. A. Casar & I. Marván (Eds.), *Reformar sin mayorías. La dinámica del cambio constitucional en México: 1997–2012* (pp. 130–222). Santillana Ediciones.

Ginsburg, T. (2003). *Judicial review in new democracies: Constitutional courts in Asian cases*. Cambridge University Press.

Ginsburg, T. (2006). Locking in democracy: Constitutions, commitment and international law. *University of Illinois Law and Economics Working Papers*, Working Paper 55. https://law.bepress.com/uiuclwps/art55/

Ginsburg, T., Chernykh, S., & Elkins, Z. (2008). Commitment and diffusion: How and why national constitutions incorporate international law. *University of Illinois Law Review*, *2008*(1), 201–237.

Gloppen, S., Wilson, B. M., Gargarella, R., Skaar, E., & Kinander, M. (2010). *Courts and power in Latin America and Africa*. Palgrave Macmillan.

González Galván, J. A. (2003a). La corte y los indígenas. *Boletín Mexicano de derecho comparado*, *36*(107), 725–33.

González Galván, J. A. (2003b). Los derechos de los pueblos indígenas en la Constitución mexicana. In Tribunal Electoral del Poder Judicial de la Federación (México), *Derechos indígenas y elecciones* (pp. 50–69). Tribunal Electoral del Poder Judicial de la Federación.

Goodman, R., & Jinks, D. (2003). Toward an institutional theory of sovereignty. *Stanford Law Review*, *55*, 1749–1788.

Goodman, R., & Jinks, D. (2004). How to influence states: Socialization and international human rights law. *Duke Law Journal*, *54*(3), 621–703.

Guerrero Lara, E. (1982). *Manual para el manejo del Semanario Judicial de La Federación*. Universidad Nacional Autónoma de México.

Hafner-Burton, E. M. (2008). Sticks and stones: Naming and shaming the human rights enforcement problem. *International Organization*, *62*(04), 689–716. https://doi.org/10.1017/S0020818308080247

Hafner-Burton, E. M. (2012). International regimes for human rights. *Annual Review of Political Science*, *15*(1), 265–286. https://doi.org/10.1146/annurev-polisci-031710-114414

Hafner-Burton, E. M., Helfer, L. R., & Fariss, C. J. (2011). Emergency and escape: Explaining derogations from human rights treaties. *International Organization*, *65*(04), 673–707. https://doi.org/10.1017/S002081831100021X

Hamilton, A. (2008). Federalist no. 78. In L. Goldman (Ed.), *The Federalist papers*. Oxford University Press.

Hart, H. L. A. (1997). *The concept of law* (2nd ed.). Oxford University Press.

Hathaway, O. A. (2005). Between power and principle: An integrated theory of international law. *University of Chicago Law Review, 72*(2), 469–536.

Hathaway, O. A. (2007). Why do countries commit to human rights treaties? *Journal of Conflict Resolution, 51*(4), 588–621. https://doi.org/10.1177/0022002707303046

Henry, L. (1929). When is a treaty self-executing. *Michigan Law Review, 27*, 776. https://doi.org/10.2307/1280325

Heyns, C., & Viljoen, F. (2001). The impact of the United Nations human rights treaties on the domestic level. *Human Rights Quarterly, 23*(3), 483–535. https://doi.org/10.1353/hrq.2001.0036

Heyns, C., & Viljoen, F. (2002a). The impact of six major UN human rights treaties in South Africa. *SA Publiekreg/SA Public Law, 16*(1), 28–67.

Heyns, C., & Viljoen, F. (2002b). *The impact of the United Nations human rights treaties on the domestic level.* Kluwer Law International.

Heywood, M. (2003). Preventing mother-to-child HIV transmission in South Africa: Background, strategies and outcomes of the Treatment Action Campaign case against the Minister of Health: Current developments. *South African Journal on Human Rights, 19*(2), 278–315. https://doi.org/10.1080/19962126.2003.11865183

Heywood, M. (2005). Shaping, making and breaking the law in TAC's campaign for a national treatment plan. In P. Jones & K. Stokke, *Democratising development: The politics of socio-economic rights in South Africa: [Proceedings]*. Martinus Nijhoff.

Heywood, M. (2009). South Africa's Treatment Action Campaign: Combining law and social mobilization to realize the right to health. *Journal of Human Rights Practice, 1*(1), 14–36. https://doi.org/10.1093/jhuman/hun006

Heywood, M., & Hassim, A. (2008). Remedying the maladies of "lesser men or women": The personal, political and constitutional imperatives for improved access to justice. *South African Journal on Human Rights, 24*(2), 263–280. https://doi.org/10.1080/19962126.2008.11864955

Hirschl, R. (2000). The political origins of judicial empowerment through constitutionalization: Lessons from four constitutional revolutions. *Law & Social Inquiry, 25*(1), 91–149. https://doi.org/10.1111/j.1747-4469.2000.tb00152.x

Hirschl, R. (2007). *Towards juristocracy: The origins and consequences of the new constitutionalism*. Harvard University Press.

Hirschl, R. (2008). The judicialization of mega-politics and the rise of political courts. *Annual Review of Political Science, 11*(1), 93–118. https://doi.org/10.1146/annurev.polisci.11.053006.183906

Human Rights Watch. 1994. Human Rights Watch world report 1995: Events of 1994. Human Rights Watch.

Human Rights Watch. 1995. Human Rights Watch world report 1996: Events of 1995. Human Rights Watch.

Human Rights Watch. 1997. Human Rights Watch world report 1998: Events of 1997. Human Rights Watch.

Human Rights Watch. 1998. Human Rights Watch world report 1999: Events of 1998. Human Rights Watch.

Huneeus, A. (2010). Judging from a guilty conscience: The Chilean judiciary's human rights turn. *Law & Social Inquiry, 35*(1), 99–135. https://doi.org/10.1111/j.1747-4469.2009.01179.x

Johnston, A. I. (2001). Treating international institutions as social environments. *International Studies Quarterly, 45*(4), 487–515. https://doi.org/10.1111/0020-8833.00212

Kapiszewski, D., Silverstein, G., & Kagan, R. A. (Eds.). (2013). *Consequential courts: Judicial roles in global perspective*. Cambridge University Press. https://doi.org/10.1017/CBO9781139207843

Kapiszewski, D., & Taylor, M. M. (2008). Doing courts justice? Studying judicial politics in Latin America. *Perspectives on Politics, 6*(4), 741. https://doi.org/10.1017/S1537592708081899

Kelsen, H. (1961). *General theory of law and state*. Russell and Russell.

Kendall, C. (2020). Avoiding international human rights law in the pursuit of peace. In A. Sarat (Ed.), *Studies in law, politics, and society* (Vol. 82, pp. 55–91). Emerald Publishing.

Keohane, R. O., Macedo, S., & Moravcsik, A. (2009). Democracy-enhancing multilateralism. *International Organization, 63*, 1–31 https://doi.org/10.1017/S0020818309090018.

Keohane, R. O., Moravcsik, A., & Slaughter, A.-M. (2000). Legalized dispute resolution: Interstate and transnational. *International Organization, 54*(3), 457–488. https://doi.org/10.1162/002081800551299

Killander, M. (2010). Judicial immunity, compensation for unlawful detention and the elusive self-executing treaty provision: *Claassen v Minister of Justice and Constitutional Development* 2010 (6) SA 399 (WCC). *South African Journal of Human Rights, 26*, 386–394. https://doi.org/10.1080/19962126.2010.11864995

Kinney, E. D., & Clark, B. A. (2004). Provisions for health and health care in the constitutions of the countries of the world. *Cornell International Law Journal, 37*, 285–355.

Knop, K. (2000). Here and there: international law in domestic courts. *New York University Journal of International Law and Politics, 32*, 501–535.

Koh, H. H. (1997). Review: Why do nations obey international law? *Yale Law Journal, 106*(8), 2599–2659. https://doi.org/10.2307/797228

Kyle, B. J., & Reiter, A. G. (2013). Militarized justice in new democracies: Explaining the process of military court reform in Latin America. *Law & Society Review, 47*(2), 375–407. https://doi.org/10.1111/lasr.12019

Landau, D. (2005). The two discourses in Colombian constitutional jurisprudence: A new approach to modeling judicial behavior in Latin America. *George Washington International Law Review, 37*, 687.

Landau, D. (2018). Courts and support structures: Beyond the classic narrative. In E. F. Delaney & R. Dixon (Eds.), *Comparative Judicial Review*. Edward Elgar Publishing.

Landes, W. M., & Posner, R. A. (1975). The independent judiciary in an interest-group perspective. *Journal of Law and Economics, 18*(3), 875–901. https://doi.org/10.1086/466849

Law, D. S., & Chang, W.-C. (2011). The limits of global judicial dialogue. *Washington Law Review, 86*(3), 523–577.

Lieberman, E. S. (2001). National political community and the politics of income taxation in Brazil and South Africa in the twentieth century. *Politics & Society, 29*(4), 515–555. https://doi.org/10.1177/0032329201029004003

Lindau, J. D. (2011). The drug war's impact on executive power, judicial reform, and federalism in Mexico. *Political Science Quarterly, 126*(2), 177–200. https://doi.org/10.1002/j.1538-165X.2011.tb00698.x

Lupu, Y. (2013). Best evidence: The role of information in domestic judicial enforcement of international human rights agreements. *International Organization, 67(3), 469–503. https://www.doi.org/10.1017/S002081831300012X.*

Magaloni, B. (2003). Authoritarianism, democracy and the Supreme Court: Horizontal exchange and the rule of law in Mexico. In S. Mainwaring & C. Welna (Eds.), *Democratic accountability in Latin America* (pp. 266–305). Oxford University Press.

Makgoba, M. W. (2000). HIV/AIDS: The peril of pseudoscience. *Science, 288*(5469), 1171. https://doi.org/10.1126/science.288.5469.1171

Marshall, M. G., Gurr, T. R., & Jaggers, K. (2009). *Polity IV Project: Political regime characteristics and transitions, 1800–2009: Dataset users' manual.* Center for Systemic Peace.

Martz, J. D. (1997). *The politics of clientelism: Democracy and the state in Colombia.* Transaction Publishers.

Maveety, N., & Grosskopf, A. (2004). "Constrained" constitutional courts as conduits for democratic consolidation. *Law & Society Review, 38*(3), 463–488. https://doi.org/10.1111/j.0023-9216.2004.00054.x

Meierhenrich, J. (2008). *The legacies of law: Long-run consequences of legal development in South Africa, 1652–2000.* Cambridge University Press.

Merryman, J. H., & Pérez-Perdomo, R. (2007). *The civil law tradition.* Stanford University Press.

Michel, V. (2018). *Prosecutorial accountability and victims' rights in Latin America.* Cambridge University Press; Cambridge Core. https://doi.org/10.1017/9781108380034

Molinar Horcasitas, J., & Weldon, J. A. (2001). Reforming electoral systems in Mexico. In M. Shugart & M. P. Wattenberg (Eds.), *Mixed-member electoral systems: The best of both worlds?* (pp. 209–230). Oxford University Press.

Montoya García, A. M. (2011). *"Si no vas al Senado no te eligen magistrado": La elección de los magistrados de la Corte Constitucional colombiana en el Senado 1992–2009.* Universidad de los Andes.

Moravcsik, A. (1995). Explaining international human rights regimes: Liberal theory and Western Europe. *European Journal of International Relations, 1*(2), 157–189. https://doi.org/10.1177/1354066195001002002

Moravcsik, A. (2000). The origins of human rights regimes: Democratic delegation in postwar Europe. *International Organization, 54*(2), 217–252. https://doi.org/10.1162/002081800551163

Morineau, M. (1997). Aguas Blancas, estudio de un caso de aplicación del segundo párrafo del Artículo 97 de la Constitución Política de los Estados Unidos Mexicanos. *Boletín Mexicano de derecho comparado, 30*(89), 795–811.

Mtshaulana, P. M. (2001). The history and role of the Constitutional Court in South Africa. In P. Andrews & S. Ellmann (Eds.), *The post-Apartheid constitutions: Perspectives on South Africa's basic law* (pp. 525–555). Witwatersrand University Press.

Nagle, L. E. (1995). Evolution of the Colombian judiciary and the Constitutional Court. *Indiana International and Comparative Law Review, 6*, 59.

Olaiz-González, J., & Bosco López, J. (2011). El rol del juez en la adjudicación de los derechos individuales de incidencia colectiva: Una oportunidad para el litigio estructural en México. In M. González Oropeza & E. Ferrer Mac-Gregor (Eds.), *El juicio de amparo. A 160 años de la primera sentencia, tomo II* (pp. 165–189). Universidad Nacional Autónoma de México.

Olivier, M. (1993). The status of international law in South African municipal law: Section 231 of the 1993 constitution. *South African Yearbook of International Law, 19*, 1–13.

Oseguera, S. I. (2009). Judicial reform in Mexico: Political insurance or the search for political legitimacy? *Political Research Quarterly, 62*(4), 753–766. https://doi.org/10.1177/1065912909346740

Paust, J. J. (1988). Self-executing treaties. *American Journal of International Law, 82*(4), 760–783. https://doi.org/10.2307/2203511

Pérez-Hurtado, L. F. (2009). *La futura generación de abogados mexicanos: Estudio de las escuelas y los estudiantes de derecho en México*. Universidad Nacional Autónoma de México, Instituto de Investigaciones Jurídicas.

Pérez Hurtado, L. F. (2010). Content, structure, and growth of Mexican legal education. *Journal of Legal Education, 59*(4), 567–597.

Pevehouse, J. C. (2002). Democracy from the outside-in? International organizations and democratization. *International Organization, 56*(3), 515–549. https://doi.org/10.1162/002081802760199872

Pulitano, E. (2012). *Indigenous rights in the age of the UN declaration*. Cambridge University Press.

Ramirez, A. (2006). Mexico. In G. Hall & H. A. Patrinos (Eds.), *Indigenous peoples, poverty and human development in Latin America* (pp. 150–198). World Bank.

Ramseyer, M. (1994). The puzzling (in)dependence of courts: A comparative approach. *Journal of Legal Studies, 23*, 721–747. https://doi.org/10.1086/467943

Reisman, W. M. (1995). Protecting indigenous rights in international adjudication. *American Journal of International Law, 89*(2), 350–362. https://doi.org/10.2307/2204207

Reyes Reyes, P. E. (2003). La facultad indagatoria de la Suprema Corte de Justicia de la Nación: Una revisión. *Cuestiones constitucionales, 1*(8). https://doi.org/10.22201/iij.24484881e.2003.8.5665

Richardson, H. J., III (2007). Patrolling the resource transfer frontier: Economic rights and the South African Constitutional Court's contributions to international justice. *African Studies Quarterly, 9*(4), 81–106.

Ríos-Figueroa, J. (2007). Fragmentation of power and the emergence of an effective judiciary in Mexico, 1994–2002. *Latin American Politics and Society, 49*(1), 31–57.

Ríos-Figueroa, J., & Staton, J. K. (2009). Unpacking the rule of law: A review of judicial independence measures. *CELS 2009 4th Annual Conference on Empirical Legal Studies Paper.* http://dx.doi.org/10.2139/ssrn.1434234

Risse, T., Ropp, S. C., & Sikkink, K. (Eds.). (1999). *The power of human rights: International norms and domestic change.* Cambridge University Press.

Roach, K., & Budlender, G. (2005). Mandatory relief and supervisory jurisdiction: When is it appropriate, just and equitable? *South African Law Journal, 122*(2), 325–351.

Rodríguez-Garavito, C. (2011). Beyond the courtroom: The impact of judicial activism on socioeconomic rights in Latin America. *Texas, 89*(7), 1669–1698.

Rodríguez-Raga, J. C. (2011). Strategic deference in the Colombian Constitutional Court, 1992–2006. In G. Helmke & J. Ríos-Figueroa (Eds.), *Courts in Latin America* (pp. 81–97). Cambridge University Press.

Roux, T. (2003). Legitimating transformation: Political resource allocation in the South African constitutional court. *Democratization, 10*(4), 92–111. https://doi.org/10.1080/13510340312331294047

Roux, T. (2009). Principle and pragmatism on the Constitutional Court of South Africa. *International Journal of Constitutional Law, 7*(1), 106–138. https://doi.org/10.1093/icon/mon029

Roux, T. (2013). *The politics of principle: The first South African Constitutional Court, 1995–2005.* Cambridge University Press. https://www.cambridge.org/core/books/politics-of-principle/C6625CF7F3EBE07DD6294A18E427429E

Roux, T. (2018). *The politico-legal dynamics of judicial review: A comparative analysis.* Cambridge University Press.

Roy, B. (2004). An empirical survey of foreign jurisprudence and international instruments in charter litigation. *University of Toronto Faculty of Law Review, 62*(2), 99–143.

Roznai, Y. (2017). *Unconstitutional constitutional amendments: The limits of amendment powers.* Oxford University Press.

Rubio, L., Magaloni, B., & Jaime, E. (2000). *A la puerta de la ley.* Cal y Arena.

Sánchez-Mejía, A. L. (2017). *Victims' rights in flux: Criminal justice reform in Colombia* (Vol. 62). Springer. http://www.springer.com/series/7888

Scheppele, K. L. (2002). Declarations of independence: judicial reactions to political pressure. In S. B. Burbank & B. Friedman (Eds.), *Judicial independence at the crossroads: An interdisciplinary approach* (pp. 227–279). Sage Publications.

Scheppele, K. L. (2003). Aspirational and aversive constitutionalism: The case for studying cross-constitutional influence through negative models. *International Journal of Constitutional Law*, *1*(2), 296. https://doi.org/10.1093/icon/1.2.296

Schor, M. (2009). An essay on the emergence of constitutional courts: The cases of Mexico and Colombia. *Indiana Journal of Global Legal Studies*, *16*(1), 173–194.

Segal, J. A. (2010). Judicial behavior. In K. E. Whittington, R. D. Kelemen, & G. A. Caldeira (Eds.), *The Oxford handbook of law and politics*. Oxford University Press.

Segal, J. A., & Spaeth, H. J. (2002). *The Supreme Court and the attitudinal model revisited*. Cambridge University Press.

Semanario Judicial de la Federación y Su Gaceta. Décima Época, Libro III, Tomo 1, Diciembre de 2011.

Shapiro, M. (1986). *Courts: A comparative and political analysis*. University of Chicago Press.

Shapiro, M., & Stone Sweet, A. (2002). *On law, politics, and judicialization*. Oxford University Press.

Sikkink, K. (2011). *The justice cascade: How human rights prosecutions are changing world politics*. W. W. Norton and Company.

Simmons, B. A. (2009). *Mobilizing for human rights: International law in domestic politics*. Cambridge University Press.

Slaughter, A.-M. (2004). *A new world order*. Princeton University Press.

Slaughter, A.-M., & Alvarez, J. E. (2000). A liberal theory of international law. *Proceedings of the Annual Meeting (American Society of International Law)*, *94*, 240–253.

Slaughter, A.-M., & Burke-White, W. (2006). The future of international law is domestic (or, the European way of law). *Harvard International Law Journal*, *47*, 327.

Sloss, D. (1999). The domestication of international human rights: Non-self-executing declarations and human rights treaties. *Yale Journal of International Law*, *24*, 129.

Sloss, D. (2009). *The role of domestic courts in treaty enforcement: A comparative study*. Cambridge University Press.

Sloss, D. L. (2020). Domestic application of treaties. In D. B. Hollis (Ed.), *The Oxford guide to treaties* (2nd ed., pp. 355–382). Oxford University Press.

Smith, R. M. (2010). Historical institutionalism and the study of law. In K. E. Whittington, R. D. Kelemen, & G. A. Caldeira (Eds.), *The Oxford handbook of law and politics*. Oxford University Press,.

Smithey, S. I. (2001). A tool, not a master: The use of foreign case law in Canada and South Africa. *Comparative Political Studies*, *34*(10), 1188–1211. https://doi.org/10.1177/0010414001034010004

Staszak, S. (2010). Institutions, rulemaking, and the politics of judicial retrenchment. *Studies in American Political Development*, *24*(2), 168–189. https://doi.org/10.1017/S0898588X10000040

Staton, J. K. (2006). Constitutional review and the selective promotion of case results. *American Journal of Political Science*, *50*(1), 98–112. https://doi.org/10.1111/j.1540-5907.2006.00172.x

Staton, J. K. (2010). *Judicial power and strategic communication in Mexico*. Cambridge University Press.

Staton, J. K., & Moore, W. H. (2011). Judicial power in domestic and international politics. *International Organization*, *65*(3), 553–587. https://doi.org/10.1017/S0020818311000130

Stein, E. (1981). Lawyers, judges, and the making of a transnational constitution. *American Journal of International Law*, *75*(2), 1–27. https://doi.org/10.2307/2201413

Stephenson, M. C. (2003). "When the devil turns . . .": The political foundations of independent judicial review. *Journal of Legal Studies*, *32*(1), 59–89. https://doi.org/10.1086/342038

Stone Sweet, A. (2000). *Governing with judges: Constitutional politics in Europe*. Oxford University Press.

Suárez Ávila, A. A. (2012). The Mexican Supreme Court as a protector of human rights. *Mexican Law Review*, *4*(2), 239–260.

Swepston, L. (1990). A new step in the international law on indigenous and tribal peoples: ILO Convention No. 169 of 1989. *Oklahoma City University Law Review*, *15*, 677.

Tate, C. N., & Vallinder, T. (Eds.). (1995). *The global expansion of judicial power*. NYU Press.

Teles, S. M. (2012). *The rise of the conservative legal movement: The battle for control of the law*. Princeton University Press.

Thompson, L. M. (2001). *A History of South Africa*. Yale University Press.

Tushnet, M. (2009). The inevitable globalization of constitutional law. *Virginia Journal of International Law*, *49*(4), 985.

Ugalde, L. C. (2001). The transformation of Mexican presidentialism, 1929–2000. *Fletcher Forum of World Affairs*, *25*, 115.

Uprimny, R. (2007). Judicialization of politics in Colombia: Cases, merits and risks (B. Whiteoak, Trans.). *Sur. revista internacional de direitos humanos*, *4*(6), 48–65. https://doi.org/10.1590/S1806-64452007000100004

Uprimny, R. (2011). The recent transformation of constitutional law in Latin America: Trends and challenges. *University of Texas Law Review*, *89*(7), 1587–1610.

Vanberg, G. (2005). *The politics of constitutional review in Germany*. Cambridge University Press.

Vargas, J. A. (1995). Mexico's legal revolution: An appraisal of its recent constitutional changes, 1988–1995. *Georgia Journal of International and Comparative Law*, *25*, 497.

Vargas, J. A. (1996). Rebirth of the Supreme Court of Mexico: An appraisal of President Zedillo's judicial reform of 1995. *American University Journal of International Law and Policy*, *11*, 295.

Vargas, J. A. (2009). *Mexican law for the American lawyer*. Carolina Academic Press.

Vidal-López, R. (2012). *Truth-telling and internal displacement in Colombia*. International Center for Transitional Justice.

von Stein, J. (2016). Making promises, keeping promises: Democracy, ratification and compliance in international human rights law. *British Journal of Political*

Science; Cambridge, *46*(3), 655–679. http://dx.doi.org.ezproxy.ups.edu/10.1017/S0007123414000489

Waters, M. A. (2007). Creeping monism: The judicial trend toward interpretive incorporation of human rights treaties. *Columbia Law Review*, *107*, 628–705.

Weber, M. (1978). Types of legitimate domination. In *Economy and Society* (Vol. 1, pp. 212–245). University of California Press.

Weldon, J. A. (1997). Political sources of *presidencialismo* in Mexico. In S. Mainwaring & M. S. Shugart (Eds.), *Presidentialism and democracy in Latin America* (pp. 225–258). Cambridge University Press.

Weldon, J. A. (2001). The consequences of Mexico's mixed-member electoral system, 1988–1997. In M. Shugart & M. P. Wattenberg, *Mixed-member electoral systems: The best of both worlds?* (pp. 447–476). Oxford University Press.

Wendt, A. (1992). Anarchy is what states make of it: The social construction of power politics. *International Organization*, *46*(2), 391–425. https://doi.org/10.1017/S0020818300027764

Whittington, K. E., Kelemen, R. D., & Caldeira, G. A. (2010). The study of law and politics. In K. E. Whittington, R. D. Kelemen, & G. A. Caldeira (Eds.), *The Oxford handbook of law and politics*. Oxford University Press.

Woolman, S., & Swanepoel, J. (2008). The Interim Constitution, the Constitutional Assembly, 34 Constitutional Principles and the certification of the Final Constitution. In S. Woolman, T. Roux, & M. Bishop (Eds.), *Constitutional law of South Africa* (2nd ed., § 2.5). Juta.

Yashar, D. J. (2005). *Contesting citizenship in Latin America: The rise of indigenous movements and the postliberal challenge*. Cambridge University Press.

Young, K. G. (2019). Waiting for rights: Progressive realization and lost time. In K. G. Young (Ed.), *The future of economic and social rights* (pp. 654–683). Cambridge University Press. https://doi.org/10.1017/9781108284653

Zamora, S. (2004). *Mexican law*. Oxford University Press.

Legal Sources Cited

Colombia

CONSTITUTIONAL PROVISIONS

Political Constitution of Colombia (1991), Articles 86, 91, 173, 214(2), 214(6), 221, 234–257, 278(5), 282(3).

CASES

Colombian Constitutional Court, Decision C-047/06 (February 1, 2006).

Colombian Constitutional Court, Decision C-141/95 (March 29, 1995).

Colombian Constitutional Court, Decision C-225/95 (May 18, 1995).
Colombian Constitutional Court, Decision C-228/02 (April 3, 2002).
Colombian Constitutional Court, Decision C-358/97 (August 5, 1997).
Colombian Constitutional Court, Decision C-454/06 (June 7, 2006).
Colombian Constitutional Court, Decision C-590/05 (June 8, 2005).
Colombian Constitutional Court, Decision C-591/05 (June 9, 2005).
Colombian Constitutional Court, Decision T-025/04 (January 22, 2004).
Colombian Constitutional Court, Decision T-318/04 (May 4, 2011).
Colombian Constitutional Court, Decision T-426/92 (June 24, 1992).
Colombian Constitutional Court, Decision T-760/08 (July 31, 2008).
Colombian Constitutional Court, Order 004/09 (January 26, 2009).
Colombian Constitutional Court, Order 005/09 (January 26, 2009).
Colombian Constitutional Court, Order 006/09 (January 26, 2009).
Colombian Constitutional Court, Order 095/10 (May 21, 1995).
Colombian Constitutional Court, Order 109/07 (April 5, 2007).
Colombian Constitutional Court, Order 116/08 (May 13, 2008).
Colombian Constitutional Court, Order 176/05 (August 29, 2005).
Colombian Constitutional Court, Order 177/05 (August 29, 2005).
Colombian Constitutional Court, Order 178/05 (August 29, 2005).
Colombian Constitutional Court, Order 185/04 (December 10, 2004).
Colombian Constitutional Court, Order 200/07 (August 13, 2007).
Colombian Constitutional Court, Order 237/08 (September 19, 2008).
Colombian Constitutional Court, Order 251/08 (October 6, 2008).

STATUTES AND STATUTORY PROVISIONS

Decree 1382 of 2000 (July 12), Colombia, Diario Oficial No. 44.082, de 14 de julio de 2000.
Decree 250 of 2005 (February 7), Diario Oficial No. 45.816, de 8 de febrero de 2005.
Decree 2591 of 1991 (November 19), Diario Oficial No. 40.165, de 19 de noviembre de 1991.
Decree 290 of 1999 (February 17), Diario Oficial No. 43.507, de 22 de febrero de 1999.
Law 1190 of 2008 (April 30), Diario Oficial No. 46.976, de 30 de abril de 2008.
Law 387 of 1997 (July 18), Diario Oficial No. 43.091, de 24 de julio de 1997.
Law 906 of 2004 (August 31), Diario Oficial No. 45.657, de 31 de agosto de 2004.

South Africa

CONSTITUTIONAL PROVISIONS

Constitution of the Republic of South Africa Act, No. 200 of 1993 (the "Interim Constitution"): §4, §§7–35 (Chapter 3, "Fundamental Rights"), §98(2)(d), §98(9), §231(3), and Schedule 4 ("Constitutional Principles").

Constitution of the Republic of South Africa Act, No. 108 of 1996, as adopted on May 8, 1996, and amended on October 11, 1996, by the Constitutional Assembly (the "Final Constitution"): §2, §§7–39 (Chapter 2, "Bill of Rights"), §7(2), §8(3)(a), §12(1)(a), §27, §§30–31, §38, §39, §74(2), §74(3), §76(1)(e), §76(1)(i), §76(1)(j), §76(5)(b)(ii), §79(4), §80(2)(a), §80(3), §167(3)(c), §167(4)(d), §167(5), §167(6), §171, §172(1)(a), §231(4), §232, §233, and §237.

CASES

Azanian Peoples Organization (AZAPO) and Others v President of the Republic of South Africa and Others, 1996 (8) BCLR 1015 (CC).

Carmichele v Minister of Safety and Security, 2001 (10) BCLR 995 (CC).

Certification of the Amended Text of the Constitution of the Republic of South Africa, 1997 (1) BCLR 1 (CC) (the *Second Certification Case*).

Certification of the Constitution of the Republic of South Africa, 1996 (10) BCLR 1253 (CC) (the *First Certification Case*).

Claassen v Minister of Justice and Constitutional Development, [2010] 4 All SA 197 (WCC) (December 8, 2009).

Fose v Minister of Safety and Security, 1997 (7) BCLR 851 (CC).

Government of the Republic of South Africa and Others v Grootboom, 2000 (11) BCLR 1169 (CC).

Government of the Republic of Zimbabwe v Fick and Others, 2013 (10) BCLR 1103 (CC).

In re: Gauteng School Education Bill of 1995, 1996 (4) BCLR 537 (CC).

In re: National Education Policy Bill No 83 of 1995, 1996 (4) BCLR 518 (CC).

Mazibuko and Others v City of Johannesburg and Others, 2010 (3) BCLR 239 (CC).

Minister of Health and Others v Treatment Action Campaign and Others (No 1), 2002 (10) BCLR 1075 (CC) (*TAC 1*).

Minister of Health and Others v Treatment Action Campaign and Others (No. 2), 2002 (10) BCLR 1033 (CC) (*TAC 2*).

Pharmaceutical Manufacturers Association of South Africa and Another: In re Ex Parte President of the Republic of South Africa and Others, 2000 (3) BCLR 241 (CC).

President of the Republic of South Africa and Others v Quagliani, President of the Republic of South Africa and Others v Van Rooyen and Another; Goodwin v Director-General, Department of Justice and Constitutional Development and Others, 2009 (4) BCLR 345 (CC).

S v Makwanyane and Another, 1995 (6) BCLR 665 (CC).

S v Williams and Others, 1995 (7) BCLR 861 (CC).

TAC v Minister of Health/MECS, March 11, 2002 (Execution Order) [2002] ZAGPHC 3 (High Court of South Africa, Transvaal Provincial Division).

Treatment Action Campaign and Others v Minister of Health and Others, Case No. 21182/2001 (High Court of South Africa, Transvaal Provincial Division) (*TAC HC*).

Zealand v Minister for Justice and Constitutional Development and Another, 2008 (6) BCLR 601 (CC).

STATUTES AND STATUTORY PROVISIONS

Abolition of Corporal Punishment Act, No. 33 of 1997, Gazette No. 18256, September 5, 1997.

Act to Amend the Constitution of the Republic of South Africa, 1996, No. 34 of 2001, Gazette No. 22853, November 21, 2001, §11.

African Charter on Human and Peoples' Rights (Banjul Charter), §16(1)–(2).

Constitutional Court Complementary Act Amendment Act, No. 79 of 1997, Gazette No. 18495, December 5, 1997.

Criminal Procedure Act, No. 51 of 1977, §294.

National Prosecuting Authority Act, No. 32 of 1998, Gazette No. 19021, July 3, 1998.

Promotion of National Unity and Reconciliation Act, No. 34 of 1995, Gazette No. 16579, July 26, 1995.

Mexico

CONSTITUTIONAL PROVISIONS

Political Constitution of the United Mexican States (with years where relevant), Articles 2 [2001], 2(A) [2001], 14, 29 ¶5 [2011], 50–54, 56, 94 [1994], 96 [1994], 97 ¶2 [pre-2011], 97 ¶3 [pre-2011], 105(2)(g) [2011], 105(I), 105(II) [1994], 105(II) [1996], 105(V) [1994], 107, 107(I) [2011], 107(II) ¶2 [2011], 107(II) ¶3 [2011], 107(IX), 107(X) ¶1, 107(XII) ¶2, 133, 135.

CASES

Amparo en revisión 1475/98. Sindicato Nacional de Controladores de Tránsito Aéreo. 11 de mayo de 1999. Unanimidad de diez votos. Ausente: José Vicente Aguinaco Alemán. Ponente: Humberto Román Palacios. Secretario: Antonio Espinoza Rangel.

Amparo en revisión 160/81. National Research Development Corporation. 16 de julio de 1981. Unanimidad de votos. Ponente: Sergio Hugo Chapital Gutiérrez.

Amparo en revisión 2069/91. Manuel García Martínez. 30 de junio de 1992. Mayoría de quince votos. Ponente: Victoria Adato Green. Secretario: Sergio Pallares y Lara.

Amparo en revisión 256/81. C. H. Boehringer Sohn. 9 de julio de 1981. Unanimidad de votos. Ponente: Genaro David Góngora Pimentel.

Amparo en revisión 269/81. José Ernesto Matsumoto Matsuy. 14 de julio de 1981. Unanimidad de votos. Ponente: Samuel Hernández Viazcán.

Case of Radilla Pacheco v. Mexico. Preliminary Objections, Merits, Reparations, and Costs. Judgment of November 23, 2009. Inter-American Court of Human Rights Series C No. 209.

Case of Fernández Ortega et al. v. Mexico. Preliminary Objection, Merits, Reparations, and Costs. Judgment of August 30, 2010. Inter-American Court of Human Rights Series C No. 215.

Case of Rosendo-Cantú and other v. Mexico. Preliminary Objection, Merits, Reparations, and Costs. Judgment of August 31, 2010. Inter-American Court of Human Rights Series C No. 216.
Case of Cabrera García and Montiel-Flores v. Mexico. Preliminary Objection, Merits, Reparations, and Legal Costs. Judgment of November 26, 2010. Inter-American Court of Human Rights Series C No. 220.
Ejecutoria CC 82/2001.
Expediente "Varios" 451/95.
Expediente 489/2010.
Expediente 912/2010.
Expediente 38/2012.
Expediente 133/2012.
Expediente Relativo al Recurso de Apelación Atraído 1/2004–PS.
Facultad de Investigación 1/2009.
Semanario Judicial de la Federación y su Gaceta, Novena Época, Tomo XVI, septiembre de 2002, página 1136, Pleno, tesis P./J. 39/2002.
Semanario Judicial de la Federación y su Gaceta, Novena Época, Tomo XVI, septiembre de 2002, página 997, Pleno, tesis P./J. 40/2002.
Solicitud de ejercicio de la facultad de investigación 1/2009.
Solicitud de facultad de atracción 8/2004–PS.
Solicitud numero 3/96 relativa a la petición del presidente de la republica para que se ejerza la facultad prevista en el segundo párrafo del articulo 97 constitucional, 4 de mayo de 1996.
Tesis 193781, *Semanario Judicial de la Federación y su Gaceta*, Novena Época, p. 10 (Tesis P. XLVII/99).
Tesis 199251, *Semanario Judicial de la Federación y su Gaceta*, Novena Época, p. 655 (Tesis P. XLIV/97).

STATUTES AND STATUTORY PROVISIONS

Ley de amparo, reglamentaria de los artículos 103 y 107 de la Constitución política de los Estados Unidos Mexicanos.
Ley Orgánica del Poder Judicial de la Federación.

INDEX

Figures and tables are indicated by page numbers followed by *fig.* and *tab.* respectively.

Abbott, K. W., 199n1

acción de tutela. See tutelas (*acción de tutela*)

activists: court behavior and, 16, 35, 39, 47, 50–52, 190; disappearances of, 160; follow-up litigation, 117–18; indigenous rights and, 168, 219n106; international human rights law and, 130; police murder of, 2; SCJN and, 156; treaty law and, 8–9

African Charter on Human and Peoples' Rights (Banjul Charter), 111

African National Congress (ANC): electoral dominance of, 93, 105, 106*tab.*, 108, 127–29; HIV treatment and, 118–19, 182, 221n2; SACC and, 49; socioeconomic rights and, 109–10

Afrikaner Volksunie, 95

Alston, P., 203n51

Alter, K. J., 34

Alvarez, J. E., 10

American Convention on Human Rights, 79–80, 89, 163

Amnesty International, 48

Apartheid: economic inequalities and, 109, 118, 131; gross human rights violations during, 121; Interim Constitution and, 92–93, 95; judicial complicity and, 102, 131; laissez-faire capitalism under, 109; parliamentary supremacy and, 100; restrictions on international law, 96–97, 131; South African transition from, 45, 92, 100, 105, 120, 126, 130. *See also* South Africa

apex courts: constitutional order and, 18, 31–33; democratizing regimes and, 6, 16; diffuse support and, 32–33; institutional settings for, 6; international law and, 5; judicial review and, 31–32; legitimacy and, 71; political actors and, 5, 31–33; procedural and institutional rules in, 5; public access to, 5, 32–33; SACC as, 102, 131, 206n20; transitional regimes and, 4–5. *See also* courts; domestic courts

authoritative legitimacy, 22, 200n2

Azanian Peoples Organization (AZAPO) and Others v President of the Republic of South Africa and Others, 121, 127

Bennett, A., 47

Bickel, A. M., 38

Botswana, 117, 209n81

Brinks, D. M., 51

Burke-White, W., 10

Burley, A.-M., 34

Bush v Gore, 199n2

Butte, W. L., 214n40

Cabrera García, Teodoro, 166

Cabrera García and Montiel-Flores v Mexico, 163*tab.*

Cacho, Lydia, 158

Calderón, Felipe, 138, 150

Carbonell, M., 220n112

Carmichele v Minister of Safety and Security, 124, 126–27

Carrillo Prieto, Ignacio, 160

CCC. *See* Colombian Constitutional Court (CCC)

Cepeda Espinosa, M. J., 202n23

Cichowski, R. A., 34, 200n5

civil society: CCC oversight and, 67–69, 72, 90; compliance monitoring, 1, 50–51, 68–69; international human rights

civil society (*continued*)
regimes and, 7; judicial orientation and, 40, 43; policy formulation and, 69; rights outcomes and, 39
Claassen v Minister of Justice and Constitutional Development, 123
Colombia: apex courts in, 5–6; armed civil conflict in, 65, 71, 74; court reform in, 48, 135; Criminal Procedure Code (2004), 79–80, 83; extrajudicial killings in, 48, 56, 73–75, 75*tab.*; FARC and ELN in, 65, 82, 91, 201n19, 203n48, 221n3; Final Agreement (2016), 83, 85; independent judiciary in, 55; inter-American system and, 46; internally displaced persons (IDPs) in, 48, 54, 65–70, 70*fig.*, 71, 71*fig.*, 72, 85, 200n1; public support for national institutions, 88*fig.*; RUPD and, 66, 202n24; as social rule-of-law state, 54; Special Jurisdiction for Peace (SJP), 83–84; in state of exception, 55
Colombian Commission of Jurists, 74
Colombian constitution (1991): *acción de tutela*, 55, 58, 62; constitutional review and, 61; elite-driven controversies, 64; enforcement of human rights obligations, 58; fundamental rights and, 63, 201n17; international law and, 46, 55, 61, 64, 66–67; judicial reform and, 77–78; military prosecutions in, 76, 78; national judicial powers, 200n2; public orientation of, 56, 200n4; review of states of exception, 58, 61, 64; strengthening of state institutions, 54; as ultimate source of law, 58; victims' rights in, 79–80, 83
Colombian Constitutional Court (CCC): activist stance of, 56; avoidance of conflict with government, 83–85; civil society oversight and, 68–69; claims against government, 1; constitutionality blocks and, 58, 67, 201n8; distinct periods of, 59, 201n9; docket control in, 64–65, 65*fig.*; embedded internationalism and, 47*tab.*, 56–59, 60*fig.*, 72; enforcement of human rights obligations, 45–46, 49, 54–59, 61–62, 66–69, 72–73, 89–91, 203n49; extrajudicial killings, 48*tab.*, 56, 73–76, 81–82, 89–90, 186, 201n15, 203n52; *falsos positivos* cases, 74, 78, 81–82, 181; FARC peace process and, 82, 205n79; institutional legitimacy and, 57, 59, 63–64; intercourt tutelas, 80, 205n73; internally displaced persons (IDPs), 48*tab.*, 56, 66–70, 72, 85–87, 89–90, 202n23, 203n49; international law and, 55–56, 58, 181–83, 186; justice terms and appointment, 59, 61–62; mandatory legislation review, 55; monist approach, 58; monitoring process, 68–70, 73; oversight of military tribunals, 76–78; policy formulation and, 69; political actors and, 61–62; political backlash and, 64; procedural flexibility and, 47*tab.*, 49, 56–57, 63–65, 72–73, 186, 188, 201n10; public orientation and, 47*tab.*, 49, 55, 57, 59, 61–63, 72, 86–88, 184–85, 187; societal actors and, 56, 200n4; states of exception and, 55, 58; strategic legitimacy and, 56; Supreme Court resistance to tutela, 62, 201n15; tutela writ, 55, 58–59, 61–63, 63*fig.*, 64–67, 72, 77, 188, 201n7, 201n10, 202n23, 215n44; victims' rights and, 78–80, 82, 204n66
Colombian Supreme Court: election of justices, 61–62; judicial powers, 200n2; resistance to tutela writ, 62, 201n15; states of exception and, 55; unconstitutionality of military courts, 76
Colossio, Luis Donaldo, 221n3
Comisión Nacional de los Derechos Humanos (CNDH): claims under treaty law, 139; on human rights violations, 2, 153, 160; investigation of Aguas Blancas massacre, 154–55; investigatory function, 159–60, 175
constitutional courts, 11, 32, 34, 55, 215n44
constitutional law: Colombia and, 58, 77; Colombian Supreme Court, 201n15; international human rights law and, 52; SACC and, 94, 101–2, 121
constitutional review: apex courts and, 31–33; diffuse review systems, 31–33; public claims and, 31–33; SACC and, 100, 102; SCJN and, 134, 142, 150, 170; tutela and, 83
Constitution of the Republic of South Africa, 92
constitutions: domestic courts and, 28–30; embedded internationalism and, 180; international law and, 28–30, 42, 180–83;

judicial power and, 11; legitimacy and, 28–29
Consultoría para los Derechos Humanos y el Desplazamiento (CODHES), 70, 203n47
content legitimacy, 22
Convention Against Torture and Other Cruel, Inhuman or Degrading Treatment or Punishment (CAT), 122, 160, 210n110
Convention on the Elimination of All Forms of Discrimination Against Women (CEDAW), 97, 124
Convention on the Non-Applicability of Statutory Limitations to War Crimes and Crimes Against Humanity (CNASL), 160
Convention on the Prevention and Punishment of the Crime of Genocide, 97
Convention on the Rights of the Child, 97, 122, 210n111
Cope, K. L., 52
Córdoba Triviño, J., 202n23
Court of Justice (EU), 34
courts: abuse of discretion and, 22, 199n1; authoritative legitimacy, 22, 200n2; balance-of-power framework, 25–26, 30, 41*fig.*; conflict with political actors, 5, 14, 23–27, 30, 38, 43; consequential, 16; constitutional review and, 31–33; covert operation of, 35; diffuse support, 23; embedded internationalism and, 27–30, 41, 41*fig.*, 42, 45, 56–57, 94; establishing legitimacy, 20–24, 28–30, 38; ideal ruling and, 40, 43; institutional legitimacy, 22–24, 27; interbranch relations, 26–27, 39; international law and, 26–27, 52–53; legal legitimacy, 21–23, 43–44, 128, 200n2; as political actors, 17–18, 20; political backlash and, 38, 40, 43–45; political insularity and, 37; procedural constraint and, 37–38, 41, 44; procedural flexibility and, 37–40, 41*fig.*, 42–45, 94, 179, 186–89; procedural rules and, 41*fig.*; public access to, 32–33, 94; public policy and, 23–24; public support orientation, 183–86; rights adjudication, 44, 181; secondary rules and, 35, 38; sociological legitimacy, 21–23; strategic approaches, 14–15, 20, 25–26, 26*fig.*, 38–39, 45; substantive legitimacy, 22–23, 200n2; transitional regimes and, 127, 211n140. *See also* apex courts; domestic courts; international courts
criminal law: citizen rights under, 120–24; corporal punishment of juveniles, 122–23; development of common law, 124–25; granting of amnesty, 121, 126, 210n97; international human rights law and, 120, 122, 124; victim compensation, 81, 124–26, 211n121

Dahl, R. A., 32, 40
decision-making: domestic courts and, 179; domestic policy space, 24–25, 25*fig.*, 26, 26*fig.*; international law and, 166, 177; judicial, 17–18, 24–25, 25*fig.*, 26; law-based, 24, 25*fig.*; legitimacy and, 26; strategic approach, 25–26, 26*fig.*
De La Barreda, Luis, 160, 217n82
Democratic Alliance/Democratic Party (South Africa), 103, 106*tab.*
democratization: apex courts in, 6, 16; constitutional courts and, 11, 32; domestic courts and, 2, 4–6, 11–12, 21; international human rights and, 7–8, 28; international law and, 5, 8, 11, 191, 199n4; political reform and, 4
Dixon, R., 38
domestic courts: claims against government, 51, 200n9; constitutions and, 28–30; democratizing regimes and, 2, 4–6, 11–12, 21; embedded internationalism and, 94, 179–80; enforcement power, 12–15, 50; government behavior and, 8; human rights violations and, 1–2, 5–6; institutional settings for, 12–15, 29; international human rights law, 4–16, 26–30, 34–35, 43–44, 50–51, 179, 181, 189–91, 199n2, 199n3, 200n5, 220n1; judicial role of, 10; legitimacy and, 21, 28–30, 38, 43; manipulation of rules, 14–15; norms promulgation and, 9–10, 16, 199n2, 199n3; passive virtues and, 38; political elites and, 30–31, 40, 43; procedural constraint and, 37–38; procedural flexibility and, 37–40, 94; procedural rules and, 33–41, 41*fig.*; public access to, 12, 31, 35–37, 71–72; public support for, 23, 26, 30–31, 44, 94; rights enforcement and, 31; self-censoring, 40; substantive norms and, 36; transitional regimes, 23, 30, 50, 122, 179; transnational activism and, 8–9; treaty law and, 7–8, 10, 16. *See also* apex courts; courts

Echeverría, Luis, 161–62
ELN (National Liberation Army), 65, 201n19
embedded internationalism: CCC and, 58–59, 72; constitutionalization and, 180–81; courts and, 27–30, 41, 41*fig.*, 42, 56–57, 94; court's ideal ruling and, 43; domestic courts and, 179–80; international human rights law and, 45, 49, 57–58, 180–83; judges and, 29–30; SACC and, 47*tab.*, 49, 94–100, 128; SCJN and, 50, 135–36, 139–42, 160, 167, 177
End of History and the Last Man, The (Fukuyama), 3
Epp, C. R., 39, 209n82
Epstein, L., 24, 25*fig.*, 26*fig.*
Escobar Gil, R., 202n23
European Court of Human Rights, 3, 34
European Union, 34–35
extrajudicial killings: binding treaties and, 89–90; CCC and, 48*tab.*, 56, 73–76, 81–82, 89–90, 186, 201n15, 203n52; *falsos positivos* (false positives), 74; Mexico, 48, 152–53; military participation in, 48, 74, 86, 153, 186; political backlash and, 186; reporting of, 74, 75*tab.*, 203n51

Fallon, R. H., 21
FARC (Revolutionary Armed Forces of Colombia), 65, 82, 89, 91, 201n19, 203n48
Federación Internacional de Derechos Humanos, 203n54
FEMOSPP (Special Prosecutor's Office for Social and Political Movements of the Past), 161, 217n72, 217n74
Fernández Ortega, Inés, 166
Fernández Ortega et al. v Mexico, 163*tab.*
Final Constitution (South Africa): application of remedies, 114–15; international human rights law and, 94–95, 97, 99–100, 104, 113; judicial review and, 100, 102; legislative claims and, 103; minimum core standard, 113–14, 209n66; procedural flexibility, 215n44; SACC and, 93–95, 97, 99–102, 113–15, 187, 207n29; socioeconomic rights and, 109–10, 113–14, 182
Finkel, J., 134, 149
Fose v Minister of Safety and Security, 126
Fox, Vicente, 150, 160, 168, 170, 217n72
Free Market Foundation, 207n43
Fukuyama, F., 3

Galanter, M., 209n82
Gauri, V., 51
Gauteng Association of Chambers of Commerce and Industry, 207n43
Gaviria, César, 54
George, A. L., 47
Gibson, J. L., 21
Ginsburg, T., 8, 34, 199n4
Goodwin v Director-General, Department of Justice and Constitutional Development and Others, 123, 127, 211n117
Government of the Republic of South Africa and Others v Grootboom, 113, 119
Government of the Republic of Zimbabwe v Fick and Others, 125
Grosskopf, A., 220n1
Guerrero Pérez, L. G., 202n43
Guiding Principles on Internal Displacement (1988), 66–67, 90

Hart, H. L. A., 35
Helfer, L. R., 34
Hirschl, R., 211n140
historical institutionalism, 18–20
HIV/AIDS pandemic: expansion of treatment coverage, 117, 117*tab.*; government rhetoric, 118–19, 209n83; mother-to- child transmission of, 111–12, 117, 119; SACC declaratory orders, 114–17, 119–20; second-generation treatment rights, 48*tab.*; socioeconomic rights of individuals with, 109–16, 119, 129; South Africans with, 111; *TAC 2* case, 111–15, 117–18
human rights: court enforcement of, 11–16, 23, 43–47, 49–50; global push for, 3–4; treaty law and, 7–8, 10, 28, 41. *See also* international human rights law
Human Rights Commission (South Africa), 113, 208n64
human rights violations: domestic courts and, 1–2, 5–6; evidentiary standards in prosecution, 34–35; impunity and, 48, 158, 164; indigenous rights and, 167–68; legal claims and, 44; Mexico, 2, 152–56, 160, 215n49; military and, 73–75, 90, 153–54, 158, 160, 164, 166
Human Rights Watch, 48, 154
Huneeus, A., 52

Ibarra, Jesús Piedra, 160
ILO Convention No. 169, 168, 171

impunity: Colombian constitution and, 79; Dirty War, 152–53; drug-related violence, 153; extrajudicial killings, 48, 152–53; human rights violations, 48, 158, 164; IACHR enforcement, 162–66; military and, 153–54, 158, 160, 163, 163*tab.*, 164, 175, 219n102; rural uprisings, 153; SACC and, 122; SCJN and, 152–53, 158, 160–63, 163*tab.*, 166–67, 174–75
Indigenous and Tribal Populations Convention (No. 107), 168
indigenous rights: collective actions for, 172–73, 220n118; human rights violations, 167–68; indigenous self-identification, 171, 219n101; international law and, 167–68; Mexican constitutional reforms, 169–73, 175; in Mexico, 48, 167–68; SCJN and, 48*tab.*, 168–69, 169*fig.*, 170–76
individuals: amparo suits, 143, 172; court enforcement of rights, 16; government persecution claims, 36–37; HIV and, 108–9, 111; human rights and, 1–4, 69; international law and, 1–2, 4, 8, 36, 59, 90, 128; liberalism and, 3; rights in criminal proceedings, 120, 123
Inkatha Freedom Party, 103, 106*tab.*
institutional legitimacy: CCC and, 57, 59, 63–64; diffuse support and, 23; domestic courts and, 5, 22–24, 27, 30, 57; international law and, 5, 59; judiciary and, 20; legal legitimacy and, 23; nonpolitical status, 42; procedural flexibility and, 39, 63–64; public support orientation and, 30, 59
Inter-American Commission on Human Rights, 2–3, 75, 90
Inter-American Court of Human Rights (IACHR): CCC and, 90; diffuse conventionality control, 165, 218n90; enforcement of human rights obligations, 163–64; on Mexican impunity cases, 162–63, 163*tab.*, 164–66, 175; SCJN and, 162–65, 188
internally displaced persons (IDPs): armed civil conflict and, 65–66, 71, 87, 89; CCC and, 56, 66–70, 72, 85–87, 89–90, 202n23, 203n49; Colombian government expenditures on, 70, 70*fig.*, 203n46; Colombian law and, 67, 69–70, 86, 202n44; Colombian population, 48*tab.*, 54, 65–66, 70–71, 71*fig.*, 200n1; growth in numbers, 70, 203n48; indigenous communities and, 66; NGOs and, 68, 70, 203n49; rights violations and, 66–67, 69, 73; RUPD and, 66, 202n24; SNAIPD and, 67–68; system-wide transformation and, 69–71; vulnerable populations, 66, 68
International Bill of Human Rights, 110–11, 208n46
International Convention on the Elimination of All Forms of Racial Discrimination, 97
International Convention on the Suppression and Punishment of the Crime of Apartheid, 96
international courts, 10, 12–13, 34
International Covenant on Civil and Political Rights (ICCPR): CCC and, 80; Colombia and, 89; International Bill of Human Rights and, 208n46; Mexico and, 139, 154, 160; South Africa and, 92, 97, 111, 122–24, 126
International Covenant on Economic, Social and Cultural Rights (ICESCR), 92, 110–11, 113, 139, 208n46, 208n47
International Criminal Court, 3, 82
International Criminal Tribunal for Rwanda, 79
International Criminal Tribunal for the Former Yugoslavia, 79
international human rights law: CCC and, 45–46, 49, 54–59, 61, 66–69, 72–73; compliance results, 7–9; constitutional law and, 52; democratizing regimes and, 7–8, 28; domestic courts and, 4–16, 27–28, 43–44, 50–51, 189–91; embedded internationalism and, 45, 49, 57–58, 94, 180–83; legalization of, 3–7, 25; procedural flexibility and, 49, 94, 179; procedural rules in, 34–35; public orientation and, 49, 94; rights under criminal law, 120–21; SACC and, 97–98; socialization and norms, 7–9, 199n2; UN Guiding Principles, 66–67
internationalism. *See* embedded internationalism
International Labour Organization (ILO), 139, 168
international law: constitutionalization and, 29–30, 42, 180–83; court access in, 34; court power and, 191; democratizing regimes and, 5, 8, 11, 191, 199n4; domestic courts and, 5–6, 8–10, 26–28, 30, 34–35, 43, 199n2, 199n3, 200n5;

international law (*continued*)
dualist approach, 27; indigenous rights and, 168–69; individual rights and, 1–2, 4, 8, 36, 59, 90, 128; monist approach, 9, 27; SACC limits on, 121–24, 126–27; soft law, 5, 199n1
international relations: domestic courts and, 189–90; global norms in, 199n2; legalized human rights and, 6, 179; substantive/procedural law in, 33–36
Issacharoff, S., 38

Jaramillo, Bernardo, 221n3
judicial independence: individual autonomy, 37; party detachment, 37; political insularity and, 37; procedural rules and, 36–37; quantifiable measures for, 38; SACC and, 105, 131; SCJN and, 149–50, 176; unbiased rulings and, 37
judicial politics: attitudinal approach, 18–19; balance-of-power framework, 24–26; comparative, 51–52; consequential courts in, 16; constructing authority, 20; decision-making and, 17–18, 24–25, 25*fig.*, 26; diffusion and, 31–33; domestic courts and, 190; elected officials and, 24–27, 30; historical institutionalism, 18–20; Latin American, 51; legitimacy and, 21, 26; strategic approach, 15, 18–19
judicial review: CCC and, 55; courts and, 31–32; government policy and, 199n4; political actors and, 31–32; procedural norms, 33; public access to, 31–32, 43; SACC and, 100–101; SCJN and, 144, 165
judicial system: Apartheid-era, 131; CCC and, 78, 84; comparative, 52; constitutional reform and, 78; diffusion and, 32; elite orientation, 40; locus of review, 31–32; Mexican, 135, 140, 142–43, 159, 166, 173, 175; procedural environment and, 34–40, 42–45; public orientation, 31, 40, 44–45, 183–84; SACC and, 102–3; tutela and, 59, 61
judiciary: abuse of discretion and, 199n1; accountability and, 21; autonomy and, 52; constitutional reform and, 11; decision-making and, 18; diffuse review systems and, 32; domestic courts and, 10; elite socialization and, 10; as entrepreneurs, 52, 190; hierarchy and, 33, 200n3; international perspectives and, 29–30, 59, 60*fig.*; perceptions of consistency, 52; personal policy preferences, 18–20, 25; procedural rules and, 34, 36–37; professional identity and, 29–30; public support for, 30; secondary rules and, 35, 38; transnational communication, 9–10, 29, 59

Kapiszewski, D., 51
Kelsen, H., 18, 32
Keohane, R. O., 34
Knight, J., 24, 25*fig.*, 26*fig.*
Knop, K., 220n1
Koh, H. H., 9

Landau, D., 39
Latin America: amparo suit in, 143; constitutional transformation in, 133, 135, 212n1; institutional flexibility and, 46; inter-American system and, 46; judiciary in, 51, 55; military impunity in, 153–54; procedural law in, 35. *See also* Colombia; Mexico
law: attitudinal approach, 18–19; courts and, 52–53; decision-making and, 17–18, 24, 25*fig.*; historical institutionalism, 18–20; horizontal effect, 33, 51, 200n4; intent and, 17–18; legal formalism, 17, 27; legal realism, 17; political concerns and, 17–18; primary/secondary, 35; procedural, 33–36; strategic approach, 18–19; substantive, 33, 36; transitional regimes and, 127, 211n140. *See also* international human rights law
legal formalism, 27
legal legitimacy, 21–23, 43–44, 199n1, 200n2
legitimacy: authoritative, 22, 200n2; constitutional reform and, 28–29; content, 22; courts and, 20–24, 28–30; defining, 21; domestic courts and, 21, 28–29, 43; institutional, 22–24, 27; judicial, 21, 26; legal, 21–23, 43–44, 199n1, 200n2; political backlash and, 38; sociological, 21–23; substantive, 22–23, 200n2
Lupu, Y., 34–35

Macedo de la Concha, Rafael, 217n74
Magaloni, B., 148
Mandela, Nelson, 92, 101

Marbury v Madison, 38
Martin, A. D., 24, 25*fig.*, 26*fig.*
Mattli, W., 34
Maveety, N., 220n1
Mbeki, Thabo, 118
Meierhenrich, J., 211n140
Mexican Constitution: adoption of, 212n2; amendments to, 212n3; human rights protections, 138–39, 145; indigenous rights and, 169–73, 175, 219n106; international law and, 136–39; *pro homine* principles, 162, 165, 173, 182; reforms of 1994, 133, 142, 144–45, 149–51; reforms of 2011, 162–63; SCJN investigatory powers, 155, 216n57, 216n61; supremacy clause, 136–37
Mexican Supreme Court of Justice of the Nation (SCJN): amparo suit, 138–39, 142–46, 148–49, 151, 157, 172–73, 213n19, 213n20, 214n25; appointment of justices, 134, 144, 148, 212n5, 214n27; avoidance of political conflict, 2, 156–57; binding precedent, 148, 166, 219n109; court-strengthening reforms, 45–46, 134–35; diffuse support and, 142; embedded internationalism and, 47*tab.*, 50, 135–36, 139–42, 160, 167, 174, 177; enforcement of human rights obligations, 50, 134–35, 152, 154–67, 176–78; human rights failures, 2, 46; human rights protections, 145–46; IACHR enforcement, 162–65, 188; impunity issue, 48*tab.*, 158, 160–63, 163*tab.*, 166–67, 174; indigenous rights, 48*tab.*, 168–69, 169*fig.*, 170–76; influence on state laws, 144, 214n28; institutional legitimacy, 174–75; international treaty law and, 136–38, 141–42, 162–65, 176; investigation of Aguas Blancas massacre, 154–57, 216n67; investigatory function, 154–58, 158*fig*, 159, 188, 216n57, 216n61, 216n64, 216n67; judicial reform and, 150, 215n43; judicial review and, 144–46, 165; jurisdiction limits, 150, 155–56, 159; jurisprudence epochs, 135, 212n8; *jurisprudencia* in, 143–44, 170, 214n26, 216n63, 219n109; justices of, 141*fig.*; LOPJF jurisdiction, 163–64; Otero formulation, 214n25; political actors and, 142–43, 145–47, 150, 152, 159–62, 176, 178; power of attraction, 165, 218n88; presidential meta-constitutional powers, 147, 214n38; PRI policy enforcement, 147–48; procedural constraint and, 46, 47*tab.*, 50, 135–36, 146–48, 150–52, 154–59, 165–67, 171–74, 177, 187–88; public orientation limits, 47*tab.*, 136, 142, 146, 160, 174, 177, 185; removal from constitutional reform, 170, 220n112; *tesis* (rulings of law), 156, 170, 173, 216n63; unconstitutionality review, 144–46, 151, 214n30
Mexico: Aguas Blancas massacre, 153–57, 216n67; anti-drug trafficking efforts, 153; apex courts in, 5–6; civil law tradition, 148–49; constitutional reforms, 133–34, 212n6; court reform in, 45–46, 48; Dirty War in, 152–53, 160–61, 164, 175, 215n49, 217n72; disappearances in, 152–54; extrajudicial killings in, 48, 152–53; federal court system, 143–44, 147, 213n24; human rights law in, 139–40; human rights violations in, 2, 152–56, 215n49; impunity in, 48, 152–53; indigenous population, 167, 219n100, 219n101; indigenous rights in, 48, 167–68; inter-American system and, 46; Jueves de Corpus massacre, 153, 161; *jurisprudencia* in, 214n40; legal nationalism in, 139–40; legislature, 214n42; party strength in post-reform era, 149, 149*tab.*, 150; *presidencialismo*, 146–47; reforms of 1994, 133–34, 212n1; San Andrés Accords, 168–69, 171; Zapatista uprising, 153, 168–69, 221n3
Michel, V., 35–36
military: extrajudicial killings, 48, 74, 86, 153, 186; human rights violations, 73–75, 90, 153–54, 158, 160, 166; impunity and, 153–54, 158, 160, 163, 163*tab.*, 164, 175, 219n102; public support for, 87–88
military tribunals: CCC oversight of, 76–78, 80; government resistance to CCC oversight, 75–78, 85–86; military jurisdiction and, 76, 204n64; political violence crimes, 76; SCJN and, 175
Minister of Health and Others v Treatment Action Campaign and Others (No. 1) (*TAC 1*), 208n50
Minister of Health and Others v Treatment Action Campaign and Others (No. 2) (*TAC 2*), 111–15, 117–18

Montiel-Flores, Rodolfo, 166
Moore, W. H., 12
Moravcsik, A., 7
Moya Palencia, Mario, 162

Namibia, 95, 117, 209n81
National Human Rights Commission (CNDH). *See* Comisión Nacional de los Derechos Humanos (CNDH)
National Party (South Africa), 103, 106*tab.*, 127
National System for Comprehensive Assistance to the Displaced Population (SNAIPD), 67–68
Nazar Haro, Miguel, 160, 217n82
nongovernmental organizations (NGOs): advocacy and, 8; on Colombian extrajudicial killings, 74–75; compliance monitoring, 68, 70; human rights and, 2, 152, 155, 158–59; internally displaced persons (IDPs) and, 68, 70, 203n49

Office of the United Nations High Commissioner for Refugees (UNHCR), 68, 203n48
Otero, Mariano, 214n25

Partido Acción Nacional, 150
Partido Revolucionario Democratico (PRD), 154
Partido Revolucionario Institucional (PRI), 134, 146–47, 149–51, 157
Pastrana, Andrés, 77
Pimentel, Góngora, 151
Pinilla Pinilla, N., 202n43
Pizarro, Carlos, 221n3
political actors: apex courts and, 32–33; CCC and, 61; conflict with courts, 5, 14, 23–27, 30, 38, 43; courts as, 17–20; court's ideal ruling and, 40; democratizing regimes and, 11; diffuse support and, 23; ideal policy points, 61; internally displaced persons (IDPs) and, 86; international law and, 11–12; judicial review and, 31–32; jurisdictional disputes, 85; SCJN and, 142–43, 145–47, 150, 152; threat of electoral loss, 23, 30; transjudicial dialogue, 9–10
President of the Republic of South Africa and Others v Quagliani, 123, 127, 211n117
President of the Republic of South Africa and Others v Van Rooyen and Another, 211n117
procedural constraint: court system and, 37–38; international law and, 43–44; legitimacy and, 41; political actors and, 189; political backlash and, 41, 43; SCJN and, 46, 47*tab.*, 50, 135–36, 146–48, 150–52, 154–59, 165–67, 171–74, 177, 187–88; self-censoring and, 40
procedural environment: access rules, 34; constrained, 33, 37–38, 41, 44; court interactions, 38; domestic judicial system, 34; expansion of enforcement, 44; first-order (explicit) deferrals, 38; flexible, 37–40, 42–45; second-order (implicit) deferrals, 38; strategic legitimacy and, 44–45. *See also* procedural constraint; procedural flexibility
procedural flexibility: CCC and, 46, 47*tab.*, 49, 56–57, 63–65, 72–73, 186, 188, 201n10; court system and, 37–40, 42–43, 94, 179, 186–89; embedded internationalism and, 45; expansion of enforcement, 44, 188; institutional legitimacy and, 39, 63–64, 186; international law and, 39, 43, 179; political actors and, 38, 44; rights adjudication and, 44, 64–65; SACC and, 46, 47*tab.*, 49, 94, 104–5, 107–8, 128–29, 131, 187–89; SCJN and, 136; self-censoring and, 40; societal actors and, 38–40, 43; tutela writ and, 201n10
procedural rules: access rules, 35–38; avoidance of conflict through, 38–39, 108; domestic courts and, 33–40; international law and, 34; judicial manipulation of, 73; judiciary and, 34, 36–37; politicization of, 172, 186; regional courts and, 34; strategic legitimacy and, 44, 179, 186; victim rights and, 35
public: access rules, 35–38; *acción de tutela*, 55; diffuse support, 23; domestic courts and, 5, 8, 12, 14–15, 26, 30–31; institutional support for judiciary, 30; judicial accountability and, 21; judicial review and, 31–32; policy goals and, 24; sociological legitimacy and, 22–23; support for CCC, 86–88; support for military, 87–88, 88*fig.*
public opinion: civil society groups and, 50–51; international human rights law and, 40; legitimacy and, 22; political

backlash and, 128; political support and, 86–87; procedural constraint and, 135
public support orientation: avoidance of political backlash, 185–86; CCC and, 49, 59, 61, 72, 87, 90, 184–85, 187; court systems and, 31, 33, 94, 136, 183–86; international human rights law and, 49; legitimacy and, 33; SACC avoidance of, 108, 128, 184–87; SCJN and, 135–36, 142, 160, 185–86

Radilla Pacheco v Mexico, 163*tab.*, 164, 166
Ramirez, A., 219n101
Ramos Cisneros, Juventino, 160
regional courts, 34
Reyes Reyes, P. E., 216n61
rights adjudication: indigenous rights and, 168, 173; litigation demand, 44, 47–48, 179, 186–87; procedural flexibility and, 44, 64–65, 174, 188–89; SCJN and, 154; socioeconomic rights and, 109
Rome Statute of the International Criminal Court, 79, 97
Rome Treaty, 34
Rosendo Cantú, Valentina, 166
Rosendo-Cantú and Other v Mexico, 163*tab.*
Ruiz Massieu, Jose Francisco, 221n3
RUPD. *See* Unified Registry for the Displaced Population (RUPD)

SACC. *See* South African Constitutional Court (SACC)
Sánchez Cordero, Olga, 137
Santos, Juan Manuel, 82, 89
SCJN. *See* Mexican Supreme Court of Justice of the Nation (SCJN)
Segal, J. A., 19
Shapiro, M., 12
Shilowa, Mbhazime, 118
Silva Meza, Juan, 173
Simmons, B. A., 8
Slaughter, A.-M., 9–10
SNAIPD. *See* National System for Comprehensive Assistance to the Displaced Population (SNAIPD)
Snidal, D., 199n1
sociological legitimacy, 21–23
soft law, 5, 199n1
South Africa: adoption of Final Constitution, 92–94, 97, 99–101, 109, 207n42; Apartheid era abuses, 96, 109, 120–21, 131; apex courts in, 5–6; Bill of Rights, 92, 94, 97, 109, 111, 114–15, 123–24; citizen rights under criminal law, 120–24; constitutional amendments, 105, 135, 207n36; court reform in, 48; criminal proceedings, 48; economic redistribution post-Apartheid, 109; Final Constitution and, 182; HIV infections in, 111; HIV treatment in, 48, 112, 115–17, 117*tab.*, 118–19, 182; Human Rights Commission, 113, 208n64; international human rights law and, 97–98; international law in legal system, 98–100; monist approach, 27; party strength in national elections, 105, 106*tab.*; rights enforcement, 1, 118, 209n82; socioeconomic rights in, 109–14, 119, 208n64, 209n66; as upper-middle-income country, 209n81. *See also* Apartheid
South African Constitutional Court (SACC): annual caseload, 107*fig.*; as apex court, 102, 131, 206n20; avoidance of political conflict, 107–8, 113, 116–17, 120, 125, 127–28, 131; common law and, 102, 124–25, 128, 189, 206n19; constitutional issues and, 102, 206n18; criminal law cases, 48*tab.*, 120–24, 130; declaratory orders, 114–17, 119–20; elite orientation, 47*tab.*, 93, 100–104, 108, 129, 131, 184–85, 187; embedded internationalism and, 47*tab.*, 49, 94–100, 128; enforcement of human rights obligations, 46, 49, 92–98, 189; Final Constitution and, 93–95, 97, 99–102, 113–15, 132, 187, 207n29, 215n44; granting of amnesty, 121, 126, 210n97, 210n104; HIV treatment and, 48*tab.*, 110–19, 182; institutional legitimacy and, 93–94, 127, 132; Interim Constitution and, 93, 95, 100–102, 121; internal court procedures, 104; international law and, 95–100, 104, 113–14, 127–28, 130–32, 182; international law limitations, 121–24, 126–27; judicial review of legislative and executive activity, 100–104; justices of, 99*fig.*; lack of public support orientation, 128–29, 131; landmark cases, 107, 207n37; limitation of government implementation, 93; presidential and legislative access to, 103–4, 207n29; procedural flexibility and, 47*tab.*, 49, 104–5, 107–8, 128–29, 131, 187–89; rights enforcement, 1, 118, 121, 126, 130; second-generation treatment rights and,

South African Constitutional Court (*continued*)
48*tab.*, 109–10; self-executing treaties, 95–96, 98, 123, 210n116; socioeconomic rights and, 109–11, 119–20, 129; structural interdicts, 114–17, 119; transition from Apartheid, 45, 92–93, 96–97; victim compensation, 125–26
South African Institute of Race Relations, 207n43
Southern African Development Community (SADC) Tribunal, 125
Spaeth, H. J., 19
Special Jurisdiction for Peace (SJP), 83
Staszak, S., 34
states: constitutional reform and, 27; democratizing regimes, 3–4, 6–8, 11, 11*fig.*, 20, 27, 32; dualist approach, 27; human rights compliance, 52–53; individual rights and, 36–37; international law and, 2–3, 9, 13, 27, 41; international tribunals and, 12–13; judicial review and, 31; monist approach, 27; norms promulgation and, 9; treaty law and, 7–9, 13, 28, 45
Staton, J. K., 12
Stein, E., 34
substantive law, 33, 35–36
substantive legitimacy, 22–23, 200n2
S v Williams and Others, 122, 127

Taylor, M. M., 51
Teles, S. M., 40
transitional regimes: apex courts in, 4–5; conditional amnesty, 122; diffuse support and, 30; domestic courts in, 23, 30, 50, 179; insurgency and, 187, 221n3; liberalization and, 12; states with, 11*fig.*, 199n5
Treatment Action Campaign (TAC), 111, 182
treaty law: CCC and, 58, 80; domestic courts and, 7–8, 10, 16; Final Constitution (South Africa), 85, 97; human rights obligations and, 7–8, 10; lock-in mechanisms, 41; SACC and, 121, 124–25, 187; SCJN and, 135–39, 142, 146; state constitutions and, 28, 45, 58, 181–82; substantive norms and, 36; transnational activism and, 8–9
Truth and Reconciliation Commission, 121
Turbay, Julio César, 76
Tushnet, M., 33
tutelas (*acción de tutela*): CCC and, 55, 58–59, 61–67, 72, 77, 188, 201n7, 201n10, 202n23, 215n44; intercourt, 80, 205n73; international human rights law, 58; public engagement and, 59, 61–63

Ugalde, L. C., 214n38
UN Committee on Economic, Social and Cultural Rights (CESCR), 113
UN Declaration on the Rights of Indigenous Peoples (UNDRIP), 168
Unified Registry for the Displaced Population (RUPD), 66, 202n24
United Nations (UN), 135
United Nations (UN) Charter, 3, 168
United States, 27, 31–32, 34, 96, 143
Universal Declaration of Human Rights, 79, 111, 208n46
UN Security Council, 96
U.S. Department of State, 48
U.S. Supreme Court: authoritative legitimacy, 199n2; conservative project for, 32; domestic law and, 42; electoral accountability and, 21; Federal Rules of Civil Procedure, 104, 207n33; institutional constraints and, 19; procedural rules and, 38

Vargas, J. A., 212n6
Vargas Silva, L. E., 202n43
victim rights: court access and, 186; in criminal proceedings, 78–80, 82–83, 204n66; military violations and, 85, 153, 167; procedural rules and, 35, 79–80; state compensation for, 125–26

Weber, M., 22
World Bank, 209n81

Zamora, S., 214n28, 214n40
Zealand v Minister for Justice and Constitutional Development and Another, 125–27
Zedillo, Ernesto, 133–34, 149–50, 155

Printed in the USA
CPSIA information can be obtained
at www.ICGtesting.com
CBHW021619110424
6728CB00001B/2

9 781512 826210